THE ART OF SOCIAL SELLING

THE ART OF SOCIAL SELLING

Finding and Engaging Customers on

Twitter, Facebook, LinkedIn,

and Other Social Networks

Shannon Belew

∆MACOM

AMERICAN MANAGEMENT ASSOCIATION

New York • Atlanta • Brussels • Chicago • Mexico City • San Francisco
Shanghai • Tokyo • Toronto • Washington, D.C.

Bulk discounts available. For details visit:
www.amacombooks.org/go/specialsales
Or contact special sales:
Phone: 800–250–5308
Email: specialsls@amanet.org
View all the AMACOM titles at: www.amacombooks.org
American Management Association: www.amanet.org

This publication is designed to provide accurate and authoritative information in regard to the subject matter covered. It is sold with the understanding that the publisher is not engaged in rendering legal, accounting, or other professional service. If legal advice or other expert assistance is required, the services of a competent professional person should be sought.

Library of Congress Cataloging-in-Publication Data

Belew, Shannon.
  The art of social selling : finding and engaging customers on Twitter, Facebook, LinkedIn, and other social networks / Shannon Belew.
    pages cm
  Includes bibliographical references and index.
  ISBN-13: 978–0-8144–3332–4
  ISBN-10: 0–8144–3332–4
  1. Internet marketing. 2. Marketing—Social aspects. 3. Selling. 4. Online social networks. 5. Social media. I. Title.
  HF5415.1265.B45 2014
  658.8'72—dc23
                                                                    2013024425

About AMA
American Management Association (www.amanet.org) is a world leader in talent development, advancing the skills of individuals to drive business success. Our mission is to support the goals of individuals and organizations through a complete range of products and services, including classroom and virtual seminars, webcasts, webinars, podcasts, conferences, corporate and government solutions, business books and research. AMA's approach to improving performance combines experiential learning—learning through doing—with opportunities for ongoing professional growth at every step of one's career journey.

Printing number

10 9 8 7 6 5 4 3 2

CONTENTS

ACKNOWLEDGMENTS

There are many people whom an author depends upon to help transition a book from concept to reality. For me, *The Art of Social Selling* would not have made it through the publishing process and onto bookshelves (or e-readers!) without the help, encouragement, and support of the following folks.

For starters, I am fortunate to have a wonderful team at Waterside Productions, led by Carole Jelen, that works hard to find a publishing home for my book ideas. And I am particularly appreciative that *The Art of Social Selling* landed in the hands of AMACOM Books, and under the guidance of Robert (Bob) Nirkind, Senior Acquisitions Editor. His patience, direction, and overall editorial vision for the book made the writing process all that more enjoyable—and provided an assurance that the final product would be all that I had intended for my readers (that's you!). I must also send a heartfelt thank you to Debbie Posner for her laser-sharp copyediting skills and for making the final editing process (dare I say) fun! And to Mike Sivilli and his design and production team, my sincere thanks for the great job and for bearing with me!

I am also extremely grateful to my family (Tom, Holden, and Wiley) for their endless encouragement and support. They help keep me motivated and on track—when I need it most.

I would be remiss not to acknowledge my friends and followers who engage with me on LinkedIn, Twitter, Facebook, Google+, Pinterest, and Instagram; they make social media both entertaining and inspiring—and I continually learn from them. Likewise, I send a very special thanks to everyone who took time to speak with me about the book and allowed me to share their expertise and experiences with social selling.

But none of this would matter without you, the reader. So thank you for trusting me to guide you through the many intricacies of the rapidly evolving concept of social selling. I am forever appreciative that you have taken time to read this book and I look forward to hearing about your social selling success soon!

INTRODUCTION

There are many possible reasons why you may be reading this book. Most likely, it's because you're a sales or marketing professional who has some level of responsibility for generating leads, closing sales, and creating revenue in your organization, and you're constantly under pressure to identify new strategies for delivering the goods. Perhaps someone suggested turning to social media as a lead source. Perhaps you've heard peers and industry leaders tout the benefits of this new thing called "social selling." Or perhaps you're an influencer within your organization who already understands the value of social prospecting and need a resource to help develop a business case for integrating social media into your current sales and marketing process. No matter why you've picked up this book, the truth of the matter is simple: Social selling is a strategy that every B2B and B2C sales and marketing professional must understand in order to increase his or her effectiveness and remain competitive in today's global marketplace.

It's a bold statement to imply that your continued value as a salesperson or a marketer hinges on successfully incorporating social media into your sales process. In reality, the decision not to adopt a social selling strategy is not a game ender; you'll certainly continue to generate leads and make sales. But you've got to wonder if what you're doing now is *enough* to not only sustain but grow revenues for your organization. Are you generating enough new leads? Are they high quality enough to continue building your sales pipeline? Can you close enough sales and do so soon enough to make quota? Consider that, on average, only 43 percent of sales professionals make their quota, according to a study from the Aberdeen Group. The same study indicated that you're much more likely (79 percent more likely, to be exact!) to hit your sales target if you're using social selling in your sales process compared to your peers who are not using it. Even so, some of you may still be skeptical of its value. After all, whether you've just begun your career or you are a veteran within your industry, you've most likely experienced some wins using traditional sales and marketing techniques. Why change now?

Think of social selling as a numbers game. Take a look at the following stats:

> ➤ Without social selling, 40 percent of sales teams make less than 80 percent of quota, on average. (Based on accumulated data from Xactly, a sales compensation management company.)

> ➤ Salespeople using social media exceeded sales quotas 23 percent more often than peers not using social media. ("Social Media and Sales Quota: The Impact of Social Media on Sales Quota and Corporate Revenue," by Jim Keenan and Barbara Giamanco, 2013.)

> ➤ In B2B organizations using social selling, 21 percent more sales reps met sales quota and 31 percent more sales teams achieved quota. (Research Brief: "Social Selling: Leveraging the Power of User Generated Content to Optimize Sales Results," published by Aberdeen Group, February 2012; distributed on SlideShare.)

> ➤ 67 percent of B2C companies surveyed use Facebook to generate leads, and 43 percent say they get leads from Twitter. ("State of Digital Marketing 2012 Report," Webmarketing123, 2012.)

> ➤ 39 percent of B2C companies receive sales from Facebook and 19 percent land sales from Twitter ("State of Digital Marketing 2012 Report," Webmarketing123, 2012.)

> ➤ 44 percent of B2B companies turn to LinkedIn to generate leads with 23 percent of B2B companies gaining sales from

LinkedIn. ("State of Digital Marketing 2012 Report," Web-marketing123, 2012.)

- 60 percent of best-in-class companies train salespeople in how to engage in online conversations with prospects and customers compared to only 19 percent of laggard companies. (Research Brief: "Social Selling: Leveraging the Power of User Generated Content to Optimize Sales Results," published by Aberdeen Group, February 2012; distributed on SlideShare.)

- Best-in-class companies are three times more likely to identify and utilize external social influencers to support the sales process compared to laggard companies. (Research Brief: "Social Selling: Leveraging the Power of User Generated Content to Optimize Sales Results," published by Aberdeen Group, February 2012; distributed on SlideShare.)

Percentages like those above favoring social selling didn't happen overnight. While I can't pinpoint an exact date that organizations first realized their prospects and customers were on Facebook, Twitter, LinkedIn, and other social networking sites, you have to understand that social media has been in existence for barely a decade. Some of today's most successful social networks, like Facebook and LinkedIn, first made their debuts in the very early part of the twenty-first century, while others, like Twitter, Pinterest, and Google+, have been around for only a few years and yet are boasting record-setting numbers of new users.

Somewhere along the way, people transitioned from using social media merely as a way to commemorate small milestones of their daily lives to using it as a medium for communicating meaningful ideas, building important business relationships, researching products and services, and interacting with brands in a very personal way. It's often said that at some point during the social media transition period, *the power shifted from the brand to the consumer.* From a marketing perspective, this means that brands could no longer send one-way messages to consumers in the form of advertising and think that would be enough. Instead, customers began talking back to brands through social media channels. Marketing has become *a two-way conversation* with the customer.

For sales, the transition to social media's use has been equally startling. Prospective customers no longer come into an organization's sales process at the top of the funnel, seeking general information or awareness of your brand, and wait for the salesperson to guide them through the company's buying process. Instead, *prospects are defining the buying process*. They're using social media to compare their purchasing options; they're turning to their personal and professional online networks to research products and brands before they even talk to a salesperson; and they're listening to what other customers say about those products and brands.

By the time a prospect finally enters your line of vision, they're most likely entering midway (or further!) through the buying process. They've already done their fact finding, narrowed their buying decision to just a few options, and most likely already *established a relationship with the brand*. As a salesperson, your opportunity to influence the sale is minimized. And should you and your organization not make a prospect's cut for consideration, your ability to compete for the deal is unlikely at best. At the very least, the social-media–savvy consumer has made the sales process an uphill battle, putting you somewhat at a disadvantage, particularly if you have not participated in the online conversations.

So how do you navigate the changing sales landscape? Adopting a social selling strategy is the first step to making sure you remain on the map.

But it's more than merely getting on Facebook or Twitter and posting your company brochures. I'm going to give away the entire secret of social selling success right here in the introduction, without you having to read the first chapter! *The Art of Social Selling* is based entirely on your ability to build relationships. It just happens that those relationships are made and developed virtually through social networking sites, blogs, and online communities. Social selling is just another tool for you to use—it's an extension of the traditional sales process that you've already mastered.

If I had to offer one reason why sales and marketing leaders are slow to adopt social selling within their organizations, it's because they've misunderstood it. Often, it's assumed that your organization must completely change to implement an entirely new sales process. But social selling is an *extension* of what *sales and marketing teams are already doing*, and integrating it becomes a matter of tweaking procedures and learning how to have persuasive conversations through social media instead of exclusively through the phone, email, or face-to-face meetings. Adopting a social selling strategy is really no different than the changes you make when incorporating any other modern sales tool.

In this book, I provide you with the resources you need to start building toward social selling success. If you're new to social media, don't worry. I'll help you understand key terms and give you a sufficient overview of the various social networking sites so that you can understand how to implement the principles and basic strategies I'll be sharing with you. Of course, you've got to go into this process acknowledging that mastering social selling takes time and persistence. So, be patient, but be diligent, and it will pay off!

As you begin building your social strategy, there's another important point to keep in mind. The only thing constant about social media is that it continually changes. New social media platforms and applications emerge, while existing social networking sites evolve to reach new and sometimes different target audiences. Likewise, the features and tools that are prominent on social networking sites today may be removed, modified, or replaced with different features tomorrow. One of the most challenging aspects of writing a book about social media is keeping pace with all of the new and improved features and sites that are continually being introduced. It's nearly an impossible task. However, I think it's important that you, as a reader, have continued access to any critical changes or updates to the social selling process. For this reason, I'm offering you a way to keep up with the most important changes through my website, www .ArtofSocialSelling.com. There, you can gain exclusive access to social selling updates and additional content (including some content that didn't make it into the book). Once on the website, look for the tab "Exclusive Content" and then enter the password: socialone. It's that simple!

Oh, there's just one more thing before you begin reading. As I mentioned, everything about social selling revolves around the relationship between you and your future customer. For that reason, it would be unfortunate if I didn't begin this book with an invitation for you to connect with me! Here are the ways you and I can start to get to know one another and for you to join the conversation:

Twitter: www.twitter.com/ShannonBelew

LinkedIn: www.linkedin.com/in/ShannonBelew

Google+: www.gplus.to/ShannonBelew

Facebook: www.facebook.com/OnlineMarketingToGo

If you have any questions or comments about the book, or simply want to engage as a sales or marketing professional, I look forward to hearing from you!

THE ART OF SOCIAL SELLING

CHAPTER 1

FISHING IN SOCIAL PONDS

Using Social Media as a Prospecting Tool for Online Sales

Why should you care about using social media as a sales and marketing tool? There are actually 1.48 billion reasons, and the number is growing daily.

If you are part of an organization that wants to grow sales, then reaching new customers is critical to your success. That means social media will become increasingly important to you. Consider that there are currently over one billion people active on the top social networks.[1] These networks include LinkedIn, Twitter, Facebook, and Google +. If you are able to make contact with even one-tenth of one percent of them, then you have reached more than one million people. When was the last time you made contact with one million potential customers—without having to pay an arm and a leg for advertising during a major televised sporting event? What's more, when was the last time that you reached out to that many people and actually had some type of meaningful conversation?

Does becoming active on social networks guarantee you will capture a million leads, or even hundreds of thousands of leads? No, of course not; but fishing in social ponds holds real potential for reaching a high number of high-quality prospects.

Before going any further, consider these two statements about sales and social media:

1. The sales and marketing process has been forever changed; if you do not adapt, then your social-savvy competitors will leave you (and your sales quota) in the dust.

2. If you want to gain new customers, there is only one way to reach them today—and that's by aggressively selling through social media channels.

One of these two statements is an exaggeration. Do you know which one?

If you chose the second statement as being an overstatement, give yourself a prize—and continue reading. If you thought the first sentence was wrong, then it's a darn good thing you are reading this book!

The sales and marketing process—the way in which you identify prospects and convert them into customers—has drastically changed with the advent of social media. In fact, you have probably heard experts make some pretty bold statements about the sales process, such as: "The traditional sales funnel no longer exists." "Solution selling is dead." "By the time a prospect first makes contact with you, they have already narrowed down the buying decision to their top choices." "Inbound marketing is critical to lead generation." "Social media marketing is a necessary evil for customer acquisition."

There is truth to all of these statements. Customers are making more educated buying decisions. They are doing their own research online. They are being influenced by peers, brands, and total strangers—and much of that influence is happening across social media channels. This really isn't a new concept, but it has taken a while for the actual sales process to evolve and catch up to what has been happening with social media.

I still remember the first time I heard about a company using social media to talk to a prospective customer. By 2010, hotels and other businesses were getting more accustomed to seeing social media used as a customer service tool, even if they didn't yet fully understand how to use that tool. Customers were talking to Twitter and other platforms to complain and businesses were struggling to find the best way to handle that public scrutiny. But some businesses were catching on and starting to see the social customer service dilemma as a social selling opportunity. I realized this when hearing the story of a customer of a fairly well-known hotel in California. In short, the hotel messed up the customer's reservation and it looked like she might not have a place to stay. Aggravated, the customer publicly tweeted her frustration on Twitter. This tweet caught the attention of a competing hotel in the area—most likely because they were either monitoring their competition on Twitter or watching for certain keywords (such as "hotel"). When this particular tweet showed up, the competing hotel was able to respond quickly and directly—and publicly—to the customer.

Did the hotel offer a free room or deep discount to switch reservations? No. It simply tweeted back that they were sorry to hear about the situation and suggested that the next time the customer was in the area, the hotel would be happy to help take care of her and make her stay relaxing and stress-free. As a result, the hotel got a lot of attention and reportedly a nice bump in reservations.

As someone who tracks online marketing trends and writes about how to use online tools for business, I was immediately captivated by the potential represented by that single tweet. Before long, I was not only doing a lot of talking about tapping into social media as a tool to reach customers, but I was using it myself as a way to generate leads for a company in the telecommunications industry. Using social media to interact with prospective customers is not really all that new. Most companies initially started using it as a way to generate brand awareness and as an extension of their customer service efforts. Only recently have companies started recognizing and regularly using social media as a sales tool—beyond simply placing ads on social networks. In particular, there has been quite a lot of buzz recently about the term "social selling." We will discuss that shortly, but first let's get back to those two statements about social media and take a look at why one is rather misleading—and why it matters to you.

TACKLING THE EVER-CHANGING SALES PROCESS

As sentence number one indicates, the companies and salespeople (your competitors) that understand the expanding role of social media in the buying process are the ones who are winning new customers and exceeding sales quotas. In December 2012, Mike Drapeau, the cofounder and managing partner of the Sales Benchmark Index (SBI), predicted that the quota attainment rate, conventionally measured as the percentage of sales reps who make their number, a rate that has traditionally hovered around 60 percent, will go up to 75 percent, permanently.[2] He believes there is a single reason for this rise in quota attainment rate: It is based on gains in sales productivity from social selling.

Mike has made a career analyzing and publishing trends in the areas of sales process, lead generation, and sales productivity (to name just a few areas). As part of the SBI team, he regularly consults for companies such as HP, Adobe, Dow Jones, Eloqua, and many more, with the purpose of helping them expand revenues. Mike has an established track record for understanding what it takes to move the needle on sales quotas and real revenue growth, so given his experience, it's particularly interesting that he placed a specific condition on his most recent prediction about the sales process. He makes the point that *only* the companies who understand social selling will bump that quota attainment rate up to 75 percent; the rest will continue to see rates closer to 60 percent.

Mike Drapeau is not the only one who recognizes the potential that social selling has within today's sales organizations. A 2012 study on social selling from the research firm Aberdeen Group indicated that sales reps who have leveraged social selling in their sales process are 79 percent more likely to attain their quota than ones who don't.[3] This research supports the contention in sentence number one that those organizations and sales professionals that adapt to the social selling process will see positive revenue and sales quota results, while those that don't find a way to fully embrace the social selling process are likely to be left behind.

You may be wondering why, if social media is so critical to the new sales process, there is anything wrong with the second statement. This was tricky. Sentence number two actually has two flaws. The first flaw? It makes the assumption that social media is the *only* way to attain new customers. But social selling is not meant to replace all other sales and marketing processes. While there is no denying that some of the traditional methods have changed, they haven't disappeared—nor should they. Mastering social selling simply means adding another tool to your sales and marketing toolkit.

The second flaw is found in the phrase "sell aggressively through social channels." It's very important to realize that potential customers who are active on social media are sensitive to the use of social platforms as delivery vehicles for blatant sales pitches. That's why *aggressive* selling techniques are likely to be ignored on social media.

So now you know what *not* to do. Let's take a look at how to do it right.

THE SOCIAL SELLING MANTRA

There has been a noticeable shift in how customers engage with companies and what, or who, influences the decision to buy. This is true whether you are selling to consumers (B2C) or to businesses (B2B), whether you are selling breath mints or accounting software. Your ability to successfully engage with customers early in the lead-generation process sets the tone for the entire life cycle with that customer. It not only comes down to how you interact but when and where you interact with customers. In this case, both the value of the information you provide to the prospect and the quality of the relationship you build are critical to getting and keeping customers. Equally imperative is that you start online conversations with prospects early. To do that, you have to know where your prospective customers are hanging out (on social media)—because this is where customer relationships start, today.

Because the process of social selling is still developing, you may hear it explained in various ways. In its simplest form, it's tempting to say that social selling is a matter of selling products and services over a social network, such as Facebook or Twitter. That's somewhat of an oversimplification of the term "social network," and is also misleading because it suggests a medium that is a one-way form of communication not much different from using advertising to sell via the television or other traditional media outlets. The process of social selling is much more robust and utilizes a two-way form of communications, where both the sender and receiver of the message are interacting and responding to each other. That's why I prefer to define the concept in this way:

> **Social selling:** the identification, targeting, and reaching out to prospective and existing customers through social media channels and social communities in an effort to engage them in conversations that result in a potentially mutually beneficial relationship.

It may also be useful to identify what social selling is *not*. Social selling is not like buying a list of leads and cold calling everyone on the list. It is not a disruptive process, where you merely spit out a series of marketing messages, lead-generation offers, or coupons and discounts.

Nor is social selling the equivalent of lead scraping. This is a big one. For some reason, when I'm working with salespeople who are trying to sell through social media for the first time, they are sometimes under the impression that you scan conversations on social networks and then pluck out the people who even vaguely reference a potential need for your product. Once you get a name, you run it through a data cleanup process to get a phone number and bam, just like that, you've scraped a lead from Twitter and dropped it into your

Customer Relationship Management (CRM) program of choice. It doesn't quite work that way. You may get lucky, but it's not best practices as social selling goes. I discuss this in detail in Chapter 4, along with the art of *un*-selling in social media.

"*Un*-selling" is something you will hear a lot about when talking about prospecting via social media. In other words, using a sales pitch and basing a good bit of that pitch on your product or service will not work anymore. Instead, social selling requires being more social (listening and conversing about the customer's needs) and much less about outright selling. It's a very soft sell, or perhaps a consultative sell. Refer back to the example of the two hotels and the unhappy customer. The competing hotel's response to the customer is a great example of *un*-selling.

At the heart of social selling is relationship building, which is based on establishing trust and offering value. For most salespeople, this should come as good news. After all, the traditional sales process is about just that—relationships. For many marketers, this should also be welcome information because social selling is based on building brand trust. In other words, these are sales and marketing concepts you should be comfortable with by now. It's only a matter of extending those concepts to a new platform—social media.

WHERE TO GO FISH

When it comes to social selling, I like using the analogy of fishing. Fishing in social ponds is very similar to the real-world art of fishing. It's relatively enjoyable, even relaxing for some, and can be a nice hobby to pass the time. But while it seems like a pretty straightforward process, professional fishers will tell you it actually takes thought, planning, and the right tools to make a lucrative haul. The same can be said for social selling. You can dabble in it and may even get lucky and get a bite after only limited effort. If you want to be good at it, and successful enough to sustain yourself in terms of sales and revenue quotas, then you need to get serious about the process. Like fishing, you need to know what kind of fish you want to catch, where and when those fish are typically biting, and what type of bait (or tackle) the fish prefer. So, where are those social ponds?

As I have already mentioned, there are some well-known social networks where lots of productive sales conversations get started. But when talking about social selling, it's important to broaden the idea of what constitutes a social gathering place. The following is an overview of the types of places you need to be social in order to start selling:

> **Social media networks:** Traditional social media networks include sites such as Facebook, Twitter, Google+, and LinkedIn. These are established outlets where lots of conversations are flowing and where the number of active users continues to rise. It's easy to start or jump into conversations on these networks, as well as to find and respond to questions or comments relating to your product or service.

> **Visual social networks:** These are what I consider second-tier social media networks that evolved somewhat later and are based more on imagery and graphics, but that have proven to be huge, active social networks. This type of network includes YouTube, Pinterest, Instagram, and Slide-Share. These networks provide a way for you to literally show what your company can offer customers, and they provide the ideal opportunity for a prospective customer to comment on and share your message with others via a visual presentation, infographic, photo, or video.

> **Blogs:** These started as online personal diaries, and have become part news and information resource and part community. Bloggers have also become sought-after influencers because they often have many loyal followers who turn to blog posts as a source for trends, product reviews, and referrals. The beauty of a blog is that it often has a narrow focus (again, it makes it easy to identify your target customer), and it's easy for you to become an active commenter on blog articles and a contributing member of that blog community. And

becoming a contributing member of the community is the best way of developing brand recognition for your company—or developing yourself as a brand in your own right.

➤ **Communities:** Similar to traditional social networks, online communities are places where people with similar interests or skills gather to discuss and exchange ideas, or participate in events based on their joint interest. A community can be based on a particular professional skill (such as a specific programming language) or a casual interest (such as gardening—or fishing!). Spiceworks™, for example, is a tech community geared to IT professionals and GreensKeeper is an online community for golf enthusiasts. Communities are great places to find and target potential customers because you immediately know they have an interest or skill that relates to your product or service.

➤ **Answer hubs and groups:** These are typically sections found within social networks or communities, but a few are stand-alone. Regardless, I think it's important to treat them as a separate entity because they take time and effort to participate in, and the conversations are slightly different from the type of conversation you may participate in elsewhere. For instance, on LinkedIn there are many groups that are based on professional skills or interests, like online marketing professionals. Within each group specific topics and conversations that may not show up on your regular LinkedIn profile feed are taking place—and if you want to participate, you may have to actively work to find them. Similarly, there are sites, like Quora, where visitors can ask specific questions and elicit responses from other members. Answer hubs are great places to look for and answer questions that may pertain to your company's product or service.

➤ **Online media/news sites:** While these websites may seem the furthest thing away from a source for social selling, they are actually lucrative places to connect with prospective customers. Like blogs, most traditional and online news sources encourage readers to register, set up a public profile, and become an active, contributing commenter on the site. News sites can attract a large audience, and may even be segmented by interests (entertainment outlets, technology or business, beauty, shopping, etc.). Again, these sites provide the opportunity for you to identify conversations that are important to your prospects, participate in those conversations, and provide a presence for your company or brand in a place where your customers are gathered.

As you can see, when talking about social networks, there are actually lots of different places and ways to get involved and start the social selling process. Although I have referenced some of the ways you may engage on these different sites, more specific details are provided in later chapters in this book. In addition to the methodologies for social selling specific to each type of site, you can also expect to learn more about the types of tools you should use to get and track results from your efforts. I also review what you should expect in terms of budgeting time and resources for an extended social selling campaign and provide tips for persuading decision makers and other team members that social selling is a worthwhile endeavor for your company.

SOCIAL SELLING IS A TEAM SPORT

There's one other detail about social selling that might be helpful for you to understand from the beginning. As an individual salesperson or marketer, whatever your position within the company, you can rack up some impressive wins when it comes to finding and selling to social customers. That said, in order to make substantial headway on social networks, you need a team to support your efforts. As already mentioned, there are lots of places where social selling works well. There are almost too many places! Trust me when I say it takes a lot of time to consistently interact on social networks, especially if you do it the right way. Don't panic. In Chapter 10, you will learn how to create and execute a plan to accomplish your selling goals. You will see how important it is to have other team members who can share in the responsibility of making your social selling plan a reality on a daily basis.

There's one other reason you need a team to help you. In this case, I'm specifically referring to a cross-functional team of members coming from sales, marketing, and customer support. This is beneficial because your customers are using social media to meet their needs, too, whether it's a place to research companies, elicit peer reviews of products or services, look for discounts and other buying incentives, get tech support on a product, or air grievances and make their frustration with a company known (just like that woman at the hotel in California). In order for you to use those same networks for selling, you need to make sure your team is working together to help clear the path for selling to occur and create a positive view of your brand—otherwise, you may end up spending your social selling time fielding tech support and customer service questions.

—

So, how do you organize your teams to boost social selling? Keep reading. In Chapter 2, we dive right into mastering the social triangle of online sales success.

CHAPTER 2

THE SOCIAL TRIANGLE OF ONLINE SALES SUCCESS

Bringing Together Social Marketing, Social Commerce, and Social Support

The on-again, off-again relationship between sales and marketing is not a new struggle. For most organizations, there is a continuous balancing act—sometimes an outright tug-of-war—that occurs between these two internal powerhouses when it comes to the customer acquisition strategy. It often results in a blame game that encompasses everything from the quality of marketing collateral and sales presentations to the effectiveness of callback strategies and lead-conversion rates.

Just when you were getting accustomed to this family feud, along comes social media to add more fireworks to the mix. The idea that you can use social networking platforms, such as LinkedIn and Twitter, to influence corporate revenue growth only increases the importance of having a strategic relationship between your company's sales and marketing teams. Yet, deciding the role each team should play within social media is yet another source of frustration within many organizations.

There's the traditional pushback from both camps. Each one claims, "It's not my job!" That attitude is typically rooted in a general lack of understanding about the importance of social media in the modern marketing and sales process. For many salespeople and marketers, there remains the perception that tweets and Facebook posts are frivolous comments about what you ate for lunch or how angry you are because someone just cut you off in traffic. For those who decide to embrace this brave new world of converting the social customer, the real challenge comes in simply figuring out how sales and marketing should collaborate.

Why bother, you ask? Resolving the issue of cross-team integration for social marketing purposes comes with a big reward. In some cases, annual company revenue could increase by as much as 20 percent when there is healthy alignment with sales and marketing, according to research from the Aberdeen Group.[1]

Before I get into how to start the collaborative process so that everyone wins the revenue game, there's one more small but potentially fatal weakness. When it comes to social selling, there is a third component that must be added to the sales and marketing mix and that's the role of customer service. Together, these three stakeholders make up the triangle of social success. Let's take a closer look to see why each has a real stake in the game.

MEETING THE DEMANDS OF THE SOCIAL CUSTOMER

There are skeptics who see social media's role in business as nothing more than serving as a public platform for customer complaints. It is true that consumers have embraced social media as a preferred method of brand engagement because it gives them a voice—often, a very loud voice. And, that very loud, very public consumer voice presents a tricky issue for your company.

Traditionally, customer service has been handled offline and out of sight of the rest of your customers. Most likely, if a customer has had a question about your product or service, or is upset about something, she would have only a handful of options: contact you (her sales or account representative) directly; call an 800 number and speak with someone from a customer support call center (which may or may not be based inside the company); send an email to a generic customer service account found on your website; or write a letter (the kind that must be delivered by the U.S. Postal Office—yes, these do still exist!). In each of these cases, you have always had the upper hand. The ball is firmly planted in your court on how, or if, you want to resolve the issue.

As a salesperson or marketer, you know that an unhappy customer translates into one less positive referral, or one fewer customer testimonials for your next slick, corporate brochure. For the customer service department, these unhappy customers may represent a minor, downward tick in one or more customer response reports. But, more than likely, in the traditional service model, that same unhappy customer would not have passed across desks in sales and marketing as well as in customer service. Unless, of course, it was a truly serious issue that had to be escalated to upper management (think food poisoning at a restaurant chain or the report of numerous pieces of faulty equipment at a manufacturing company). In which case, the issue was likely to jump from a low-level entry point, like customer service, straight to the CEO or legal department before trickling down to everyone else's desks. That was then.

Today, social media has turned much of that staid, stale customer service process on its head. Suddenly, everyone in the company must care, every time.

In its "Social Media Report 2012," Nielsen reported that 47 percent of social media users engaged in "social care," or the use of social media for the purpose of customer service.[2] Additionally, 70 percent of those customers claimed to access social care on a monthly basis. Granted, that last number may seem like a red flag, possibly signaling a small group of active customers who are abusing the access that social media provides to companies. However, social care can mean a lot of different things, from a prospective customer asking for product information or other types of product research to a prospect asking to be put in touch with one of your salespersons. The point is that not all social care incidents are complaints. These new interactions also are not limited to your company's Facebook page or Twitter account. Social customers look for support everywhere, from YouTube videos to non-company blogs, such as industry-related blogs and forums.

As the Nielsen report so nicely sums up, the new reality is that, "Customers choose when and where they voice their questions, issues and complaints, blurring the line between marketing and customer service." I would add that social care not only blurs the lines, but it brings with it the potential to impair your entire sales process, both online and offline.

Here are the challenges that social care presents to your company and, ultimately, to your sales pipeline:

- ➤ **The curtain is pulled back:** No longer can you hide problems behind a phone line. If a customer puts an issue out on social media to be addressed, then it's the equivalent of broadcasting it through the radio. Anyone tuned in to that channel has the potential to hear it. That means prospects, customers, and competitors have equal access to your customers' comments; how you responded to or handled the issues; and whether or not the issues were successfully resolved. And if you choose not to reply at all? Well, ignoring a customer is never a good idea, and is handily rejected in any customer service playbook. When it happens on social media, your lack of response is all that much more visible. To sum it up, the power has shifted from you (the company) to the social consumer.

- ➤ **Competitors gain behind-the-scenes access:** As I mentioned above, everyone who cares to listen now has access to this public customer service channel. It's great information to have, too. A competitor can swoop in on an unhappy customer and initiate a conversation about the alternatives to your company's solution. Similarly, competitors use social care as an opportunity to spot your prospects, those potential customers who may have you on the short list as a product or service provider.

Almost as important to point out is the access that social care gives to seemingly harmless information. For instance, perhaps a customer simply asks whether your product supports a particular device or application, or wants to know when an updated version of your solution will be available. Whatever information you provide is visible; and if that means chatting about a future product release, then you may inadvertently give away some key corporate data that wasn't officially ready for public consumption.

➤ **Immediacy is expected:** Social care warrants a faster response than you may be able to provide. Edison Research shows that 25 percent of customers expect a response within one day when contacting a company via social media, and 12 percent expect to hear back within thirty minutes.[3] While about one-third of those surveyed were generous enough to allow "a few days or so," it's clear that serving your customers through social media channels can easily become an around-the-clock initiative, especially if you have customers in other countries.

What happens if your customer service team can't keep pace? The worst-case scenario, according to results from Oracle's recent "RightNow Customer Experience Impact Report," shows that consumers will stop doing business with you if they don't receive a response within a week.[4] It isn't that customers who engage with you online are more impatient or less forgiving than other customers. It's simply the nature of the beast. Social media is a channel for fluent, often real-time communications and consumers, and your customers have become conditioned to expect a rapid response.

➤ **Established, internal processes are interrupted:** Perhaps one of the biggest—and, often most frustrating—parts of social care is that it doesn't fit neatly into your current customer service procedures or customer support guidelines. This is where the lines really begin to blur. Who is responsible for managing and routing customer issues that originate out of social media? Who is supposed to respond—and how or through which channel? What if the issue requires a more complicated technical answer? Is it appropriate to contact the person outside the social network?

Technical support questions can pose particularly unique challenges for companies that have paid support models in which customers must pay to have access to some level of support for particular products or services. I have also seen the challenges social care presents for technology companies that have open source, or free, products. These companies are often strapped for resources and struggle to provide support through traditional customer service channels, even before social care is added to the mix. The problem boils down to trying to merge the "process" of social care issues into your traditional methods of customer service. Does "square peg, round hole" ring a bell?

➤ **Lack of information to meet system requirements:** Finally, consider that many companies now use Customer Relationship Management (CRM) software or third-party solutions to track all sorts of customer interactions. As you may already know, in customer support these solutions basically allow you to create "virtual" support tickets and to log responses. Or, in sales, they let you create a lead that can be tracked from the top of the sales funnel to the very bottom, whether the prospect buys or doesn't. CRM solutions are often used by both customer service and sales and, increasingly, by marketing teams, but there may or may not be one solution used across all departments. You don't have to be part of a big organization to do battle with a CRM. Because CRM solutions are now more affordable and easy to manage, they are becoming widely used by all sizes of businesses. This includes even very small, one-person operations.

What do CRM solutions and their adoption rates have to do with social care? These solutions often require a certain amount of information about the customer in order to bring it into the system and create a lead or support ticket. With social media, you may not even have access to a person's full name, let alone an email address or phone number. Like your internal processes, the software systems that you use to support those processes are traditionally not set up to support social care.

In Chapter 7, I cover lots of other types of tools and applications that are helpful as part of the social selling process, including some innovative CRM solutions. Here I will simply point out that there are CRM solutions that are beginning to provide a formal way to introduce into the system the customer who originates from social media. This initiative with CRM systems is still in its infancy, however. So the challenge remains—for now.

CAPTURING THE CUSTOMER EXPERIENCE

No matter which, if any, CRM solution you use, and regardless of your company's processes for tracking customer service issues, handling social care presents some interesting opportunities. It's also clear that customer service is an important link in the social selling chain. As an example, think about the challenges I detailed above, and then consider the following social care scenario.

Imagine a customer asks your company a question, using Twitter. To make it really interesting, let's say that an intern from the marketing department is the one who first sees the question and then sends it in an email that's copied to the entire inside sales team. One of the salespersons reads it and determines the question is a support issue. She then forwards the email to customer service. All the customer service representatives are busy taking calls and ignore the in-house email, considering it to be a lower priority. Sometime the next day, the email gets someone's attention in customer service. It turns out to be a simple question that merely required directing the customer to one of the company's online support pages. The customer service representative responds to the intern's original email, sending her the response, which includes a link to the website. Unfortunately, the intern only works three days a week and is out of the office until the following Monday.

In the meantime, the customer's original question is still hanging out in the public sphere, awaiting an answer. And, anyone who sees the question in Twitter can also see that no one has responded to it, at least not publicly. As a reminder, the marketing team has set up your company's Twitter feed so that it automatically populates on the sidebar of every page of your website and company blog. That means the latest tweets about your company are constantly in view to your website visitors, even if they don't normally follow you on Twitter.

Obviously, there are many problem points within this scenario, and marketing, sales, and customer service each contributed to the poor handling of the customer request. By the way, while this may seem a worst-case situation that would rarely occur, I can assure you it's not all that uncommon. I've even witnessed this one firsthand! Here are the highlights of what went wrong:

- **Slow response:** It took far too long to get an answer to the customer.

- **Wasted time:** Too many people were unnecessarily included in the process, making it a potential time waster, especially for the sales team.

- **Faulty process:** The hand-off process was broken. The lack of a defined path made it impossible to provide what should have been a quick answer to a simple question; at the very least, the intern should have acknowledged the tweet and let the customer know someone from the company was working on a response.

- **Lack of ownership:** No stakeholder, or anyone with actual authority, had ownership of the process. This made it easy for

the request to slip through the cracks, and go too long without a response.

As a result of a situation like this, your customer walks away with
a negative experience that she is likely to share with hundreds or
thousands of her social media connections. Potentially, the delay in
response also gave one of your competitors the opportunity to start a
conversation with the customer and show that they are actively
engaged in the process of social listening. At the very least, both competitors and prospective customers have seen you drop the ball and
may see it as a reflection of how you treat customers.

On the flip side, I recently experienced a similar situation on
Twitter that was handled almost flawlessly. It's a great example of
how easy it is to respond to a social media request. Figure 2–1 shows
my brief exchange on Twitter with the company, LivePerson. In a
happy coincidence, they had tweeted results of some research about
how quickly customers expect to receive help when making online
purchases. In case you skim over the tweets, allow me to point out
that five minutes (yes, five!) is all the time that customers are willing
to wait for assistance before leaving and going somewhere else,
according to their research. Because I was writing about this very
topic when I received the tweet, I felt compelled to ask a question
and test their own social media responsiveness. I was pleasantly surprised to have my tweet acknowledged within a minute or two. While
LivePerson's social media team couldn't provide an immediate
answer to my question (I really wasn't trying to stump them, I was
simply curious—I promise!), they did offer to hunt down the answer
and get back with me. Though I flirted with the possibility that I
would never hear back, LivePerson followed through on their promise. It took a full day to hear back, but I got my answer—and I felt
good about the interaction.

That said, when critiquing LivePerson's interaction, there is
something they could have done better. Most definitely they get an
A+ for "active social listening"—that is, monitoring their social
media channels for comments and questions related to their brand. I
give them another A+ for a quick initial response and for following

FIGURE 2-1

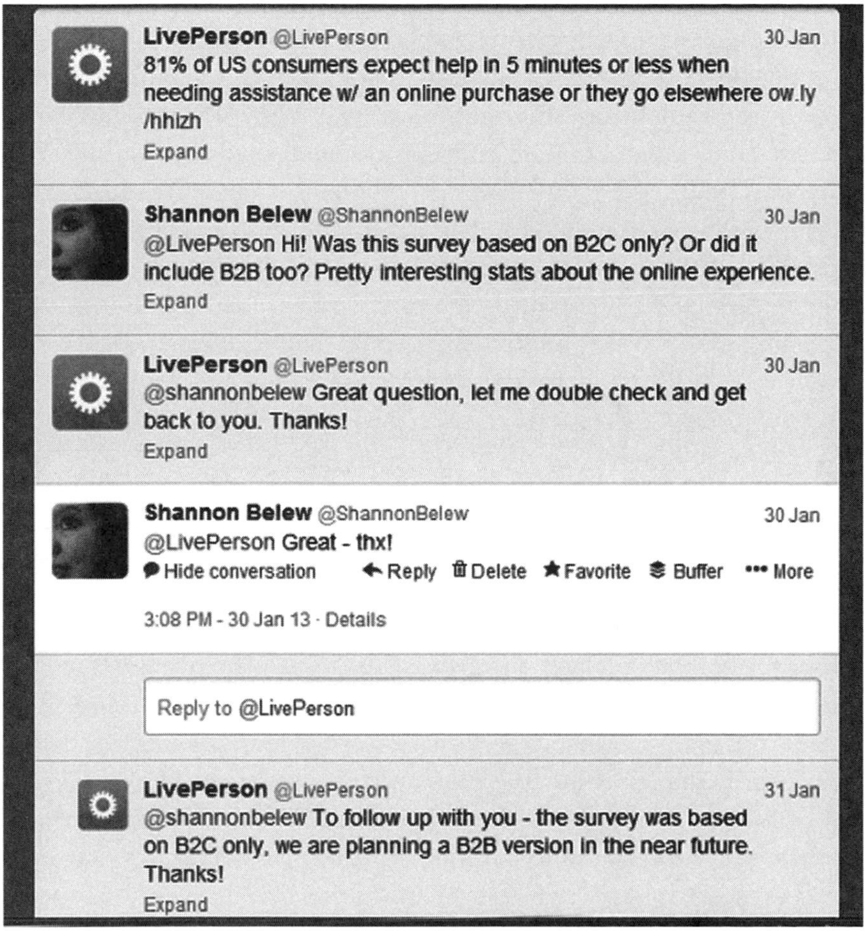

LivePerson @LivePerson   30 Jan
81% of US consumers expect help in 5 minutes or less when
needing assistance w/ an online purchase or they go elsewhere ow.ly
/hhizh
Expand

Shannon Belew @ShannonBelew   30 Jan
@LivePerson Hi! Was this survey based on B2C only? Or did it
include B2B too? Pretty interesting stats about the online experience.
Expand

LivePerson @LivePerson   30 Jan
@shannonbelew Great question, let me double check and get
back to you. Thanks!
Expand

Shannon Belew @ShannonBelew   30 Jan
@LivePerson Great - thx!
♥ Hide conversation   ← Reply 🗑 Delete ★ Favorite ⧉ Buffer ••• More

3:08 PM - 30 Jan 13 · Details

Reply to @LivePerson

LivePerson @LivePerson   31 Jan
@shannonbelew To follow up with you - the survey was based
on B2C only, we are planning a B2B version in the near future.
Thanks!
Expand

through and providing an answer to my question. After that, however, their performance falters *because they didn't successfully flag me as a potential lead*. In other words, the hand-off to sales didn't happen.

From a prospective customer's viewpoint, LivePerson did everything right. But they missed an opportunity—a social selling opportunity. Don't misunderstand. It would not have been appropriate for

LivePerson to ask me if I wanted to see a demo of their solution—that would have been a bit too much, too soon. However, I expressed an interest in what they were saying, and I was asking for specific information. Because they let me know that information would be available in the near future, it would have been perfectly reasonable for them to offer to send me the information once it was obtainable. This way, they would potentially capture my name and email address. Or, they could have asked if I would like to be added to an email list to get updates about this or similar research—again, capturing my contact information and transitioning me out of social media and into their internal sales process so that they could begin to nurture me as a lead.

TAKING SHAPE AND CONNECTING ALL THE DOTS

While this chapter could very easily focus only on the importance of taking care of your customers through social media, there's obviously much more to it. After all, the crux of the book is learning *how to sell through social media*. And doing that successfully requires a united front from your customer service, marketing, and sales teams. As the previous examples show, it's easy for the sales process to get overlooked when marketing is busy educating prospects without also focusing on pulling them through the sales funnel; or for the sales process to get halted when poor customer service impedes the opportunity to sell socially. It's also possible that each of your teams may be doing their respective jobs well, and yet, collectively, you're not excelling when it comes to increasing conversions and growing revenue through social media channels.

Collaboration is often easier said than done. Whether you're in sales or marketing or customer service, there is a risk in deciding to work with others. Each group has something to gain or lose and a change in any process can negatively impact a myriad of goals by which each is measured. For sales, there is often concern with how process impacts commissions and pipeline; marketing may be fighting for a bigger budget and more control over systems; and customer support may be wrapped up in protecting recurring revenues and meeting already tight customer service metrics. It's hard enough to fight your own battles. It can become particularly frustrating when you are told that your welfare is now closely tied to another group's performance. But as the saying goes, with great risk comes great reward.

I might argue that bringing together these three groups to attempt social selling is hardly risky. But I have heard plenty of horror stories to the contrary! This is usually the point where I might insert one of those horrifying stories of the clash of the sales and marketing titans, and try to put a humorous spin on it. Instead, I want to share an interesting fact about hawks.

Have you ever watched a hawk circling its prey? If so, you probably saw not only one hawk, but several of them hovering in the skies. I used to think the large number of birds meant a large animal had already bitten the dust and it was now easy pickings for all the feasting creatures in close proximity. It turns out that's not the case, at least where the breed of Harris hawk is concerned. This type of hawk exhibits a rare form of social behavior when it comes to pursuing its food source. Harris hawks are quite organized, and work together in groups of at least five or six when hunting prey. This socialized hunting strategy has earned them the nickname "wolves of the sky." It's also earned the Harris hawk the reputation as one of the best hunters. You might see one or two of the birds in a group watch for or track a likely target, while the others implement an orchestrated flight focused on pursuing and capturing the prey. Hunting in a group also allows the hawks to watch out for and protect against other competitors that may want the same prized prey.

Notice any similarities between the social hunting strategy of the Harris hawk and the collaborative approach to social selling? While I'm not suggesting you or any of your colleagues go after a prospect in social media like a predator going in for a kill, I am pointing out that it's possible to devise a strategy for effectively working together to both generate more leads across social networks and to deter competitors from taking advantage of poorly handled social interactions with your customers and prospects.

Social selling barriers are often rooted in an organization's internal chaos, or a lack of formal commitment and structured plan. These barriers not only lead to poor customer support and missed sales opportunities, but to a diminished amount of trust in the brand by the company's customers. How do you bring together sales, marketing, and customer service to combat these barriers?

Successful integration across departments for a social selling model requires the following:

> ➤ **Buy-in from key stakeholders:** Rarely does any type of corporate change get approval for launch, let alone have staying power, without the backing of key executives. When it comes to a structured, integrated social selling plan, this means getting buy-in all the way up to the vice-presidents of each team, and possibly the stamp of approval from the CEO. That's because many companies are still contemplating how much time to spend on social media in general, let alone considering using the time of top-performing salespersons. It's also helpful to also have a champion, someone who is passionate about the opportunity social selling holds, to help sell the idea to all the stakeholders.

> ➤ **Clearly defined roles across each of the teams:** Especially in the beginning, it's probably not necessary for every person in all three core teams (marketing, sales, and customer service) to be involved with social selling. Identify one or two people from each team who can take the lead. Make it clear what each person's role is and create a written definition of those roles to ensure everyone agrees with the plan.

> ➤ **Development of a formal process:** This really comes down to defining the hand-off between divisions. Once you know the individual roles, it's much easier to map out a formal process. It must spell out who will be responsible for different points in the process, how social media leads will be identified and passed to sales, how social care issues will be responded to, the acceptable time frame for response for

each, and when and how these customer support issues and lead opportunities will be integrated into your other CRM solutions or other in-house processes/applications.

> **Shared resources across departments, when necessary:** In reality, especially in smaller organizations, there may not be unlimited resources (time, people, budget) to dedicate to social selling. This is where integration across teams becomes particularly important. You may need to share resources.

  Yes, share! That may mean that a team member from customer service is loaned to the marketing department to help monitor social media channels and route requests and responses. Or, it may be that a member of your sales team is needed to help not only respond to sales requests, but also to participate in social conversations (something that has been traditionally assumed to be a marketing role).

> **Commitment of adequate resources, including budget and time:** There are never enough resources to go around. But when developing an integrated social selling strategy across multiple departments, it's very important to formally allocate adequate budget and staff and get all stakeholders to agree on it.

> **Agreement on the social media platforms to receive your focus**: Often, various teams (or team members) will have a favorite social media network, the one where they feel most comfortable. You may be the same way. If you spend most of your time on Facebook, you want to make sure that's where you start your social selling endeavors. While there is an advantage to being familiar with the social media outlet, you also want to make sure it is the right place for your company to start selling. Is it really the network where your customers are? How many social networks can your team reasonably manage to monitor and engage? You can't be everywhere— and you don't need to be. So agree ahead of time which social media platforms are right for your business and ripe with your active prospects and customers.

➤ **Ability to identify and transition the social "hand-off" to the appropriate team:** Knowing when and how to hand off a sales lead is critical. Set aside time for your integrated team to discuss what qualifies as a warm lead in social selling and how and when it should be passed to someone (and decide to whom) for follow-up outside of the social network where it was identified.

➤ **Implementation and use of tools that assist with the process**: There is a wide range of tools, from social monitoring tools to CRM solutions, that your team can use to make social selling easier. I go into various tools in detail in Chapter 7, but for now, know that it's important for you to identify which tools your teams will use and make sure everyone has access and knows how to use them.

➤ **Integration or modification of existing processes and tools with new applications and procedures**: It's very likely your teams will need to bring in new tools that are more specific to monitoring and managing customer interactions on social media. Take time to discuss how you can marry the new tools with your existing applications and processes.

➤ **Flexibility to make modifications if the approach isn't netting the anticipated results:** Perhaps this is one of the most critical steps when working with an integrated team approach. The social selling process will present some hits and misses for each and all of the sales, marketing, and customer service teams, especially early in the process. Publicly recognize that there will be some trial and error and that things may not go just as you planned. Most importantly, agree that when that happens you won't immediately bail on the process, but will instead work with the teams to make necessary adjustments and tweaks to find a better process for everyone.

Once you, along with the major stakeholders in the organization, have made the commitment to an integrated approach to social selling, the real fun begins! It starts with learning some basic rules of online socializing. No matter how organized and dedicated you are within your company, you can deter or offend even the best prospects if you are not adept at talking with customers on social networking channels. Are you ready to dive into the ten most important rules for social conversations? In Chapter 3, I review everything you need to know to be comfortable chatting online to ensure you are part of a winning conversation.

CHAPTER 3

SPEAKING A NEW LANGUAGE

The Ten Most Important Rules for Online Social Interactions

Finding and targeting prospects on social networks is new territory for everyone—salespeople and marketers alike. For some social media purists, the idea of anyone selling into or making money from social networks is offensive. Other social networking users don't really mind the concept of social selling, but they're still trying to figure out exactly what it means and how it impacts on them. For example, when is it okay for companies to reach out to them (as users), and when does it feel a bit too intrusive or commercial? Because the process of selling through social channels continues to be defined, it's even more important to understand the new language of social networking sites and the rules that go along with social engagement.

There are probably a hundred different rules that I could share with you about having appropriate and positive social interactions as they relate to social selling. The list of things you should do is as long as the list of things you absolutely should *not* do. However, I've narrowed it down to the ten most important things for guiding you through positive online conversations that promote trust and brand loyalty.

This isn't just my list. True, I've spent much time on social media and learned some of these rules through trial and error (or, in some cases, through trial by fire!). But I've also spent a great deal of time interacting with other social media experts, with community managers, and with active users of social networks. I've invested time researching, analyzing behaviors, prodding interviewees and taking notes, and outright asking for feedback. Granted, it wasn't formal research, but I stand by it. The resulting list is focused on the top-level rules of engagement that generally apply across any social network.

In case you're wondering, this list offers pretty good advice, no matter what reason you have for jumping into social media–infused interactions. That said, I have developed this list with an emphasis toward social selling. You will find that these "rules" aren't all that different from the ones you are used to with traditional selling strategies. At first, it may seem that social media is part of a strange new world where people speak in short spurts of acronym-laced partial sentences. In reality, the social media lingo is easy to pick up, and the rules governing this new language are rooted in basic common sense, the same common sense that you already apply to your other customer and prospecting conversations. The guidelines are simply adapted ever so slightly to spur positive interactions when forming online customer relationships.

As you may have noticed, I frequently use the term, "positive interactions." You may also hear the term "engage" or "social engagement" when people talk about social media. That's because industry professionals use engagement as a barometer of success. Simply put, did you get some type of response when you reached out to a person online? Essentially, the goal with online conversations is to engage, or interact. It's no different than making a call to a prospect. If you phoned a prospect, did they answer your call? If you sent an email to a prospect, did they open it and respond to it in some way? In social media, when you reach out to a potential prospect or customer, you want them to acknowledge you and respond in some way. Preferably, you want it to be a positive interaction. The following ten rules are focused on eliciting positive interactions. And while this list is short, it can have a huge impact on your social media efforts.

RULE #1: BE GENUINE

Remember when you were growing up and struggling to make friends for the first time? Adults usually doled out the same advice each time, "Just be yourself." This tried and true advice applies to your interaction on social networks as much as it does in face-to-face situations. For some reason, that golden advice often gets thrown out the window when you are suddenly forced to communicate via a keyboard and hidden behind an avatar (the picture or graphic you use to represent yourself and it shows up next to whatever text you tweet or post). When jumping into social media conversations, people sometimes forgo their otherwise good judgment and decide that this is the time they are going to try their hand at being a stand-up comedian or a political pundit. But let's be clear: *Your social networking persona should be an extension of your actual personality.* And, being yourself is the basis for having genuine exchanges that lead to those positive, lasting interactions that translate to potential customers.

Another term commonly associated with the idea of being genuine in the world of social media is "authenticity." Social media experts are quick to suggest that brands need to "be authentic." I'd like to expand upon that advice, just a bit, in terms of how you develop your personal brand and in turn, the way you represent your company brand. For example, let's say you are known for having an outrageous personality, and have an endless stream of one-liners and jokes that regularly make your boss blush. Even though it's an authentic representation of your personality, there is some value in toning down that wit while on social networks (unless that's how you make your living).

Of course, this example is pretty clear-cut. Sometimes, it's trickier. Authenticity can involve religious and political views that, while authentic to who you are, may get in the way of appealing to and interacting with a diverse social network. Dan Cathy, president and chief operating officer (COO) of the fast food restaurant Chick-fil-A, is an example of an executive who has struggled with the issue of authenticity in social media on more than one occasion. In 2012, Cathy made public statements speaking out against same-sex marriage and admitted that the popular chicken restaurant chain made donations with corporate funds to groups that shared his beliefs on the topic. Within days, the public backlash began to grow and the company used its Facebook page to reassure its fans (and the rest of the social media world!) that it did not discriminate against customers for any reason. But the brand's effort was not enough to put out the social media firestorm that Cathy's words ignited, nor did it stop the nationwide protests that forced loyal customers to choose sides. Less than a year later, the COO was at it, again. In 2013, Cathy tweeted what was considered an anti-gay response to news of a controversial Supreme Court ruling in support of same-sex marriages. The tweet was eventually deleted from Cathy's personal Twitter account; and Chick-fil-A was put in the position of trying to separate the brand's core message from the opinions of its executive.

On one hand, the company and its founding family have always been clear that they maintain "personal and business philosophies based on biblical principles" and conservative values.[1] While Cathy's statements may seem to some in keeping with an ultraconservative outlook, his words are also considered offensive to many of the customers who regularly patronize Chick-fil-A restaurants. As a result, the tweet, which was probably authentic to Cathy, put his business at risk of losing millions of dollars.

The challenge with authenticity on social media can also stem from something much less controversial than Dan Cathy's explosive tweets! In my case, I tend to be very sarcastic in my offline interactions. I quickly learned that sarcasm often doesn't translate well, online. For me, being authentic and genuine means maintaining a balance between my bent toward sarcasm and my ability to generate meaningful, positive conversations with people who only know me through a computer screen.

RULE #2: LISTEN, LISTEN, LISTEN

What makes a salesperson successful? You'll surely get a wide range of responses, including everything from having a passion for what you are selling to having the ability to persuade others. One fairly consistent trait is having the ability to listen—to truly hear what your customer is saying so that you understand her problems and can then present her with a viable solution. The same trait is incredibly valuable when it comes to social networking, but there are a couple of different layers to what I refer to as "active social listening."

As part of the listening process, you first have to monitor conversations. This means you are actively on the lookout for comments coming across social media channels that relate to your company, your products, your competitors, or common industry-specific topics.

In addition to monitoring, or being on the lookout for conversations, once you enter into a conversation with someone on social media, you want to be able to keep that conversation going. You certainly don't want to walk away from the conversation in midstream—just as, if you were having a conversation with someone in person, you would not suddenly walk away from her while she continues to talk, because that would be rude and unprofessional. The same rules apply online. Unfortunately, conversation threads in social media move rapidly, and sometimes you can end up dropping out of a conversation and not even realizing it because you overlooked a response or forgot to get back to it. That's why it's critical to follow the conversation from start to finish and pay attention—to really listen to what the other person or persons are saying. Active social listening gives you a distinct advantage in social selling. It means you are more likely to:

> ➤ Use the monitoring process to find conversations that relate to you.

> ➤ Identify your prospective customer's needs, concerns, and interests.

> ➤ Remain relevant to your prospective customer.

Listening is a powerful sales and marketing tool. I cannot put enough emphasis on the need to practice online listening and put it to use every chance you get.

RULE #3: BE RESPONSIVE

Generally speaking, communication is the act of sending and receiving a signal (or message). However, that communication isn't effective unless the signal is understood and elicits an appropriate response. When it comes to positive social interactions, you certainly hope that people are seeing the information you are sending out over Twitter or your company blog, for example. Most important, you hope that it triggers the desired response. Unfortunately, you don't have control over whether or not that happens. Part of the reason is because there are so many signals going out across social networks today. The sheer volume of messages being sent prevents or decreases the odds that your messages are received every time.

But let's flip that scenario and put *you* on the receiving end of the signals. As I mentioned, a part of your listening goal is to actively monitor so that you receive relevant messages that are being sent out. That means it's then up to you to understand and respond to those messages. There are lots of ways to be responsive. You can answer questions, congratulate someone when they post an achievement or award, comment on articles that someone posts or links to, or simply "Like" or "Favorite" a post. The point is that *you* have the power to identify and engage, and ultimately create a positive social interaction.

When it comes to being responsive, there are three vital qualities, and you must have them all. The first is listening for messages and then responding to them, as I describe above. The second is perseverance—staying active and responsive once you are in engaged in a conversation. The third revolves around customer service. As you recall, in Chapter 2 I discussed how many customer-related complaints and concerns are voiced across social media channels. Being responsive requires you to identify and understand those customer concerns and help find *resolutions*. Whether you are in customer service, sales, or marketing, all of these conversations influence your ability to sell, so it's critical that you (and the company or brand you represent) are responsive to customer issues.

RULE #4: FOLLOW THE LEADER

There are all types of social networks in which to participate, including blogs, forums, professional groups, and other communities (where people gather online, based on common interests). And, as with other social networking sites (such as Twitter or Facebook), all of these social and professional gathering spots usually have rules and guidelines. For example, when participating in some Groups within LinkedIn, the person or organization that created the Group typically have a set of guidelines you must follow. This can include dos and don'ts covering everything from posting job openings to how often you should comment.

As you become involved in the different social networking communities, take a moment to find out what rules or guidelines they have for participation. If you don't see guidelines posted, or don't receive any when joining a community, do a little research. Identify group leaders or other active community members and follow their lead—watch how they participate, try to identify when they have a successful conversation, and use that as your guide.

RULE #5: TAILOR THE CONVERSATION

Communicating with people, whether in person or over social media, isn't rocket science. It's about finding common ground and sharing information that is relevant to your audience. Talking with people is usually very easy, certainly for those of us in sales. However, for your message to be received and understood, it must be meaningful to the person you're trying to reach. That means you want to match both the type of content you have and the tone or structure of your message to your target audience.

This can be illustrated by looking at vertical markets. Perhaps you sell a product that can be used by school systems, retail stores, and hospitals. You may have a particular piece of content, perhaps an article that discusses your product in general terms, and you want to share it over social media. Let's say you take that single article and decide to post it in a LinkedIn Group dedicated to clothing retailers, and a Group dedicated to healthcare executives, and post it in another Group made up of secondary school administrators. In each case, you post a link to the article using the same message: "Here is a great article that describes the power of a Coverall Health-Based Cleaning System. Please read it and let me know if you have questions." Chances are pretty good that you are going to get zero response, except some criticism for posting a message that borders on spam! That's because the message and the article are so general that they don't have any meaning or relation to those Groups or their members.

A better option is to find several articles, or other pieces of content that relate to members within each of those vertical markets. Even if you don't have vertical-specific content, you can still tailor the message you that use to post the article. For example, you might say: "Schools are increasingly challenged with keeping classrooms clean to help prevent the spread of illnesses. Are you using an updated cleaning system, like the one in this article, to help prevent the spread of common germs in your school?" By using a more personalized message, you are much more likely to get a response.

Keep in mind, when you are tweeting, you have to be much more succinct: "Losing money to student sick days? See how an updated cleaning system helps prevent the spread of germs. bit.ly/11mTips" Notice that the use of a link-shortening tool allows you to use fewer characters by shrinking the original URL for your website address (www.coverall.com/about-coverall/detail.aspx?id = 117) to a special miniature URL address (bit.ly/11mTips).

It's important to take a similar customized approach when sharing information across different social media channels. The type of content or tone of message you use on Facebook can often be much more lighthearted and fun. That same approach might not work on your LinkedIn company page, where posts are typically framed with a more professional tone. Again, the idea is to tailor your message to each audience so that it is more likely to be received and understood—and you get a positive response.

RULE #6: BE HELPFUL

When you think about a social networking site, such as Twitter, think about its origins. It was intended to be an open system for sharing information with others by using short messages. Most social networks are based on that same concept of sharing information, events, and images that are meaningful to your circle of contacts. That's why one of the ten rules for having a positive interaction is about helping others. When it comes to social selling, being helpful can mean offering educational opportunities, or general support, or even inspiration.

One of the brands that I follow on Facebook and Twitter regularly posts tips that relate to their particular industry—in this case, it's online marketing and search engine optimization. Probably three out of every four posts they share are pretty general, and don't relate to or reference any of the products or services they offer. Nevertheless, the information is extremely helpful and often includes valuable tips of things I can do to help my website get found more readily in Google so potential customers can learn about me. Because of this company's helpful posts, I choose to continue to follow them and I make a point to turn to them when I need additional information. In fact, the information they shared helped position them as an expert in their industry. When I began looking for a tool to assist with optimization, I went to their website, first—and, yes, ultimately purchased from them. Additionally, I share their informative posts with everyone in my social networks. Being helpful goes a long way in the rapidly expanding world of social media networks.

RULE #7: IDENTIFY THE ENTER AND EXIT SIGNS

This rule is a bit tricky. When it comes to having positive social interactions, you not only have to identify relevant conversations to participate in, but you need to understand how to gracefully enter into and exit out of those same conversations. I like to refer to this as how *not* to be awkward. For starters, you may pick up on an existing conversation that is between two or three people. Perhaps they are going back and forth about a problem which you know your product can solve. The temptation is to immediately insert yourself into the conversation; to send a tweet or post a comment directly to the person with the problem and tell her you have a product that will solve her problem. Unless you already have a relationship with this person through other social interactions, she will have no idea who you are, and no reason pay attention to you or your recommendation. Even worse, she may view you as a nuisance or be offended by your outright sales pitch, when all she wanted was someone to provide her with helpful information. She or others may even push back and challenge your statement, possibly even mentioning one of your competitors as a better solution. So what do you do?

As with in-person gatherings, when entering a new social conversation it's helpful to introduce yourself or provide a valid reason why you have something worthwhile to offer to the conversation. For instance, you might say something like, "I happen to work in that field and I'm always interested in hearing what problems pop up when dealing with this" or "I totally agree. I've worked with others who had that same complaint." Even though many social networks are open and conversations between just a few people are completely visible to the public, it can still be poor form to intrude on a somewhat private group conversation. In that case, you can often enter the conversation simply by starting with an apology for interrupting: "Sorry to intrude, but I couldn't resist sharing an idea that may be helpful."

Along these same lines, you do have to monitor social media conversations and make a call on whether or not the person is open to hearing from you. This is especially important if they are engaged in a conversation with your competitor, in which case directly entering the conversation may appear too aggressive. If entering the conversation doesn't look promising, instead of openly commenting on the conversation thread you could be more subtle and Like or Favorite a comment that is made and then come back at a later time and engage with the person.

Knowing when to exit a conversation over social media is equally important. Sometimes you can engage with a person who does not want the conversation to end. Or the conversation could start to get heated or uncomfortable for some reason. (This really does happen.) While an easy out is always to simply stop responding, that too can be awkward. Again, as with face-to-face conversations, it's perfectly acceptable to "sign off" and let the person know you need to go. Or be honest and say you don't have answers to the questions being asked and you need to go research the matter. Be sure to follow up on any promises you make, even when using it as an exit strategy.

RULE #8: MAINTAIN THE SEPARATION OF PROFESSIONAL AND PERSONAL

When using your social media presence for both professional and personal purposes, it can lead to a struggle. The challenge becomes trying to balance two very different identities. After all, the things you discuss in your downtime from work may not always be appreciated by or appropriate for people you interact with professionally. The easy answer is to maintain separate social media accounts—one for personal use, one for work. This reduces the likelihood of you getting carried away and posting something you shouldn't. But sometimes it's not feasible to maintain multiple accounts. For example, Google+ is increasingly trying to tie all your online identities together. LinkedIn is also structured for a single account per user. And, sometimes, you simply prefer not having to worry about managing duplicate accounts or spending twice the effort to build followers and connections for both work and personal accounts.

If you do end up using a single social media account for multiple purposes, be cognizant about the information you share. It's certainly preferable to stick to information that is suitable for both of your audiences. Of course, you do want to be genuine and true to your personality (Rule #1!). Having a professional profile doesn't mean you have to be robotic and devoid of personality; find a comfortable balance. Because you are also using social media to find customers, your social profile descriptions will likely mention the type of work you do and for whom you work. It's important to make it clear that all of your comments do not necessarily represent your company or brand. You may want to state that right up front. (You often see reporters, analysts, and executives of high-profile brands state that they work for Company X, but the opinions they express on social media are their own.)

RULE #9: BE CONSISTENT

Have you ever followed a company or a celebrity on social media because you look forward to the information they share? Then you quickly discover that the amount and types of posts they share are hit and miss, at best. It's disappointing. More important, it becomes incentive for you to disengage. Even though you may not have celebrity status, once you start networking across social channels and building relationships with followers, it's critical to keep up communication. Maintaining a social media schedule is helpful to keep you on track, and I give you some guidance on how to set one up in Chapter 8.

Along with maintaining frequency, you also want to be consistent with the type of information you send. You want people to have a clear expectation of who you are and what your area of expertise is so they think of you when they need assistance in that area. Recall the Internet marketing company that steadily sent out helpful information. They were consistent, and it paid off for them—I became a customer.

RULE #10: ADMIT WHEN YOU'RE WRONG

Truthfully, this rule doesn't require much explanation. Simply put, be ready to admit when you make a mistake and apologize for it, whether you say something you shouldn't, put out information that is wrong, or don't do a good job taking care of your customer. When those things come to light on your social networks, the right thing to do is to own up to your mistake. The good news is that, in most cases, information moves fast across social networks and the social ramifications of your mistake are likely to pass quickly. In addition, people are usually very receptive to apologies and are happy to share with others that you made good on the issue, which can lead to more positive social interactions.

Now that you understand the basics for successfully communicating on social networking sites, it's time to find out how to turn those positive social interactions into potential customers—without pushing your solutions.

CHAPTER 4

MORE THAN LEAD SCRAPING

The Benefits of *Un*-Selling in Social Media

Lurkers Beware! While you won't see this warning officially posted on Twitter or LinkedIn, or any other social media platform, it has become one of the underlying rules for online prospecting. If you want to use social networking as a sales tool, then you must actively participate in conversations and the exchange of ideas. It may seem an obvious declaration, but you would be surprised to learn how many experienced sales professionals (and marketers!) are content to sit back and silently hover, like vultures patiently eyeing their prey.

To be fair, not all Lurkers are vultures. In my definition, a Lurker (as it pertains to social selling) is someone who joins one or more social networks but isn't really active on those networks. Instead of participating in and creating online discussions, and adding value to social interactions, the Lurker remains passive. Although he is only observing online conversations, he also expects to benefit from those same conversations—by capturing information that can be used to create a lead. Lurkers are all too willing to sit back and let their peers, and even their competitors, do the work of starting and holding online conversations, sharing information, and building relationships. While this may appear to be a savvy strategy for time-crunched sales professionals, the problem is that social networks are just that—social. If you are gathering information about your target customers on social networks without first having had any positive interactions with them, then it has basically the same value as cold calling. The idea of social selling is to build relationships and create warm (sales-ready) leads based on your prior positive interactions.

Of course, if Lurkers are silently sitting at one end of the social extreme, then the Pushers are whooping and hollering at the other. The Pushers (as I've chosen to call them) are those social media sales enthusiasts who are genuinely eager to share—share their product pitches. Instead of initiating conversations and participating in mutually beneficial interactions, Pushers serve a one-way stream of marketing propaganda that steadily flows out to no one in particular.

Similar to Lurkers, Pushers think they have earned the right to gather information and create leads simply by showing up on Google +, Twitter, or LinkedIn. Sure, the Pusher has been active, but her effort has been self-serving. The information she distributes is focused only on her company, her brand, her products, and her messages. She hasn't considered how those messages influence her target customers. Even worse, the Pusher assumes that she has an audience. In actuality, she has no idea whether or not anyone is even paying attention to her never-ending product pitches.

The days of relentlessly pushing out your sales messages and quietly stalking your prospects from afar are over, at least if you want to be successful in social *"un*-selling." That is to say, the reality is that social prospecting is less about selling and pushing out messages and more about having normal conversations, participating in communities, and building genuine relationships. If this all sounds familiar, it's because these are the same elements that you already use to contribute to the sales process, offline. Now it's a matter of transferring these skills to building online relationships.

BOOSTING YOUR ONLINE LIKEABILITY

"Prey." "Propaganda." "Stalking." I realize these are strong words for a salesperson to hear associated with their profession. But before you start sharpening your darts, hear me out. First and foremost, I know you are not a vulture (at least I don't think so!). The objective, however, is to ensure that your fellow social media users don't think so, either. You want to focus on changing any bad habits that might seem vulture-like and instead build up what one social media expert refers to as "likeability." Dave Kerpan, founder of Likeable Media, coined that term in relation to a brand's approach to social media. The more likeable you are, the more likely you are to have the results you want. I think it's a simple and accurate gauge for companies and individuals to use when choosing their online actions. In terms of *un*-selling, think of it as a better approach to help boost your likeability.

As both a reformed Lurker and renounced Pusher, I can attest to the importance of choosing your social prospecting behaviors carefully. After all, social media is brimming with quality leads for your business. It is a phenomenal resource. According to global research from Nielsen, 46 percent of people surveyed in late 2011 said they turn to social media when making purchasing decisions.[1] In other words, they are using social sites like LinkedIn, Facebook, Google+, and even Pinterest with the intent to connect with and research your company or that of your competitors. If you're not familiar with all these social platforms, in later chapters I will introduce you to each of them and help you weigh their pros and cons. To start, let's take a look at what those prospective customers are really like. Here's a hint: They care about and talk about a lot more than what they ate for lunch today or which TV show is their favorite.

Your prospective social media leads are savvy, knowledgeable consumers. They are comfortable researching their options online, and they frequently seek input from their peers before making a final buying decision. Today, active social media users readily turn to online product reviews as part of the buying process. A whopping 70 percent of social media users say they trust those online consumer opinions, even more than they trust editorial content in newspapers or content on a company's website.[2]

And here's where it gets tricky. The same consumers who are actively using social media to aide their buying decisions tend to be skeptical of marketers and salespersons lurking and pushing from within their social networking circles. To be perceived as a Pusher can be a deal breaker when it comes to building social currency as a trusted online resource.

The good news is that once you develop a trustworthy relationship, and up your "likeability" rating, there is a big payoff. Social customers are known for being fiercely loyal to brands they support and will gladly sing your praises as long as you continue giving them reason to do it. If you think about it, since you don't use vulture-like sales behaviors offline, it should be easy to let your non-vulture personality shine online, too. No vultures here!

LEAD SCRAPING OR LEAD GENERATION?

Vultures, Lurkers, Pushers . . . are they all really lead scrapers in disguise? And, what's wrong with that, anyway? The social sellers I have described so far may utilize different tactics, but the goal for each is usually the same: prospecting. You want to *use social selling to generate real, workable leads*, and preferably *by increasing the flow of inbound leads* (that is, those leads that come *to you* rather than you having to find them). Wait. You may be asking yourself, if you have to go out on social networking sites to search for leads, then how can those be *inbound* leads? I'll get to that in just a minute. My main point is that lead generation is a goal shared by everyone who wants to sell through social platforms, but the success rate varies substantially. The difference is often in the *process* that you use to prospect: lead scraping versus lead development.

When searching for leads online, the idea is to find sufficient information about your target customer, such as a real name (not a social moniker), an email address, a phone number, or a company website. You want to identify enough usable data that allows you, as a salesperson, to capture that person as a lead so that you can reach out to them in other ways (offline). Lurkers and Pushers believe that you can simply pluck this type of information about prospective customers from social networking sites in order to help fill the always-starved lead pipeline. Generally speaking, this is referred to as "lead scraping." It's a lead-generation tactic that's been around for a while and one you have undoubtedly used for yourself.

Lead scraping, by itself, isn't a bad thing; and it's sometimes necessary and helpful. In social media, you will use lead scraping as a way of gathering all types of information, but you shouldn't depend on it as a way to get your best results—that is, to increase inbound leads. Lead scraping uses social networks to create a lead record you can use *today*, but lead development uses those same social networks to build online relationships and generate a flow of incoming leads *over time*.

I'm just old enough to have firsthand experience of lead scraping the old-fashioned way, long before the Internet made it seem effortless. While working my way through college, one of my part-time jobs was working for a women-only fitness center selling annual memberships. I remember the first time I sat down with a big, thick local phone book, going page by page through the residential listings picking out potential names and numbers to call and offer a free week of Jazzercise classes. My sales manager taught me to narrow the process by first focusing on the section of names in the zip codes closest to our gym, then by looking for listings that had only a woman's name or that listed both husband and wife. This was a way to help ensure the likelihood of reaching our target market. Chances are, even if you haven't had the joy of scraping leads from a phone book, you have probably done something similar using a membership directory from your Chamber of Commerce or another organization. Once upon a time, using this technique to find leads was almost like a rite of passage every salesperson had to experience.

Fast-forward a few years to the booming online marketplace and that same process of lead scraping was applied to information found across the Internet. This time around, software was developed to replace the tedious manual process. Instead of searching through a phone book, lead-generation software was able to riffle through thousands of virtual pages of websites and online directories, guided by a set of search criteria you defined. Unfortunately, as you may already know, this system wasn't much more foolproof than the phone book approach. The automated process was clunky and the search criteria were either too broad or too specific to return a quality list of leads. In addition to concern over list accuracy, depending on the quality of the lead-generation software, the emails sent to addresses in the resulting list sometimes got flagged as spam and never even made it to your recipients. There have always been plenty of companies around who handle the tedious backend details of lead generation and then sell you the semi-qualified leads, but the price of these leads can range anywhere from $20 to $150 (or more) per lead. Often, you are sharing the leads with at least two or three competitors as well. For many businesses, paying someone else for leads just isn't financially feasible. And that brings us back to today's process of lead scraping on social media networks.

MOVING BEYOND LEAD SCRAPING

In a way, lead scraping has come full circle. The goal is relatively unchanged, and like those first efforts of culling through a phone book, page by page, social media lead scraping is somewhat of a manual process. At the very least, it is a hybrid version. That's because with social media lead scraping, you can spend hours at a time reading through tweets, Facebook feeds, blog post comments, updates in LinkedIn groups, and questions and answers posed in various online communities. There are tools to help, but it is still not an automated process. That said, the nuggets of information you discover through social media are often much greater than any lead-scraping program of the past!

Unlike the days of phone books and software programs, when searching through social networks you actually get contextual clues by way of the social media conversations that tell you a particular person may be your target customer. This assumption is not only based on demographics and psychographics (such as zip code and marital status), but on real conversation threads.

Not only can you identify someone as a target customer, but sometimes, through these social media conversations, you get additional clues about their buying preferences, such as specific product needs, purchasing time frame, budget constraints, technical barriers, and much more. It's as if that phonebook that I once used for cold calling could have instead revealed the intimate story behind every name I searched in the White Pages. Instead of only showing me that Mrs. Barbara Little lived two blocks away from my fitness center, it might have also told me that she had a baby six months ago and she's struggling to take off her pregnancy weight. To boot, it might let me know that her best friend is getting married in the fall. And, she's agreed to be a bridesmaid, so she is desperately looking for weight-loss tips. When looking for leads on social media and following and engaging in conversations, that is exactly the type of details you could potentially uncover. The trick is finding all of this information about Barbara Little in time to provide her with the solutions she indicates needing.

In the reality of today's sales landscape, by the time a prospect becomes a lead for you, that customer has already narrowed her decision. In the case of Barbara Little, she is already pricing options for a six-week diet program from both Weight Watchers and Slim-Fast. By the time your fitness center gets to her, she may have decided a traditional gym may not meet her needs, unless the price is right.

During the process of social selling, instead of assuming that the prospect is entering at the top of the sales funnel and open to receiving very broad, general information, realize that the lead (or prospect) may instead already have your company or product on her short list. She's made the decision to buy, and it's just a matter of where or from whom she will make her purchase. The information she wants is very product- or service-specific, and possibly focused on price alone. It's the type of information that is typically shared at a stage much later in the sales process. Thus, the opportunity to influence this lead's buying decision is greatly limited at this point.

Even the best salesperson may struggle to keep the lead warm. So how do you change this scenario and flip it to your advantage?

First, you start by moving away from the idea that simply scraping information out of social networks is the only answer. Why?

> ➢ **Generic lead scraping is no better than cold calling:** You may have some basic facts about the prospect, but you have had no previous engagement. There is no existing relationship or other interactions to build upon when trying to contact the lead outside of the social channels.

> ➢ **When lead scraping, you miss the opportunity to add value:** Typically, if you are only scraping information, then you have not actually entered into the social conversation. The lead doesn't know you. You haven't had the opportunity to establish trust, value, or credibility for you or the brand you represent.

> ➢ **Lead scraping often occurs late in the buying cycle:** More than likely, you are plucking information at a point when the lead is already toward the end of the decision process. That means you have less opportunity (if any at all) to influence or change the final purchasing decision.

Considering that lead scraping and other traditional (direct) sales methods may not net you the best results, it's time to turn to lead development and *un*-selling to help you prosper.

THE TRUTH ABOUT *UN*-SELLING

When I talk about the concept of *"un*-selling," I think of it in terms of putting value on building relationships first and foremost as opposed to forcing a sales transaction. As with any relationship, it takes time to build. But, as you are establishing and growing these connections, you are developing not only relationships, but potential leads. In his book *The Thank You Economy*, Gary Vaynerchuk explains how he started "selling" wine through social media. Instead of jumping in and talking about what types of wine his store offered, or how good the prices were, or that he could offer free shipping, he looked for conversations about wine. He participated in those conversations by offering help—suggestions, opinions, and answers to basic wine questions. In the process, he developed a social following and a reputation as a trusted wine expert. What followed were not only leads, but customers. As he says in his book: "Social media relationships and personal relationships work exactly the same way—you get out of them what you put into them. You can't buy them, force them, or make them into something they're not ready to be."[3]

That, in a nutshell, is the essence of *un*-selling in social media. First, you must make a connection, and then you have to invest time and effort into building the relationship. As a result of this process, you are able to establish credibility and trust, which, in turn, generates leads. As you tackle the idea of *un*-selling, here are the key points to remember:

- ➢ **Exhibit patience:** Sorry to break the news, but the social selling process is not instantaneous. *Un*-selling is a process that occurs over time; it requires consistent interaction with your prospects via social media so you can establish credibility for yourself as a good resource.

- ➢ **Utilize contextual (lead) scraping:** Instead of looking for basic information about a prospect in order to fulfill the data requirements to call them a "lead," look for other meaningful information to identify someone with whom you should connect. Contextual signals might include: industry, job status, general interests that could relate to your product or expertise.

- ➢ **Track customer sentiment:** Like contextual signals, customer sentiment is meaningful because it's an indication of how a customer feels about a particular brand, company, product, event, etc. It can be positive (reflects a good experience; indicates a brand supporter or enthusiast), negative (indicative of a poor experience), or neutral (interested but doesn't have a personal opinion or association, yet). By identifying social conversations that exhibit customer sentiment about your brand or competing brands, it provides a good opportunity to enter the conversation and start building a relationship.

➤ **Brand yourself:** Heeding the recommendations from Chapter 3, get active networking across the social platforms. Even though you may represent a company or product/service other than your own, it's still important for you (as the sales professional) to become the trusted expert. After all, people don't really interact with a company or brand, but with the people within the company!

➤ **Engage with existing customers:** As with traditional sales, in social selling you can benefit from the network of others. That's why, as you start building your own social circles online, you should reach out to people you know first—especially existing customers. Use social networks to thank them for their business, check in with them, and send them helpful information and tips related to your products and services.

➤ **Identify industry influencers:** In addition to reaching out to customers, look for respected social influencers within your industry, whether they are bloggers, analysts, designers, trendsetters . . . you get the point. These are great people to connect with to help expand both your prospect base and your knowledge base!

➤ **Interact and give back:** While you want others to listen to you, like you, follow you, and hang on every word you send out across the social networks, there's something even more important when it comes to building online relationships—giving back. A big part of *un*-selling is having positive interactions with your social connections without being a Pusher or a Lurker. But you don't have to wait for others to take action.

You can be the one that gives someone a $+1$ (in Google $+$) or retweet something they said, share or Favorite an article they posted, or comment on their blog. Remember, successful communication is a two-way street.

➤ **Be a thought leader to build social influence:** Another component of *un*-selling is being able to discuss and share information that reaches beyond your core products or services. If you sell premium household paint, you can certainly brand yourself as an expert in paint, providing tips and answering questions about your product. To truly build social influence, you also want to become a thought leader. Write blog posts, articles, and other social media posts about bigger issues or trends that relate to your industry. Sticking with the paint example, you might discuss design trends based on paint colors or how economic conditions impact the decision to redecorate a home or buy a new home.

Becoming a thought leader also exposes you to other social influencers (reporters, bloggers) who may want to interview you. That, in turn, exposes you to a wider audience, affirms your credibility, and helps expand your online social connections—all while *un*-selling!

➤ **Embrace consultative sales:** As an established sales professional, you may want to always compare the consultative approach to the short-term transactional sales process. You may even be convinced that your product only lends itself to the transactional process—it's about a price point; it involves a quick decision; you only need to drive traffic to your appropriate Web page and start the e-commerce process. However, there's really not a product or a service or a type of business that cannot benefit from *un*-selling over social networks if you embrace the consultative sales approach. Consider it a longer cycle, one in which you are developing conversations that educate and assist the prospect throughout the buying process. Sure, you may not have a complicated product, but the key to *un*-selling is building relationships—and that naturally takes time to do it right.

EXPANDING CIRCLES, INFLUENCE, AND RECOMMENDATIONS

Another benefit of *un*-selling is that it really does open the door to an increased amount of sharing by those who follow you, whether you have reached the level of thought leader or you simply become adept at being helpful and sending out quality information. This is particularly true when you think about sharing with existing customers. As you interact with them, you are also exposed to contacts in *their* networks and it provides more opportunities to demonstrate your credibility and build new relationships.

—

How much influence does an existing customer have over potential customers in the world of social selling? What's the worth of a +1, a Like, or a four-star review? In the next chapter, I show you how and why peer-to-peer influence matters to your brand.

CHAPTER 5

TWEETS, LIKES, COMMENTS, AND RECOMMENDATIONS

Understanding the Value of Peer-to-Peer Influence in Social Sales

As a salesperson or marketer, you are most likely accustomed to using customer references and testimonials. What could be better than an existing customer offering a glowing recommendation of your business to a prospect? The only thing better than a recommendation is when a prospect has a corporate mandate that your product must be used! In which case, no level of external influence is going to make a difference in the buying process. While these types of top-level purchasing mandates do occur (this happens with tech products, in particular), they are rare; this brings us back to what *is* far more likely to influence the buying decision: customer recommendations.

In the past, you have typically been able to control or manage the recommendation process by helping shape the quotes used in a testimonial, determining where and when to use them, and by deciding which customer references to send to which prospects. In modern peer-to-peer influence, the power is shifting to your customers, competitors, and critics. Using social media, these groups now impact your brand's image through the power of public sharing— offering endorsements or rejections of your product, and deciding where (and how) those recommendations are used. Even more important is that both friends and strangers are actively listening— and responding, accordingly.

ONLINE REVIEWS: WORD-OF-MOUTH MARKETING ON STEROIDS

When explaining peer-to-peer influence, it's helpful to discuss it in terms of good old-fashioned WOM, or word of mouth. There has always been value in word-of-mouth marketing (WOMM), but the Internet has given it the power to spread and influence at an exponential rate. I have worked in the food industry for many years, and WOMM was considered a critical factor in the success or failure of a restaurant. My boss used to constantly remind everyone of the damage one person could do if she had a bad experience. In what I started referring to as the "WOM multiplier effect," it seems that if one person received a bad meal or poor customer service, you could count on her telling at least ten of her friends. And, each of those friends would tell ten more of their friends, and so on.

On the other hand, a positive experience was expected to net about half (or less) of that WOM multiplier effect. That shouldn't come as a surprise. Bad news has always spread faster than good news. The same holds true online and in social media. Think about the last time you saw a tweet used to thank a business for doing something well versus airing a complaint.

I don't think any businessperson has ever doubted the power of WOM. As e-commerce (online shopping) grew, several industry leaders found a way to capitalize on the WOM multiplier effect, understanding that consumers have opinions and are willing to share them so freely. I can't say with certainty that Amazon.com is the absolute first online retailer to allow customer reviews of a product to be posted on their website; but they are definitely recognized as an early adopter and a current leader in this effort. In some ways, Amazon .com is the best example of WOM on steroids.

Not only do they provide the means for buyers to rate and review products, but they encourage it. If you buy something from Amazon.-com, they send you e-mail reminders to post a review of the product. As you probably have seen for yourself, they also actively promote and display customer reviews to shoppers. I think it's safe to say that Amazon.com (arguably the world's leading online retailer) has not only seen industry data supporting the persuasiveness of online product reviews, but has experienced it firsthand. Amazon knows how frequently a recommendation from a customer can convert another shopper into a buyer.

Online product reviews have spread well beyond Amazon to nearly every industry and genre, from travel sites to medical equipment sites, from large luxury retailers to small mom-and-pop businesses. As a consumer, there is so much emphasis placed on the value of customer reviews that websites often let you sort reviews by the best, or the worst, and by the most or least helpful. That's right, you are now asked to review the reviewer—to rate the value of the customer recommendation! And the power of online reviews and peer influence continues to grow thanks in large part to social media.

For starters, consider that globally nearly one in every five minutes spent online is spent on social networking sites, according to a state of social networking report by comScore.[1] In their opinion, this makes social networking "the most popular content category in engagement, worldwide." Then, in research from Nielsen, 59 percent of survey respondents in the United States indicated they were "much more" or "somewhat more" likely to buy a new product after learning about it online.[2] In that same survey, 30 percent of people said they were "much more" or "somewhat more" likely to buy a product after learning about it through social media. As Rob Wengel, senior vice president at Nielsen Innovation Analytics stated about that report[3]:

Social media can also be an effective soundboard to hear about potential issues or to identify future innovation opportunities. As reliance on social media continues to broaden for CPG (consumer) products, it is especially impactful when used in combination with TV to enhance recall, facilitate one-on-one consumer engagement and dialogue, and listen to what consumers are saying.

The Nielsen research found that the Internet impacts purchasing decisions 81 percent of the time which it comes to electronics and 77 percent of time with appliances. Purchasing decisions for books, music, cars, clothing, personal hygiene products, and even food and beverages are also greatly influenced by online research. While purchasing decisions of consumer or B2C products are often thought of as being most susceptible to online reviews and peer-to-peer influence in social media, B2B products are also proving to experience similar influence. A study in late 2012, commissioned by LinkedIn from Forrester Research, confirmed that social networks are a "critical source" when it comes to buyers of IT (Internet Technology) related products.[4] The report broke down the typical IT buying process into five parts (awareness, scope, plan, select, and implement) and discovered nearly half of the IT decision makers were influenced by information shared on social networks, and this occurred in each of the five stages of the buying process.

When it comes to peer-to-peer influence across social networks, there is something even more fascinating than the what, why, or where. It's not the realization that peer-to-peer influence is occurring, or why it all got started, or in which product categories you see the most dramatic influence. It's the matter of *who* it is that buyers are listening to that is particularly interesting. It turns out that social shoppers are persuaded not only by their friends and family, but by perfect strangers, too! This certainly helps clarify why online reviews are so popular; buyers trust them, regardless of who writes the reviews—more than they trust your advertising.

How much do they trust and whom do they trust most? According to recent research from Nielsen, the online consumer review comes in as the second most trusted resource for any type of information about your brand or even brand messaging.[5] A whopping 70 percent of buyers, worldwide, said they fully trusted online reviews. This is a full 15 percent bump in just a few years. Perhaps less surprising is that your buyers also trust their personal network. The same research indicated that 92 percent of consumers put their trust into "recommendations from friends and family," above any type of advertising or paid brand endorsement. If you happen to sell to a younger audience, you may want to know that a survey from Bazaar-Voice discovered that those buyers 18 to 34 years of age, also referred to as "Millennials," said they trusted the online opinions of strangers *more than* friends or family.[6]

The ultimate question becomes how can you, as a salesperson, take advantage of the online product review? Is there anything you can or should do? After all, if your existing customers are already out there leaving a trail of virtual comment cards, there's really nothing more you need to do than sit back and watch the good reviews come rolling in, right? Then again, if the feedback is a bit slow, or nonexistent, you may be tempted to help the process along by writing your own review (under an anonymous or fictional name) or prompt your own friends, coworkers, and family members to add their signatures to a few reviews, on your company's behalf. Neither one of these is a good idea—mainly because it is simply wrong and misleading to do so. But popular sites that deal with lots of product reviews, such as Amazon and Yelp, are starting to identify and crack down on reviews that don't seem legitimate, or that appear forced (for example, restaurants that encourage patrons to complete an online review from their mobile device while still at the business location). Even the search engine powerhouse Google is getting into the game and trying to make sure phony online reviews don't mislead organic search results.

So, what can you do to use online reviews in a positive way to support the social selling process?

> ➤ **Ask your best customers to participate:** While you don't want friends and family submitting reviews, there's nothing

wrong with encouraging happy, satisfied customers to provide a positive online testimonial. You can reach out by
phone, online, or in-person; it really doesn't matter. However,
it is always helpful to follow up any conversation with an
email, thanking them for agreeing to provide the review and
offering brief instructions on where and how to submit the
review.

By the way, if you have multiple places where online
reviews reside (your website's product pages, Amazon.com or
another reseller website, in LinkedIn product pages, etc.),
only ask your customer to complete the review in one place.
Not only does that keep from overwhelming them, but it is
more effective if one customer isn't submitting multiple
reviews.

➤ **Include links on thank-you pages and emails:** Sometimes
it is preferable to reach out to specific customers personally,
similar to asking for a sales reference or a marketing testimonial. You can also automate the process. The same way that
Amazon sends emails following a purchase, you can ask for
customers to complete reviews by adding it to an online product "thank-you" page (or order confirmation page). You can
also add it to a shipping invoice or set up an automated email
that goes out a certain number of days after purchase or
installation.

Of course, when automating the process of asking for an
online review, you risk encouraging unhappy customers to
document their experience too. In my opinion, this is perfectly okay. It's better to know that a customer is not satisfied
and have the chance to correct it (even if you find out along
with thousands of other online shoppers).

➤ **Respond to negative reviews quickly:** Should you end up
finding an online review from an unhappy customer, it's best
to respond to it—and fast! While you may want to avoid getting into a public back-and-forth exchange for all to see, you
do want to have at least an initial response that is open

because it lets prospective buyers know that you are paying attention to customer concerns, and that you have attempted to resolve the issue. It's also been my experience that when you do successfully resolve the problem, most customers go back online to acknowledge it and publicly thank you.

In Chapter 2 I talked about the importance of sales, marketing, and customer support working together to help the social selling process. Negative online reviews are great examples of why that is important. However, as a salesperson or a marketer, you don't have to wait for your company's customer service to get involved. You can leave an initial response to a negative review with instructions for contacting support, or with a note letting the customer know you are taking the action to get customer support involved.

➢ **Thank customers publicly for positive reviews:** If you spot a positive review, particularly one that is especially descriptive, take a moment to thank the customer for his business and for taking time to share his experience with your company. If it makes sense, a positive online customer review can also be the perfect place to suggest other products or services your customer might appreciate, or to ask him to connect with your company on other social networks so he can stay informed with the latest news and product updates.

➢ **Actively search for reviews:** Although you may know the official places where you are likely to receive customer reviews, online customer feedback can appear in lots of different locations, from your company Facebook page to an obscure ratings website. In addition to paying regular visits to all the sites you know, collect customer reviews. I suggest using a search engine like Google or Bing to see what search results are returned when you search your company name. There are other tools that can help you monitor this, and I share those with you in Chapter 6.

➢ **Regularly check legitimacy of reviews:** As you read online customer reviews, keep your eyes open for feedback that seems odd or untruthful. Unfortunately, fake negative reviews do happen. Indicators that a review is not legitimate can include: references to products or services that you don't even offer (it happens!); an excessive number of misspellings or poor grammar; and mentions of your products being used or purchased in geographic areas that you don't sell into (perhaps outside your region or country). With many review sites, you may have the option not only to reply to the review, but to flag it as inappropriate or as spam, or to contact the review website and ask them to remove the view upon verification of it being false.

> **Use good reviews in your sales and marketing process:** As you spot positive reviews, take note of where they are and refer prospective customers to them as examples of satisfied customers. You might also contact the customer and ask permission to use parts of the review in other sales and marketing material, or to serve as a source for a more formal or in-depth customer case study.

> **Monitor competitors' online reviews for helpful information:** One of the wonderful things about online customer reviews is that you can see what others have to say about your competition (of course, they can do the same with you!). From a social selling perspective, this is a terrific way to get a glimpse into your competitor's world. You can see what customers think of your competition and of their products and services; how they use them; and if there are problems— either with the product or with the support.

There are times when it may be appropriate for you to respond to a negative review, sympathizing with the customer's problem and suggesting that if she ever need help in the future or care to try another product, you are available to assist. While this can be a wonderful social selling opportunity, it's always advisable to use it sparingly.

In the end, whatever information consumers glean from online reviews, good or bad, it ultimately influences buyers' final decision-making processes. It's possible that your social prospects are actively seeking the opinions of their online peers, specifically asking what others think about your products. If buyers really like you, they just might share the love on social networking sites and give you two big, virtual thumbs up.

LIKES, FAVORITES, FOLLOWERS, AND OTHER POSITIVE SOCIAL INDICATORS

In social media, there are lots of different ways for customers, fans, and prospects to show they care about you and to interact with you. Compared to the online customer review, many of the other positive social indicators are a bit more subtle, but they are equally useful in the social selling arena.

Today, many companies use growth indicators, such as the increase in the number of their social media fan base or followers, as a way to measure both social success and return on investment (ROI). The thinking is that if you are increasing your Facebook fans by 20 percent every week, then you must be doing something right and it must be paying off (literally and figuratively). Many brands have these types of "earned media goals" associated with social media campaigns. The most popular measurements of success are the number of Facebook Likes, Facebook fans, Twitter followers, number of retweets on Twitter, and number of comments received. These types of figures are also simple and seemingly clear-cut metrics that can be used to justify social spend, whether it's the budget dollars allotted for social media ads or the investment of employees' time spent on social networks.

However, if you have lots of followers but they aren't responding to you or engaging with you, then it doesn't do you much good, especially when it comes to trying to sell into these social channels. The lack of social engagement, regardless of number of fans or followers, would be similar to having a customer walk into your retail store and then walk out without buying anything from you or without even telling other friends about their visit to your store. You could have 300 people come through your store and, essentially, do nothing. Obviously, it doesn't help you with revenue goals. There's always a chance they will remember you at some point in the future and come back to make a purchase—but there's no guarantee.

With social selling, when customers or prospective customers interact with you in some way, it's like receiving a vote of confidence for your brand; and it's a potential opportunity to move a prospect, and their friends, closer to a buying decision. As with the old-school version of word-of-mouth marketing, when you get at least one fan or customer to interact with your brand using one of the social indicators, that positive interaction can spread to their network of friends and followers. The more interactions, the more your brand or product is likely to be seen by their friends. And, the more likely you are to convert their friends into your prospects. This is the social media version of the WOM multiplier effect, but it's based on using various social signals to engage with you.

If you have spent any time on social networking sites, then you are probably familiar with the social signals or indicators that a customer uses to interact with you. Here is a brief list of the most often tracked networks, along with their associated social signals:

- ➤ **Facebook:** Social signals include the number of fans and number of times a post or picture receives a Like, or a comment, or is shared with others.

- ➤ **Twitter:** Social signals include the number of followers, the number of retweets (when your tweet is shared), and the number of times your tweet is marked as a Favorite (similar to a Facebook Like).

- ➤ **LinkedIn (personal profile):** Social signals for your personal profile include the number of connections, recommendations, and endorsements you receive.

> **LinkedIn (brand profile page):** Social signals for your company's brand page include the number of people who follow your page; the number of recommendations your products or services receive; the number of times that updates on your company profile page are Liked, commented on, or shared; and the number of people who belong to any LinkedIn groups you manage that are related to your brand or products.

> **Google +:** Social indicators include when someone gives your comment or update a + 1 (the equivalent of a Like or Favorite), and the number of people who have added you into their circles (or groups).

> **YouTube:** Social indicators include the number of times an online video has been viewed, Liked, commented on, or shared.

> **Pinterest:** Social indicators include the number of times one of your company or product images have been "pinned," which is a method of virtually attaching an image to a section of someone's Pinterest account, also called a "board." Think of Pinterest as a place that showcases virtual corkboards, where images and documents from around the Internet can be "pinned" to those boards. The act of pinning or repinning is a way of sharing in this social network, In addition, someone may also Like an image that you have shared. (More, much more, on Pinterest in Chapter 14.)

> **Communities/Blogs:** Social indicators for various communities, groups, or blogs that your company manages, sponsors, or participates in usually include the total number of followers or group members, the number and frequency of comments and questions received, or the number of Likes or shares your posts receive.

You may be wondering if there is anything you can do to encourage people to use these social signals. There are definitely a few ways you can help improve engagement—including everything from the type of content you use (which I discuss in the next chapter) to how often you post information to your social media channels. One of the best things you can do is make it easy for customers and prospects to share. This can be as simple as enabling social sharing buttons on your website, blog, or community. Make sure the social icons for Twitter, Facebook, Google+, and others are readily seen and actually work so that people can share information from you at the click of an icon!

Another surefire way to help increase engagement is to ask people to leave comments to your blog post, to "follow" you or Like you, or to retweet one of your tweets. Asking your target audience to participate is pretty powerful, and you may be pleasantly surprised to discover how often it works! To find more details and tailored tips to help increase the activity and response rates you receive, check out Chapters 11 through 14; each chapter covers a specific social media platform or group of social networks.

BLOGS, FORUMS (GROUPS), AND COMMUNITIES MATTER, TOO

You may have noticed that I have mentioned blogs, groups, and communities several times in this chapter. For the purpose of social selling, know that I include these as part of the larger, online social hemisphere and consider them to be an important component of the social selling process. Typically, however, analysts and researchers treat these categories as being separate or different from social networking sites, so you may you see them broken out separately in some social media research. Much like online customer reviews, blogs and industry- or product-specific groups and communities can be very influential. A 2013 report from Technorati Media finds that consumers do turn to blogs when making a purchasing decision.[7] Further, the survey indicated that blogs are the "third-most influential" digital or online resource, and they were the "fifth-most trusted" resource on the Internet. YouTube, Facebook, and Google+ were also included among the most influential social media sites that buyers turned to for information as part of their purchasing decisions.

One interesting point is that 54 percent of those surveyed believe that the smaller a community is, the greater its influence on the buying process. It's reasonable to assume this happens because consumers are able to form closer relationships in groups and communities that are smaller. So as you begin to identify blogs and communities to get involved in, don't overlook those with a smaller membership base because they could turn out to be a better source of influencers and prospects.

Even though there are lots of different social networks and online communities where you can play, it's highly improbable that you can be active in all of them and do it well. A better plan is to determine where your customers and prospects are most likely hanging out and participating, and then invest your time and energy in those social networks.

Likewise, it's helpful to identify industry influencers and develop relationships with them. Influencers are the bloggers, community leaders, industry analysts, and very active influential customers who have a large (or active) audience and are respected for the information they share and the recommendations they offer. If you are a marketer, these are ideal people to help share your success stories. As a salesperson, your interaction with influencers can be important for several reasons, including that they may:

➤ Tag you as an expert in your field and use you as a resource for articles and blog posts.

➤ Promote and share to their audience any information that you post to social networks.

➤ Publicly recommend you and your products to their followers.

To make it easier to reach out to your key influencers, keep track of them using a list that also includes notes about their specific areas of interest, expertise, or other pertinent details. This list is also a handy way to keep a record of when you last engaged with them and what information was shared or topics discussed. In the next chapter, I will show you how to use different types of content to aid the social selling process and target the content toward both influencers and prospective customers.

Oh, there is one other thing to consider before moving on. While I talk a great deal about your company, and the products or services offered, you—as a representative of that brand—are greatly intertwined with your company's image. There will be plenty of times when you, as a salesperson, benefit from the strength of that brand. By participating on your company's social networks, you not only help the company but you also help build your own social influence. For example, it may be that your company's Facebook page has thousands of fans, while you personally may have only a few hundred (or less). You can and should still engage and comment on the company Facebook page, even though you don't already have a large following. Posting meaningful comments and responding to others helps you build credibility and make more social connections. You don't have to broadcast the fact that you are a salesperson or marketer for the company every time you comment on a post; instead, your profile description should reference that you represent the brand or work in that particular industry. The suggestion for engaging and commenting on your company's Facebook page also holds true for LinkedIn, Google +, and the many communities and groups. When it comes to Twitter, however, you are more likely to be able to build a strong presence with lots of followers of your own.

As I shared with you in Chapter 3, there are rules to follow to improve your positive connections—for both you and your company. It is to be expected that consumers want to connect with brands online, but they will build relationships with the actual people (salespersons, marketers, and others) who represent the company. Remember that both you (as a salesperson) and your brand need to stay active online in order to maximize the benefit of peer-to-peer influence as it relates to the social selling process.

Now that you know the importance of interacting with fans and followers on social media, let's look at some of the best ways to keep the conversation going.

Spoiler alert! The secret to starting and holding online conversations ultimately comes down to *content*. In the next chapter, you'll discover the different types of content you can use to engage prospective customers and how to match your content to the buying stage of your social prospect.

CHAPTER 6

CONTENT, ENGAGEMENT, AND BUILDING A RELATIONSHIP

Pulling the Social Customer Through the Online Sales Funnel

Social media, along with other revolutions in mass media and modern marketing, have without doubt altered the way consumers make purchasing decisions. Today's B2B and B2C prospects are self-educated, savvy shoppers who are increasingly influenced by their peers, turning to online reviews and social media channels for information and product recommendations. Particularly in the B2B market, the sales process, and especially its classic sales funnel, has been permanently altered as social consumers have redefined how they move through the buying stages.

The change in purchasing behavior has increasingly put more pressure on sales and marketing to use content to reach and persuade buyers long before they officially enter your system as a lead. Even with these changes, when you are accurately able to map the right content to both the buyer persona and to the purchasing stage of that buyer, you are often rewarded with shorter buying cycles and increased revenues. Content is used not only to educate prospects about your business, but also to engage them, or to provide the prospect with a reason to interact with or start a conversation with you. Sharing high-quality content through your social channels is the foundation for building a relationship with your prospective customers.

UNDERSTANDING THE CHANGING SALES FUNNEL

The sales funnel is dead—and content is king! This is the mantra now spreading throughout sales and marketing organizations everywhere. However, while there's a great deal of truth to this contention, it's only partially correct. The traditional sales funnel is by no means dead—but it is outdated. Representing the buyer's journey through your sales process, the long-standing model of the sales funnel is illustrated as an inverted pyramid. In the traditional model, the largest number of leads (albeit unqualified) enters at the wide top of the funnel. As they are pulled through the linear sales process from one stage to the next, more and more leads drop out along the way until only a small portion actually make it to the bottom, narrow part of the funnel to become loyal customers.

The traditional sales funnel, as illustrated in Figure 6–1, generally has four stages, starting at the top with the *awareness stage* (unqualified leads); then moving on to the *evaluation stage* (qualified prospect); and finally, as prospects make the decision to buy, entering the *purchase stage* and then becoming part of the *loyalty stage* (as customers). It is important to note that in the traditional funnel, it is the salesperson who controls or guides the lead through the sales process, educating and qualifying the prospect along the way until the purchasing decision is finally made. So what has really changed about this process?

For our purposes, the names of the stages will remain the same. But the behavior surrounding those four stages is markedly different. Perhaps the biggest change is that research indicates *customers are*

FIGURE 6–1

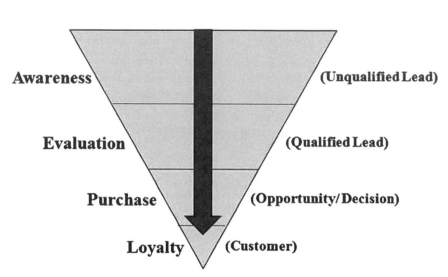

Traditional Sales Funnel

Awareness   (Unqualified Lead)

Evaluation   (Qualified Lead)

Purchase   (Opportunity/Decision)

Loyalty   (Customer)

In the traditional sales funnel, the buyer moves through the four stages of the sales process in a linear manner.

now 57 percent of the way through the sales process before ever engaging with a salesperson.[1] In some cases, depending on the product type and whether it's B2B or B2C, prospects could be as much as 90 percent through the buying process before contacting a salesperson.[2] This is indicative of the level of consumer self-education that is occurring, or rather, it shows how (and how much) information is being consumed prior to a prospect making the first personal contact with a company representative. Remember, your prospective customer now has access to endless streams of branded and non-branded content, research, and opinions from websites, social networking sites, peer-to-peer virtual conversations, and even competitors. These highly educated consumers now enter the buying process much closer to the bottom of that traditional sales funnel as qualified prospects ready to *purchase*, which brings us to the other significant change.

The salesperson is no longer in charge of the buying process and no longer the gatekeeper of the information that would typically move the buyer from one stage of the funnel to the next. Instead, your customer defines the buying process. She may want to engage with you early on, or she may not want to talk with you at all before making her decision to buy. In fact, the only time you may engage with the prospect is during very late-stage activities, such as providing product demos and price quotes. At this point, you may be one of several companies being considered by the buyer, yet your ability to influence the purchasing decision has long passed—without your ever having had contact!

For these reasons, experts say the traditional sales funnel has been phased out. There is no longer a linear movement from unqualified lead (at the top of the funnel) to loyal customer (at the bottom of the funnel). Even so, there has not been a consensus as to what the new, online-driven sales funnel should look like. I have seen it illustrated as a sort of French horn, a series of circles, and as a neuron (as in a neuron or synapse from your brain) with a central hub and lots of little tentacles sprouting from it. Although a replacement for the traditional funnel is difficult to envision, experts seem to agree on the following changes to the buying process:

- ➤ Buyers no longer depend on salespeople to provide information and educate them on products or solutions.

- ➤ Buyers have extended the number of places they get information and the way they consume it.

- ➤ Buyers are entering the sales process much later and salespeople have less opportunity to influence the purchasing decision.

- ➤ Buyers have increased the type of and the frequency of activities they complete before engaging with a salesperson.

➤ Buyers are influenced by content prior to becoming a recognized lead in the sales process.

The last point is particularly important to understand. Content, if delivered soon enough, often enough, and through the right channels, still provides sales and marketing the opportunity to engage and influence prospective customers before they officially enter your sales cycle.

DEVELOPING BUYER PERSONAS FOR YOUR SOCIAL CUSTOMERS

Ultimately, being successful in the social selling process requires you to *build a relationship based on positive interactions with the buyer.* Content is at the crux of the formation of that relationship. As a tool, content allows you to start a conversation, which may lead to a trusted relationship, which may turn into a sales transaction. But as you've seen from the changing sales funnel, this process can take much longer than it previously did. As analysts from Forrester Research have described it: "Engaging, throughout the customer's buying cycle, requires completely different thinking. B2B marketers must nurture prospects for months or years before they turn into sales opportunities, so it is critical to know how you are connecting with each buyer at each interim stage that buyer goes through."[3]

As you put all of these pieces of information together, you see that in order to build a relationship and pull a buyer through today's online sales funnel it takes using content in the following five ways:

1. Promote constant top of mind awareness.

2. Provide useful information.

3. Establish trust and credibility as a legitimate resource.

4. Capitalize on peer-to-peer influence.

5. Target each buyer stage, each buyer persona, and each social network.

Understanding your typical buyer behaviors, or having buyer personas identified, is also helpful when it comes to knowing what content to use, and on which social networks, in order to pull your prospects through the online sales process.

Having a buyer persona, or profile, for your targeted prospects helps with the selling process. A buyer persona provides a demographic snapshot of your typical buyer. It can include descriptors such as job title, industry, or vertical market in which the buyer works; level of expertise; and geographic region in which the buyer is located. A buyer persona can also include gender, income, or level of discretionary spending; shopping preferences (where he likes to shop, or how frequently); and what most often influences her decision to buy (peer recommendations, advertising, discount offers, etc.). You most likely have multiple buyer personas for your products or services because there are many different types of customers, especially when more than one type of product or service is offered, and each of those buyer types is motivated by and responds to different influences and prompts. Your buyer personas will also be unique to your industry and your company (there is no one-size-fits-all model across all industries and brands). Understanding these subtle differences is key to providing the right information, at the right time, and to the right buyer.

Is a buyer profile different for an online customer than for a traditional buyer? Not necessarily. Instead, where or how the buyer prefers to shop, including her online social behavior, becomes one more piece of information that makes up the complete persona. The more you understand a particular persona's online preferences and activities, including information about their social networking behaviors, the easier it will be for you to engage with that buyer in his or her preferred communities (or networks) and build a mutually beneficial relationship. I suggest that you consider every one of your buyer types to be a social consumer, and be sure to include the details of online preferences as an important part of every buyer persona.

If you don't already have buyer personas identified, I would encourage you to take some time to tackle this project. It's a fairly easy task for a salesperson or marketer to complete. In most cases, creating a buyer persona involves interviewing a mix of existing, former, and prospective customers. Ideally, it's preferable to speak with a customer over the phone. It only takes ten or fifteen minutes to ask the buyer a few questions, including why he chose your product and what factors influenced his final decision. You can also put the same questions into a quick survey that can be emailed to both customers and prospects. The goal is to get enough information that you are able to form a clear picture of who your buyer is, but without so many questions that it is off-putting or overly time-consuming for the person taking it.

When developing buyer personas, a good tip is to always include a picture or image that reflects the buyer. For example, in the telecommunications industry where I work, we usually have two buyer personas that happen to be segmented by job roles: the IT professional, and the business executive or owner. But perhaps you sell video games in the B2C market. You may have one persona that reflects a preteen male buyer; a second persona of a teenage female buyer; and a third persona, the mother of the intended consumer. Having an image that represents each of these buyer types isn't necessary, but it often helps you, and your sales and marketing teams, better visualize the person to whom you are talking so that you better choose the type of content that is most fitting for each of these personas. You can use clip art or stock photography (images someone else takes and makes available for your use for free, or for a small fee) to go along with the written description you complete. Once you have buyer personas nailed down, you can begin creating content that is more likely to influence your specific buyer personas in each of the four buying stages that make up the online sales funnel.

CREATING CONTENT TO FEED THE ONLINE SALES FUNNEL

If content is indeed king, then you may wonder what makes it so special. Think of it as a tool. If done well, content has great persuasive power. As mentioned earlier, it is a device that is used to pull a prospect into or through a particular stage of the buying process. As a salesperson, you have been using content for years, whether it is a company brochure, a customer testimonial, a technical datasheet, or a product description. Content is the message inside an email, a call to action on your website, a case study, a white paper, or a chart comparing your solution to that of your competitors.

In addition to using social media to distribute the content mentioned above, pure social content can come in the form of a status update on your Facebook page, a 140-character message sent out on Twitter, a blog post on your website, a picture shared on Pinterest, a comment left in response to an online article, or a video uploaded to YouTube. The point is that content is *everywhere*.

Today, quality content is considered critical. Simply creating content doesn't make it good, and if it's not good it doesn't have value in the eyes of your prospective customers, or to the search engines that are responsible for sorting and ranking your content for online users. Most important, content that is not good is not very effective in the sales process. Poor content is a dull tool that just isn't capable of getting the job done!

What makes content good? It should be a given that text-based content must be well written and free of grammatical errors. Similarly, images and illustrations should be clear and easy to understand, and videos should be short and to the point. Content, in whatever format you choose to use, should also serve a purpose, which may include being informational, instructional (how to), entertaining, humorous, or inspirational.

In terms of creating content that helps you build relationships and ultimately sell, then "good" content is best described as that which resonates with your target audience. What are their concerns, problems, or interests? Share content that matters to them. For instance, think of the types of questions the prospect needs answered about your type of products or services. Or, consider the problems or desires your prospect might have that would lead them to want to buy from you. Develop and share content that addresses these issues and establishes a need.

Of course, content shouldn't always be based on your business.

Since you are using content as a way to establish a relationship and build trust and interest, good content is also that which speaks to broader topics. For example, you might create content around industry news and trends, interviews with experts, obscure or silly facts, celebrity happenings, or current world events. Ultimately, in the world of social selling good content is not only that which your prospect wants to consume, but it's also something that she or he is then willing to share with their network!

As you hear experts talk about content, or as you think about the types of quality content you can create, there are several terms (or names of content types) that you want to know. You are most likely familiar with content such as a standard article, or blog post, or a video, but there are some other common types of content that can be useful to you as well:

- ➤ **Evergreen:** An evergreen is content—often an article or blog post—that never becomes dated. The information is as valid and accurate today as it was a year ago; and it will still be valid in the foreseeable future. That means it doesn't contain dates or other time-sensitive references (such as a coupon that expires or an event or holiday associated with a particular time of year).

- ➤ **Topical:** The opposite of an evergreen, topical content is often based on current news or world events. Because it revolves around a specific point in time, it may have limited shelf life and only be useful for a few days or weeks.

- ➤ **How-to:** Any material that is instructional, or provides information that trains you in a particular skill or process, is considered how-to. How-to content is often very popular online.

- ➤ **List:** Whether you use bullets or numbers to rank details or items, you are creating a list. You often see this type of content online as a "Top Five" or "Top Ten" list of what to do or not to do. In fact, I am using a list right now to describe the different types of content you can create; but when used online, the list (and perhaps an introductory paragraph) would comprise the entire article.

➤ **Testimonial:** A testimonial can be something as simple and brief as a single quote from a customer or much more in-depth, like a customer case study. Testimonials are meant to give you or your product credibility based on someone else's experience or opinion.

➤ **Q&A:** Content that provides direct answers to questions are referred to as Q&A, or Question and Answer. This type of content is used most often for reference. You might even have an entire page of content dedicated to answering a single question. This technique is often used to help your site rank better in search engine results, too. For example, a common question for a cooking site may be "How do I thaw a turkey?" You can create content that answers this question, thus potentially bringing more visitors to the site.

➤ **Polls/Surveys:** Considered to be one of the easiest types of content you can create, quick polls and surveys are a favorite for use online. That's because many of the social networks, like Facebook and LinkedIn, have built-in tools that let you easily create a poll to share with your network of fans and followers. If you use a blog platform, like WordPress, it also has this built-in capability for creating, distributing, and tabulating polls and surveys.

➤ **Infographic:** An infographic, a popular type of content, takes text and displays it in a visual manner using images. An info-graphic can also be easily shared by others on their websites or on their social networking channels, giving it the potential to "go viral," the latest way of saying your content spreads rapidly across multiple social networks.

➤ **eBook:** An ebook is an electronic format for sharing almost any type of content—including images but not video (yet!)—and then delivering all of it in an online book format.

> **Repurposed:** One of the best parts of creating content to share is being able to take one piece, such as a white paper or case study, and then reusing, or repurposing, it in other types or formats of content, such as a YouTube video or a blog post.

> **Curated:** The best way to describe curated content is any type of digital information that is pulled together from multiple sources and then displayed to your target audience. Rather than providing the complete content, you summarize it and provide links back to the original source. For example, if you sell luxury travel packages, you might curate any type of content having to do with travel, such as planning a vacation, packing for exotic locations, or securing your valuables while traveling. Essentially, it is any related content that would be interesting or timely to your prospects; you are gathering the content from different sources and making it available in one place.

> **User-generated:** Similar to curated content, user-generated material is not created by you. You may have existing customers, vendors, or other partners and resellers who are able to contribute original pieces of content for your use. Often, you might see this used as a guest post on a blog.

> **Decision making:** Content that falls in this category is usually focused on pushing the prospect to make the choice to buy. Sometimes referred to as "convincing" content, it usually tries to overcome any final objections a buyer has or answer common questions that may be all that stands in the way of the prospect making her final purchasing decision.

> **Credibility:** Similar to decision-making content, credibility pieces focus on overcoming potential objections, but usually where those objectives are about the brand. This type of content is designed to show your brand or company is viable and trusted.

➤ **Thought leadership:** This type of content takes an in-depth look at a specific topic or trend that impacts your industry. As a subject-matter expert in the market you sell into, you may have an insightful view on a particular topic that could be useful to both your customers and your prospective buyers.

As you decide on which type or types of content to use for a specific purpose, you also have to choose whether or not the content will be branded or unbranded. In this case, I don't mean whether or not you include your company logo on the content, but whether or not the content is written about your company. Do you want the message in your content to be product- specific? Should it be information that is focused on only your business or services? There are times when you need this type of content because it may help create consumer confidence. Branded content can show that your company has been around for quite a while and that you have legitimate experience.

At the same time, if you only create branded content, or create too much branded content, the information becomes all about you and less about how your products or services can solve a problem for your prospective customer. As I mentioned previously, just as you want to create a mix of the different types of content, you want to strike a balance of how much branded content you create.

MAPPING TYPES OF CONTENT TO THE SOCIAL NETWORKS TO ENGAGE AND BUILD RELATIONSHIPS WITH PROSPECTS

Now that you are familiar with the most common types of content you can create, I want to show you how content, social networks, and the various stages of the buying process relate to one another as part of your overall social selling strategy. And it cannot be said enough that effective social selling is rooted in quality content. It is your content that allows you to make an initial connection with your prospect, prompts continued positive interactions (i.e, engagement), and eventually serves as the foundation of an ongoing, trusting relationship. In essence, your reputation as a social salesperson is built on the content you choose to distribute and share!

To begin building relationships with your prospective customers, you want to first consider your buyer personas and how each might search for or consume content depending on where they are in the buying process. Remember, today's buying process is still focused on these main stages: awareness, evaluation, purchasing, and loyalty. However, your buyer does not necessarily pass through these stages in a linear manner, so you have to provide lots of content, over and over again, and make it available in all the places where your prospect may be looking for it (social networks, online communities and websites, and peers). After matching personas to the buying stage, you can then identify *the most appropriate social network* in which to distribute the content.

As I show you which social networks best match up to which stages of the buying process, understand that each of these social networks could influence your prospects, regardless of which buyer stages they are in at any given moment. But when matching social networks to buyer behavior as part of the updated online sales funnel, there are some buyer stages that are *most likely* to be influenced within each of these social networks. These include:

> **Twitter:** Twitter makes it easy to introduce yourself and your products to other members of this social network. The ability to easily search by keyword and track trends means it is ideal for the early and mid-stages of the buying process—awareness and evaluation. Because users of this social network are already utilizing Twitter for customer service, it also makes it a natural fit for ongoing customer support once your prospects become customers.

> **Facebook:** Especially useful during the purchasing stage, Facebook can be used to offer content that triggers final buying behaviors for existing fans, or can be used to reach and engage new fans as part of the awareness stage. Facebook is

also a good venue for increasing engagement over the lifetime of the customer.

➢ **LinkedIn:** LinkedIn groups are particularly useful in both the awareness and evaluation stages of the sales process because LinkedIn gives the buyer the ability to ask specific questions that can be answered by you, your customers, and your partners.

➢ **YouTube:** The visual component of YouTube is particularly helpful for product demonstrations (used during the evaluation and purchasing stages). Videos are also ideal for post-sales training, which can be beneficial to customers long after the decision to buy has been made (as part of the loyalty stage).

➢ **Google +:** Google + Hangouts On Air are live video chats that bring people together in one virtual room, and are particularly useful as content for both the evaluation stage and post-purchase stage. You can invite a small group to participate; but once your live Hangout is over, Google automatically posts the recorded version to your Google + page and your YouTube channel, making it easy to reuse the recorded version as much as you like. You can use Hangouts to conduct real-time training classes, hold real-time Q&A sessions, discuss product and service updates, provide product demonstrations, interview satisfied customers for video testimonials—I could go on.

➢ **Pinterest:** The nature of Pinterest is that it is full of window shoppers, but it is also conducive to impulse shopping. For this reason, Pinterest works well in both the early and late stages of the buying process (awareness and purchase).

➢ **Communities/Forums:** Communities and forums are set up to establish a network around a particular topic or theme, so they are made up of members with a similar interest. This means that any buyer stage—from awareness to loyalty—that is susceptible to peer influence can be influenced by these types of social networks.

➤ **Blogs:** Similar to communities, blogs are often created around a particular theme or brand (such as your company blog). And like communities, blogs have a great deal of influence in almost every buyer stage, including awareness, evaluation, purchase, and loyalty.

Now that you know which social networks are conducive to which buying stages, you want to ensure you are also accomplishing the goal of using content to pull prospects through the buying process (or online sales funnel). To do this, first take an inventory of all the content you have. Next, map the types of content on a chart to identify which buyer persona is targeted and in which social network it is most appropriate to distribute the content. To make it easy, I suggest using a visual icon or image of each buyer persona in place of using an "X" or a check mark in the appropriate columns. This gives you a quick visual of which buyer personas you are targeting. You can find a sample "Buyers' Personas" chart on the website for this book (artofsocialselling.com), under the tab at the top of the site's homepage, called *Exclusive Content.*

You can also create content map for each month or quarter to help you fully track your content and evaluate how you are using it. This also helps you to see where there are holes, or where you may need another type of content to ensure you are reaching all of your prospective buyers at all the critical buyer stages. You can also find a sample Content Map on the website, by clicking the *Exclusive Content* tab, which features not only this map, but other content and tools you can download. By mapping your content this way, you are creating a content *strategy* for where and when and to whom you should distribute content.

Chances are, you will quickly realize that you need *a lot* of content to build relationships and keep the sales funnel fed! Repurposing the content you already have will certainly help, but you may be surprised to discover how quickly even repurposed content is consumed.

One of the ways you can create more content is to outsource it, or pay someone else to help create new pieces of content.

There are tools you can use to make it easier to generate more content. In the next chapter, I show you these content creation tools, along with tools that help you find and engage the social customer.

CHAPTER 7

TOOLS OF THE TRADE

Using Online Services and Applications to Help You Find, Track, and Engage Social Customers

The modern sales and marketing machine thrives on data. From analyzing customer profiles to tracking pipeline growth, it's easier than ever before to gather, sort, crunch, and make use of numbers that provide a data-driven snapshot of how you and your business are performing at any given point and time. What's truly exciting is that it's no longer only Fortune 500 companies that have access to this level of detail. Even if you are a small company, or flying completely solo, you have access to a great deal of information that can help you be more successful. As an added bonus, accessing data is quite affordable—and often free. With so much information available at your fingertips, the questions that businesses of all sizes eventually ask is which data (and how much of it) do you use, and how do you make it meaningful.

When it comes to social selling, it may be somewhat easier to answer those questions compared to other areas of your business. Data points taken from social media typically serve as indicators of how well you are reaching and engaging the people who mean the most to your brand. Tracking this type of data, usually referred to as *analytics*, tells you whether those who matter are actually responding to your messages, or social conversations.

But not all of the data collected as part of your social media analytics is based on raw numbers—such as how many followers you have, or how often someone Likes or shares your posts. In social media, the "who" is sometimes just as important as the "what." You not only want to track and analyze how often you reach people, but you also need to identify *who* you are reaching and who else is influencing those you have reached.

SOCIAL INFORMATION THAT MATTERS

To discuss social information that matters, I first need to briefly discuss a couple of terms that have become buzzwords in the business world—and it starts with *big data,* or what is considered excessive amounts of data that is complicated to process and filter. When you think about data that is typically collected, it's often in terms of *structured data*, or information that can be easily processed and managed in a database (mainly, lots of numbers!). However, *unstructured data,* a generic term for information that has no identifiable structure (for example, text, images, and video files) is increasingly becoming of interest. In part, this is because of the rise of social networking sites, blogs, forums, and online communities. A healthy dose of the information that makes up unstructured data comes from, or is associated with, the conversations you are having through social media.

Why does any of this matter to you? One day, in the not-so-distant future, companies are going to get really good at collecting and analyzing big data (structured and unstructured) in a way that helps create a very clear picture of what each individual consumer looks like and how he or she behaves. This information can, in turn, be used to benefit those companies. Insurance companies already use structured data to indicate that drivers of a particular age or sex are more likely to have wrecks, so those customers have higher premiums.

But what if the insurance company is able to gather unstructured data about you, largely collected from your social media profile, data that indicates you partake in a lot of high-risk behaviors (perhaps you enjoy stock car racing for a hobby)? The company may then use that information to raise your insurance premiums, regardless of that high-risk category based on age or gender.

As a salesperson, you can see how this same type of information could be used not only to increase premiums, but to sell that high-risk client a different or an additional type of insurance product (perhaps a life insurance product with a larger payout but at a higher rate!). Whether you are selling insurance or cars, social media is littered with bits of unstructured data that can help you match prospective buyers to your products or solutions. The trick is in knowing how to find and use all of the data that is available to you today.

When you are looking for information that matters as part of the social selling process, you want to know more about that unstructured data—those individual bits of information, or *social indicators*, that, when pieced together, can tell you how best to identify, reach, and engage with your ideal prospects. These social indicators are found throughout social networking channels, blogs, forums, and groups—basically, anywhere public conversations occur online.

Social indicators often contain enough information to help point to the *why* in the sales process. They can provide guidance on why a prospect needs your product, why a particular vendor is being considered, why another vendor didn't make the short list of possible solution providers, and so on. Or, social indicators may simply act as a signal that there is a need or an interest in your product (or type of product), without providing much additional detail. Depending on what clues these social indicators reveal, you can try to engage the prospects with the best conversation starters and the most appropriate types of content to help pull the prospect into your social sales funnel.

Before discussing some of the tools of the trade you can use to help spot social trends, here is a list of some of the important indicators you should you look for in social media:

- ➢ **Mentions:** A mention is any time that your name, product, or company is referenced in social media. It can be as simple as someone tweeting, "I learned a lot from the book *The Art of Social Selling.* Or, it could be someone posting to Facebook, "Not much to do on this rainy morning, so I finished reading *The Art of Social Selling.*" (This is a good time to mention that I personally monitor and respond to social mentions, so I encourage you to share your thoughts about this book!) A mention can be found within any social channel or blog.

- ➢ **Feedback:** Generally speaking, feedback consists of detailed comments about your brand or product. While a mention may be neutral, feedback is more likely to contain an opinion (good or bad), or be a review of your service. Feedback may also be part of a conversation that is looking for information or support, or asking questions about your products or services. Although you may think of feedback as being more in-depth, it can just as easily occur in the form of a short, 140-character tweet ("Finished reading *The Art of Social Selling* today. Loved it!"). It doesn't have to be a lengthy 300-word post on a blog or a two-minute video posted on YouTube. Feedback comes in lots of different formats and is often rich with useful, unstructured data to help you better understand how to market and sell your products or services.

- ➢ **Sentiment:** Typically, you are most concerned with *customer* sentiment, which helps indicate how an existing customer feels about you. But whenever your name is mentioned or there is feedback on your company or product, it can be perceived as having a positive, negative, or neutral (indifferent) sentiment. Public relations professionals have tracked sentiment for quite some time, particularly in reference to a company's mention in a newspaper or magazine article. For a salesperson, tracking social sentiment is a good way to gauge not only how someone feels about your company, but to give you a better idea of how to enter a conversation online and how you may be able to steer the conversation, based on that initial sentiment.

➤ **Competitor mentions and sentiment:** It's not enough to understand when and what something is said about your company. To increase your social selling effectiveness, you also want to pay attention to conversations that mention your competitors. If the sentiment is negative, that is an indicator that you may have an opportunity to provide an alternative solution for an unhappy customer.

➤ **Influencers**: Potential customers are not the only ones whose opinions matter in social media. Influencers are those who have the ability to engage and persuade others. Influencers typically have a large audience or following, are active and vocal with their online commenting, and their opinions are usually respected or trusted. Mommy bloggers are a great example of influencers. As the popularity of blogs increased, companies who marketed and sold products targeted to babies and young children discovered dozens of influential parents (usually moms) who maintained blogs. The "mommy bloggers," as they have been labeled, review and recommend products to other parents. Some B2C companies spend a lot of time and effort (and sometimes money) finding and wooing these highly engaged influencers to help them promote their products.

While you still want to find and engage influencers, giving away gifts may not be the way to do it. As a result of the bonanza of gifts mommy bloggers received over the last decade, there have been some restrictions put in place on the way companies now provide sample products and other compensation to influencers.[1] Even so, tracking influencers also provides you an opportunity to monitor feedback from their audience and find prospects who may be searching for (and researching) your products. Prospects often respond to an influencer's blog post, article, or tweet with comments that are filled with lots of unstructured data or details about their situation.

➤ **Friends, followers, and defectors:** Although it's not the only indicator to watch, you still want to keep track of how many people are taking action to follow you on all the social networking sites where you have a presence. Also worth tracking is the number of *defectors*, people who choose to disengage with you on these networks. A significant decrease in number of followers, or the inability to significantly grow your fan base, could be an indication that you are not having the right type of conversations. Or, maybe you are not offering the right mix of content to attract and keep your audience of customers and prospective buyers.

➤ **Social demographics:** Increasingly, more social media networks are providing analytics specific to each platform. There is a decent amount of data that you can access about your Facebook fans, followers on Pinterest, or the groups you belong to in LinkedIn, for example. With this increase in data, you can start to learn more about the people who are behind the numbers. In some cases, you may not only see gender and age, but you may be able to tell in what part of the world (or in what part of the country) the majority of your followers live. You may be able to see which level of job role seniority—senior executive, managerial, or entry-level—engages most, or which job functions—marketing, sales, IT—are most active. Some of the social platforms also make it easy to see what topics, current events, comments, or posts your followers Like or are discussing at any given moment. These are all social indicators that not only help you better understand who is interested in you, but help you determine how to converse with them and how to target others like them, who may be your most likely prospects.

As you can see, when it comes to social selling, there are other types of data beyond Likes and +1s that you need to capture in order to help you reach, engage, and convert. There are, however, plenty of tools available to help you track and use social data in a smart way.

FINDING PURPOSE WITH SOCIAL TOOLS

If you're not a natural-born number cruncher, or you aren't part of the marketing operations team, whose job it usually is to turn raw data into *dashboards* that visually illustrate key performance metrics for the CEO, then why should you care about analytics or social tracking tools? For starters, it isn't necessary for you to delve into all levels of data and social indicators. To be perfectly honest, if you spend too much time digging into the numbers—if you fall into the data hole—then you will not have enough time to be an effective salesperson. However, it is still important to understand what types of social data exist, and which tools are available to help you analyze it. From there, you can decide which indicators are most important to you and choose when and where it's worthwhile to invest your time.

When it comes to using data to paint a picture of your social land-scape (your customers, influencers, and engagement), you also have to consider content. As discussed in Chapter 6, content is used to spark social interactions and build relationships. Fortunately, there are some social tools to make it easier to create and distribute content across your social media channels. Even better, many of these content tools have the ability to track analytics as they pertain to your content. For example, was your content viewed by someone, or did they view it and then download it? Perhaps they shared your content, or commented on it. Sometimes, your content creation tools will give you that view into your prospects' behavior, which makes it helpful in gauging the effectiveness of your content. (Getting some level of active engagement, such as having it shared, is always better than just viewing it.)

Some of the tools I am about to introduce to you, including those to help create content, are more likely to be meaningful to marketers, while others may be of better use to you as a salesperson. Considering that marketing teams often own the social media process, particularly social monitoring, they usually pave the way, deciding which social tools the company officially adopts. This is particularly true for more expensive, enterprise-level applications. If the tool requires a significant investment, you can bet that it will be vetted and approved by the CMO (Chief Marketing Officer) and possibly even the CTO (Chief Technology Officer).

Unfortunately, the sales team may be the last to hear about a new social media tool. The good news is that social media makes it possible for you, as an individual salesperson (or marketer), to have your own tools as well. Many social tools are free or low cost, making them affordable. There have even been cases when tools get adopted by the broader organization only after an individual has discovered, tested, and proven them to be useful. The takeaway? Don't be afraid to experiment!

As you consider which types of tools are important to your role as a salesperson or marketer, consider how social tools can help you most. The best social tools should:

- ➤ Make you more efficient.

- ➤ Help you identify and find influencers.

- ➤ Make it easier for you to find and engage with prospects and customers online.

- ➤ Improve your rate of response to social mentions or requests.

- ➤ Provide useful feedback on who is interacting with you, how often, and in what way.

- ➤ Increase your ability to share information quickly.

- ➤ Offer a better way to create and deliver content to use in the social selling process.

- ➤ Manage your company image or brand reputation online.

- ➤ Increase your reach and (positive) social influence.

With these benefits in mind, I have put together lists of tools for the types of social media, along with descriptions of those that are most likely to be of use to you. Keep in mind, each of these categories probably has a dozen or more tools that could be listed, and new ones pop up every day. In order not to overwhelm you, I mention only a few tools in each category, but know that your options are almost limitless.

Also factored into the tools that made this list is cost and ease-of-use. There are thousands upon thousands of social media tools available; but for the average small business or individual salesperson, the price range and complexity puts many of them out of reach. Most of the tools listed here have a free or very low-cost option that is billed either monthly or annually. Since prices fluctuate frequently, I am leaving those specific details off; but the paid versions of many of these tools are often less than $10 per month, and often not more than $20 per month.

Further, there are some social tools that are specific to individual social media platforms (like Facebook, Twitter, and LinkedIn). You will find those tools referenced in later chapters when I discuss each of those top social networks and the features and tools that make them so useful in the social selling process.

MONITORING TOOLS

Conversations move rapidly in social media, and often occur in real time. Granted, it's possible to manually sort through all the interactions happening across the different social channels and find mentions of your company or products. But it certainly isn't efficient to do it this way! And you simply cannot sit at your computer twenty-four hours a day, every day, and watch for your name to pop up somewhere. This type of manual social surfing is going to take you much longer to find and respond to someone when your name surfaces—and that's not going to help you sell. Luckily, there are lots of social tools available to make social monitoring more efficient.

➤ **HootSuite:** This social listening tool is a workhorse that allows you to monitor, track, and manage social mentions (and more) using a Web-based dashboard. You can manage multiple social media accounts and track multiple social platforms (included Twitter, LinkedIn, Facebook, Google+, and WordPress) by creating "streams" of segmented data based on keywords, hashtags, or mentions, all in real time. HootSuite allows you to respond to messages without having to leave the dashboard, and you can preschedule messages to send or post at later times on your different social networks. It also includes detailed analytics.

➤ **Mention:** Another monitoring tool, Mention, provides real-time alerts of your brand or product mentions across social platforms and other online resources. In addition, it allows you to respond and engage directly from the application. It can also monitor in multiple languages, forty-two to be exact. While there are extensive analytics and reporting features, they are not available with the free version of Mention.

➤ **Google Alerts:** A free tool, Google Alerts notifies you via email when your company or products are mentioned online. You can set alerts for any term, including those of competitors, and you decide how often (daily or weekly, for instance) you want to receive alerts for each term. This is a super simple way to monitor important terms online.

INFLUENCE TRACKERS

With millions of people using social media and millions of blogs and online magazines, how do you find the sites and the people who are going to most help your cause? What qualifies someone as a high-quality influencer? For starters, you want to find influencers who are active in your market space. They may be trusted bloggers, active social media enthusiasts, or passionate customers turned brand advocates. The important thing is they have the ability to help spread positive messages about your brand effectively and often.

You'll probably know or discover some of these influencers on your own, but there are also a few accessible tools to help you do this. Many of the more sophisticated tools used to find and monitor social influencers are fairly expensive. Traackr, for example, costs nearly $2,000 (annually) for the enterprise edition. However, there are a few tools that individual salespersons and marketers are able to afford.

> ➤ **Wefollow:** Self-described as a directory of online social influencers, Wefollow lets people register and identify the subjects that they are most likely to influence. The application identifies and pulls in experts from across social networks as well. With more than 1.3 million users in its database, Wefollow uses a "Prominence Score" to help you determine how valuable or influential a person may be in your area of interest. You can conduct a search using keywords to identify those who are engaged in that subject matter. Their profile also shows their Prominence Score.

> ➤ **Socialbro:** Designed to help you get more from Twitter, Socialbro helps you search for, identify, and target influencers in your key areas of interest by using different filters and search tools.

> ➤ **Trackur:** A social monitoring tool, Trackur has a tool within a tool, called InfluenceRank. Using the InfluenceRank service for approximately $27 per month, you can determine if someone is discussing you (or your product), and how influential that person is. In addition, Trackur automatically tracks and analyzes the sentiment for every item on your Trackur dashboard so you can further determine if the sentiment of a particular social mention is positive, negative, or indifferent.

SOCIAL SHARING TOOLS

At the heart of social media, and at the root of social selling, is the ability to share information and start conversations. Any tools that can help you do this better, or more quickly, is certainly worth using. The primary benefits of these particular sharing tools is that they either offer an abbreviated linking URL (the website's address), or a linking URL that provides tracking information. Like some of the other social media tools, these tools also provide analytics that track what content was viewed, and how and where it may have been shared with others.

➤ **Bit.ly:** What happens if you have a piece of content you want to share on your social networking sites, but it has an extremely long and complicated URL (that is basically the equivalent of alphabetical nonsense)? Bit.ly (also displayed as Bitly) is a free tool that automatically shortens your link to something much more manageable. This is especially important with sites like Twitter, where your messages, or tweets, are limited to a certain number of characters. Bit.ly also tracks the number of clicks, shares, and saves that your shortened link receives, along with more in-depth analytics about how and where the shortened link was viewed or shared.

➤ **SharedBy.co:** Similar to Bit.ly, on the surface SharedBy replaces long, complicated URLs with shorter versions, but it's much more than that. It allows you to frame your brand around any piece of content shared, using a special "Engagement Bar" at the top of the Web page being shared. Let's say you want to share an article from an online newspaper with your followers. When they click on the link, they see not only the article, but a special bar across the top of the page that contains your name or company name, logo, contact information, and other brand details that you can choose to include in the bar. Additionally, it includes detailed tracking information about your shared links and those who are viewing them.

➤ **Google URL Builder:** This is one of many tools available to create unique URLs for link tracking using UTM parameters. "UTM" is short for Urchin Tracking Module, but you are most likely to hear it referred to as "UTM parameters." This free online tool from Google allows you to add special tags, or descriptors (such as an ad campaign name or source), to any URL. The special code is tracked by Google Analytics to show that you received visitors to your website because of a particular link associated with an ad campaign or piece of content. The only downside to this tool is that because it is tracked as part of your website analytics, it may require some help from your IT department (or whoever manages your website statistics) to get final tracking results.

CONTENT CURATOR TOOLS

Sometimes, you want to easily scrape content from across the Web based on topics you are interested in, and bring those articles, blog posts, and other online content into one place for easy access. As a salesperson, this helps you keep up to date on trending topics or articles and keywords that are important in your industry. Some curator tools are publishing platforms as well and allow you to assemble and spread this content online and in social networks.

- ➤ **Feedly:** As you may know, RSS (Really Simple Syndication) readers allow you to subscribe to and receive updates from your favorite websites or blogs. A true curator tool, Feedly collects information and lets you organize important content from many different sources and then makes it easy for you to get to them from one place. Feedly is also a very visually pleasing RSS reader, which assembles the information as a deck of cards and then lets you share, engage, or respond to articles and blog posts from the application.

- ➤ **Paper.li:** Billed as an online newspaper publisher, this social tool provides the means for collecting articles, blog posts, and videos of interest to you (or your prospects), perhaps based on industry topics or subjects that match or reflect your buyer personas. You select the sources you want the app to pull from, you customize the template (how the information is organized and displayed visually), and then when everything is collected and formatted, you have a nice piece of content to share.

> **Scoop.it:** Similar to other curators, Scoop.it lets you enter keywords and phrases that are of interest to you. Scoop.it goes out to social media sites and other online resources to collect content that matches your subject preferences. You can pick up or "scoop" the content you like and format it into an online magazine. Your followers or readers can suggest topics for you to include, and you can share the final product across your social media channels. Plus, Scoop.it includes analytics that tracks your readers' engagement.

APPLICATIONS FOR CREATING CONTENT

In many companies, content is often created for you, from company brochures and product tutorials to white papers and case studies. All of these are great pieces of content to distribute to your social networks, but there never seems to be enough of it. Whether you are part of the team responsible for developing new content, or you're an individual in need of extra information to share, there are some creative tools that can help with the ongoing challenge of content creation. This is a larger category, because some of these tools help with visual content, too, such as infographics, videos, and other presentation formats.

> **Visual.ly:** Infographics is a visual format for sharing content, and uses mainly graphics and images as opposed to only text. This is an increasingly popular type of content to share through social media. Unless you happen to be a graphic artist, creating an infographic from scratch isn't easy. There are some tools, like Visual.ly, that provide you with some standard templates and auto-generated information (gathered

from your social networks) that is developed into an info-graphic. Visual.ly has a limited number of free templates, but you can also hire from their network of designers to create a customized infographic.

➤ **Infogr.am:** Another tool for creating infographics, Infogr.am provides a larger variety of templates, or themes, from which to choose. You can upload your own images, and even video, and you can create new charts using your own data that you upload into Infogr.am. The free version of this tool has plenty of options and flexibility for creating a professional-looking infographic to share online.

➤ **Prezi:** This tool makes it a snap to create animated presenta-tions. Think of it in terms of a modern version of a Power-Point presentation. In fact, you have the option to import directly from PowerPoint. These short online presentations are created from templates provided by Prezi, then you add text and video (if you like) and choose special effects for emphasis. The finished presentation can easily be distributed via social media.

➤ **SlideShare:** A sort of hybrid between a content creation tool and its own social platform, SlideShare lets you create visual online presentations based on your existing content in a slid-ing image format. You can base a SlideShare presentation on a PowerPoint presentation or create it from a PDF or a video. The great thing about this tool is that it lets you insert a call to action, or form, to create a lead and collect the viewer's contact information. You (or the viewer) can easily share the presentation on your social networks, or on the SlideShare network, which has grown quite large.

➤ **Animoto:** Creating videos is easier for some than others, but Animoto makes it very easy for all skill levels. You basically select and layer components to build a thirty-second to full-length video. It starts with the selection of your preferred templates, and can even include sound clips or music. The finished product is pretty decent video that presents your message in a more engaging manner.

➢ **Present.me:** For a salesperson, Present.Me is a simple way to combine a traditional presentation with a video of yourself. All you have to do is upload your finalized presentation, which can include PowerPoint or any other standard file. Then you use your computer's webcam to record yourself going through your presentation, just as if you were at a live event or a face-to-face meeting. It also includes some simple editing functions in case you need them. Once you are finished recording yourself giving the presentation, you are ready to share your new video-style content across your social media channels.

➢ **Scripted:** Videos, shared presentations, and infographics often start with other plain text pieces of content. If writing a blog post, white paper, or even your own promotional tweets is challenging, Scripted has developed a quick, online process to have independent writers do the job for you. Although most of the process is handled via a Web-based form, the writing and editing process is handled by real writers. You decide the topics, content format (blog post, Web page, tweets, etc.), tone, and writing style, and you can even identify keywords to include or avoid. Although this service is not free, it's still very affordable and quick—you can have a piece of content created and finalized in just a few days, and for less than a hundred dollars.

SOCIAL INFLUENCE MEASUREMENT TOOLS

Does your level of social acumen help promote your company's brand or impact your ability to persuade prospects to choose your products and services? These tools are designed to measure your influence, as well as those of others. Each creates a numerical score that represents your social reach and influence.

> **Klout:** Using a scoring system of 1 to 100, Klout monitors your activity and interactions with others across several social networks and then determines your amount of influence. It also provides a quick overview (along with an actual photo!) of each person who engaged with you and to which post, tweet, or image they interacted with you. It then summarizes of which topics you have expert-level knowledge based on these interactions. Some of the other social monitoring platforms and CRM tools actually pull in Klout scores so that you can see the Klout score of a particular prospect or customer and know whether or not they have influence within their networks.

> **Kred:** Similar to Klout, this tool also measures social influence (how people engage with you) and reach (how you engage with and share other people's messages). Its scoring system ranges from 1 to 1,000 for influence and from 1 to 12 for reach across social media networks and other online communities. In addition, it uses a visual dashboard to let you search and identify content from other influencers.

MOBILE APPS

Many of the tools mentioned offer a mobile application, or app, for your phone. In most cases, the apps are available for the iPhone and Android devices, and sometimes for the Blackberry. The importance of a mobile app is that it allows you to stay alert while you are away from your office and makes it easy to respond and engage, no matter where you happen to be at any given time. As a sales professional, this probably isn't a new concept. You already appreciate the need to respond quickly to sales inquiries. Social media has introduced that same, and possibly greater, sense of urgency to everyone else.

Online chatter happens quickly, and in some social networking platforms, the discussions are tracking in real time—and almost everyone has equal opportunity to view and engage. Unlike the old days, when a prospect would leave a message on your phone with a question and you would have at least a little bit of time to return the call. Today, your prospect is posing that same question to everyone—across social media channels. Your ability to respond quickly (and sometimes instantaneously) can make all the difference in making the sale. In social selling, time is of the essence. Mobile apps allow you to better compete for the online prospect.

—

After going through this list of tools, you may feel exhausted just reading about each of them. But I promise that these tools are social boosters. These social media tools are simple, effective, and fairly inexpensive—and designed to make your social sharing life a little more manageable. Even so, it can be time consuming to do everything you should with social media in order to be effective in social selling. There's no time to stress about it, simply keep reading. In the next chapter, I help you sort through all the potential time synchs and develop a feasible schedule that keeps your social (media) life on track, and supports—not distracts from—your professional goals.

CHAPTER 8

TIME IS MONEY

Building Social Selling into Your Schedule

If you could improve a single part of your overall sales process, what one factor would potentially have the biggest impact on reaching your sales quota each month? More than likely, you would want to change the part of your process that influences either the quantity or the quality of your sales leads. Perhaps you need a larger number of leads coming into your pipeline, or you want more qualified prospects, or maybe you could benefit from prospects that are further along in the buying process and ready to purchase—sooner rather than later. Sadly, I don't have a magic wand to grant your wishes, but I can assure you that adopting a solid social selling strategy can have a positive impact on each of these areas. There's just one catch—it takes time. But rooting around in social media doesn't have to be a drain on your time, if you plan accordingly.

IDENTIFYING CURRENT TIME CONFLICTS

Before adjusting your schedule to make room for social selling, it's important to understand where most of your time is currently being spent with regards to the sales process, and why it's being spent that way. A benchmark report from CSO Insights examined how a typical salesperson's time is spent.[1] A whopping 19 percent of the day is eaten up with (non-customer) meetings and administrative functions, including CRM tasks that help with organization and data cleansing (to tell you more about a particular customer). Another 16 percent of the day is spent on service calls and training. And then about 24 percent is spent searching for leads. This leaves only 41 percent of the day for selling either face to face or over the phone.

Even though finding leads is a legitimate function, many sales managers, and their sales teams, would rather see a bigger portion of that time focused on selling. In the CSO Insights report, sales professionals admitted to being frustrated with the process of finding and researching leads and viewed it as a time waster. In other research, from InsideSales.com, the salespeople surveyed said that having problems contacting leads or identifying the proper decision makers were among their top barriers to selling.[2] Also flagged as problematic was the fact that even after researching leads, they didn't have the right information before making a call to a prospect. This is disconcerting because typically, the better quality of information you have for a lead before your first contact, the more successful you will be in pulling it into the buying cycle and ultimately winning the deal. This is one reason that LinkedIn has been such a critical tool for savvy salespeople. In Chapter 11, I explain exactly how you can use LinkedIn to improve the quality of your conversations with prospects.

So, to summarize, more than half of your day is likely spent on activities other than your primary goal—selling—and even then you may not possess the right information to have a good, quality conversation with a prospect. If this describes *your* typical day, you may find it hard to believe that it's worthwhile to add yet another set of tasks, or another lead pool in which to fish. But there are many reasons why social networks are lucrative for prospecting. With the proper use of social media, you can increase your efficiency and improve the quality of information available to you before picking up the phone for that first call to your prospect or before going into the initial sales meeting.

SPENDING YOUR TIME IN FISHING HOLES, NOT RABBIT HOLES

Time wasters are much like falling down rabbit holes. You become distracted and disoriented, and can easily lose your way. Some people, maybe even you, have previously thought of social media this way. I've met plenty of skeptics who think using social media for business is simply an excuse for otherwise well-meaning employees to waste time sifting through their friends' status updates on Facebook, or viewing and sharing the latest viral video craze on YouTube. For sales and marketing professionals serious about social selling, this simply is not the case.

By spending as little as six hours per week in social media, 68 percent of marketers reported gaining benefits in the area of lead generation; additionally, 40 percent of those surveyed also realized an improvement in sales. These are a sample of the findings from the 2012 Social Media Marketing Industry Report.[3] The annual report surveyed nearly 4,000 marketing professionals to see how they used social media to grow business. It's worth mentioning that the survey participants were split almost evenly in their target markets of B2B (51 percent) and B2C (49 percent), indicating that it's likely you can benefit from social media, whether you are selling to businesses or to consumers.

To reap these benefits, you may be wondering how much time you really need to devote to social media. Is six hours really the magical number if you want to find new leads? The feedback from this survey (which is one of the best reports I have seen on the topic of increasing business through the use of social media) indicates there are two time-related factors that make a difference. Whether you are looking for new leads or trying to improve overall sales, these objectives benefit from the combination of total weekly hours devoted to social selling and the number of years you have been using social media.

In general, those marketers who have spent anywhere from six to eleven hours weekly in social networks gained a significant increase in leads and improved sales, and were able to build new business partnerships. This is in addition to increasing awareness, or exposure, to their business. Marketers who had been using social media for one to three years saw the greatest benefits, significantly more than those who had been using it for six months or less. Small businesses, companies with twenty employees or fewer, often realized the most benefit across several of the categories, or objectives, specified.

The takeaway from all this data is that spending time in social media does have a tangible payoff that makes it a viable place to fish for leads and build business relationships. But you have to be willing to invest a solid number of hours each week, and commit to being patient—because the results improve over time (in this case, meaning a minimum of six months!).

CONQUERING THE SOCIAL SELLING CONFLICT

As you can see, social media presents an interesting challenge for sales professionals. On one hand, it holds the potential for providing more—and more direct—access to better quality prospects. These prospects have often already invested a good deal of their own time researching product options, which means they are typically closer to making a final buying decision. What's not to love about a lead source that delivers higher-quality results? On the other hand, how do you find the amount of time and effort needed, that block of six hours or more per week, to get that big payoff from using social networks as a lead source? Time management, after all, can be an Achilles heel for many salespeople.

In addition to trying to figure out how to make time for social selling within your own schedule, you may also need to convince a sales manager that it's truly worthwhile. It's possible that you will be met with resistance—after all, time is money. The first time I suggested the idea of letting our team of inside salespeople fish for leads online, specifically through social media, there was some hesitation. I was prepared for the sales manager to balk because he didn't view social networks as legitimate sources for finding leads. But his low-level resistance was based on two very different factors: time and compensation. He was worried about how much it might pull his team away from their normal sales call activities, and how this new lead source would fit into the sales compensation model for his team.

Like most small, inside sales teams, the group already had a lot of responsibility, from answering phone calls and responding to online chat requests (triggered from the company website) to qualifying new leads and following up with existing leads and passing them to an account executive. If you are an independent salesperson, you can probably relate to the pain of juggling so many balls in the air at once while relentlessly chasing leads to close the sale. You can certainly understand the sales manager's concern for how the team would possibly find extra time in the day to devote to foraging the social networks for leads. Of course, it's my personal belief that if ever there was a person on this earth who could figure out how to cheat time and squeeze more than twenty-four hours out of a day, it is bound to be a salesperson—a really good salesperson. With that in mind, we compromised and managed to find some spare time to *test* the idea of social selling.

The sales manager started by agreeing to let one of his newer team members serve as the guinea pig, so to speak. Because she was not yet fully in the sales call rotation, she had some extra time available; and since she was still on a draw rather than normal commission, he didn't have to worry about adjusting commission structures. As well as resolving the two primary concerns he first had about social selling, the sales manager thought that by using the newest team member, she would be the most hungry for a sale and possibly more aggressive in finding prospects from an untested lead source.

To ensure she wasn't completely flying solo, she was paired with a marketing specialist, from the internal marketing team. The two women shared the responsibility of monitoring several social networks and online communities for any mentions, feedback, or conversations that allowed a salesperson to engage. The marketing specialist even helped provide the salesperson with content in order to feed all of her new social interactions. (By the way, this is a great example of how easy it can be for sales and marketing to work together in an effort to further social selling goals, as discussed in Chapter 3.) And as a result of these initial efforts, we made definite headway in proving the merits of social selling, at least enough to win approval for the continued investment of time and resources.

While our internal social selling process has matured since that first attempt, there were many good ideas that developed out of it—and several important lessons learned, especially concerning time management. These lessons in social selling efficiency created the basis for the social media time management strategies I'm about to share with you. Not only can they help you make the most of your time spent in social media, but they may help you convince sales managers and marketing executives that you can make time for social selling.

SETTING CLEAR OBJECTIVES

Before spending your first hour perusing a social network, it's critical that you know what you are looking for and what you want to achieve. As part of a sales and marketing team, you are usually focused on hitting specific targets, and closely monitored metrics are used to determine how well you are meeting those goals. The amount of pipeline created, number of leads generated, total value of deals closed, and number of certain products sold are among the many common goals you either set for yourself or are expected to accomplish as part of a larger organization.

Social selling is no different—you need to identify not only a broad purpose, but the specific goals that support that purpose so you can avoid wasting precious time randomly surfing from one social network to the next, unsure of what you're actually hoping to find.

One overarching objective, for example, may be to increase sales pipeline generated through social media. Specific social selling goals to support that purpose might include:

> ➤ Engage in a set number of social media conversations per month that contain late-stage buying indicators (for example, asking questions that compare specific vendor solutions).

> ➤ Use LinkedIn to identify a certain number of decision makers in one or more of your target verticals and invite them to a Webinar, product demo, or other online sales presentation.

> ➤ Identify how much content you want to distribute on a weekly basis, for instance, and then identify to which specific social media channels each piece of content should be posted. You may want to match the types of content to the audience found on each social media channel, in line with your content strategy, as discussed in detail in Chapter 6.

These are sample goals, but you get the idea. Your initial purpose can be general, but your social media goals should be specific and should be set weekly, monthly, or quarterly. When possible, be sure to use the tools introduced in Chapter 7 to help you find the right social conversations to engage in and to track which content and conversations produce results. This is helpful in making sure you are meeting your goals and not wasting time on the wrong activities.

DESIGNATING BLOCKS OF TIME

You have already seen how a typical day is spent for many salespeople. The research indicated that at least two hours out of an eight-hour day are dedicated to searching for new leads and digging up information about prospective customers. Yet salespeople admitted to not being satisfied with the results. What if you took at least one hour of that time, or the time already being spent on administrative tasks, and dedicated it to specific social selling actions that align with your social media goals? To help keep you on track, take it one step further and actually schedule time for it on your calendar.

There is a generally accepted practice that if you repeat an action enough times it will eventually become a habit, but getting started is the challenge. Placing social media activities on your calendar ensures you spend a designated amount of time on it as part of your daily routine. One hopes that it will become a habit, something you do automatically, but if it's on your calendar or part of your official to-do list, then it's *guaranteed* to receive your attention. Plus, allotting a certain amount of time on your calendar helps prevent you from falling down one of those rabbit holes and wasting a disproportionate amount of your time.

Be strategic about defining the blocks of time to be carved out of your daily schedule. Instead of putting "Get on social media from 8:00 to 9:00 a.m." on your calendar, schedule small time slots that detail specific activities or specific social networks, providing details on what you plan to accomplish. You might, let's say, allot a thirty-minute block of time from 8:00 to 8:30 a.m., saying: "Post new Social Selling white paper to Twitter and LinkedIn and check the list of trending topics in Twitter and new group discussions in LinkedIn for opportunities to make comments." The more specific you can be, the less likely you are to waste time.

PRESCHEDULING POSTS

One of the best ways to make the most of your time on social media is to plan ahead for the comments and information you want to share in the different networks. Make a list of topics each week and then identify helpful content that supports each topic. Then write the actual comments you want to post each day for each social media channel in one or two sittings. It's ideal to compose a minimum of two or three comments daily. To manage this process, I find it is easier to keep up with the information by placing it all in an Excel spreadsheet, with columns labeled by social network, message, links, and time of post. An example of what a "Social Postings" spreadsheet might look like can be found on the website for this book (artofsocial selling.com) under the tab *Exclusive Content,* at the top of the homepage.

After you have created your comments and links for the corresponding content, you are ready to load, or preschedule, the posts. Refer back to Chapter 7 for a list of tools that allow you to do this. I like to use HootSuite but there are many others that let you do this, too. There are a couple of things to keep in mind with prescheduling posts. While this is a great way to make the most of your time, when it comes to something as time consuming as posting comments, it does not alleviate the need to make real-time comments during the week. Real-time engagement offers a better level of interaction with your social media audience, and lets you have more natural conversations (just as if you were talking face to face). It also reduces the likelihood that you might miss responses to your comments. When using prescheduled posts, you may have them set to go out when you are not available to respond to feedback and this can be a frustrating experience to your fans and followers, especially if it happens frequently.

You may want to use a three-to-one ratio as a guideline to get started. For every three prescheduled posts you use, make sure to have one real-time post. As you get more experienced with social selling and more comfortable with managing your time commitment, you will want to reverse that ratio, making it three real-time comments for every one post you schedule. But, that doesn't mean you have to use completely unique content or feature links to a new piece of content. Remember, "real-time" posts include retweets, mentions, and responses (such as a "thank you" to a new follower).

Prescheduling your posts is not the same as *automating* them. This is an often debated topic among social media experts. Essentially, the idea of automated posts or responses in Twitter means you *have no other engagement or real-time activity.* Deciding in advance what to say and when it will post and *then walking away* from it is a big no-no. You will be taking the "social" out of social media! Pre-scheduled posts should never be a replacement for real-time interactions in your various social networks.

Because some tools make it easy to automatically post information or comments for you, they remove a level of control. For example, HootSuite offers an "AutoSchedule" feature that will decide (on your behalf) the best times to post your prescheduled tweets; you write the tweet, but you don't get to decide *when* it should be posted. So you can't make it your business to be available for real-time interaction with your followers.

Another problem of using an automation tool is that you may have the option to have each new blog post automatically shared on your designated social networks. This would mean that the same exact post would appear on Twitter, Facebook, and LinkedIn, and at the exact same time. And your blog software (or specific design template) may not have the feature allowing you the option to add or customize a message; instead, it automatically grabs only the blog title, or a portion of the title, and uses that with a shortened link. As you know from the example of the Coverall cleaning product for schools (discussed in Chapter 3), it's important to create tailored messages for your various audiences—this absolutely applies to the various social networks, as well!

In sum, while automation can be a time-saving tool, many social media experts (myself included) believe these types of automation are not a best practice. You want to fully control the information you post, including when it is posted, in which network it is posted, and what message accompanies the post. Prescheduling—not automation—allows you to easily manage this process.

LIMITING YOUR EXPOSURE

Just as you want to manage when and where your comments are posted, you may also want to limit *how many places* you "network," or try to engage with others on social media. There are a handful of primary social platforms that most people associate with social media, including Facebook, Twitter, LinkedIn, Google +, and Pinterest. When it comes to social selling, there are potentially hundreds of other platforms where you can become active, from blogs to community forums. Once you begin identifying all the places you could ultimately engage in conversations, you'll see that your entire day could be dedicated to these networks and you still wouldn't get to all of them.

More than likely, you'll find that there are certain networks where your target audience is most likely to congregate. A simple way to manage your time is to pick a few of those that are most appropriate to start with—the ones with the highest concentration of active prospects. Concentrate on one or two, maybe three, and give up the idea of trying to be everywhere. It's not an effective approach to social selling, nor is it the best use of your time. In the earlier example about my company's first approach to social selling, the limited resources and minimal amount of dedicated time forced us to concentrate on only two networks, and it quickly became obvious that this was a smart approach (even if we had stumbled onto it by accident!). The first network we focused on was LinkedIn, particularly a couple of groups within the network that revolved around topics pertinent to our solutions; the second was an online community geared toward our target audience of IT professionals. Concentrating our time and effort in those two networks to start with helped us achieve our goals.

USING YOUR EXTENDED RESOURCES

One of the components of social selling that takes up the most time is developing content to feed the social machine. As shown in Chapter 5, a great deal of effort (and time!) goes into producing and coordinating content. One way to minimize this investment of time is to turn to others for help; tap into any and all resources you may have available.

If you are part of a company with an active marketing team, ask them to help you sort and organize content so that it's easy for you to quickly identify which pieces are most useful in which networks.

You could even make a list of topics or ideas that would aid your social media strategy and suggest having those pieces of content developed by the marketing team. Similarly, look to customer support, product marketing, and any other departments in your company for content that already exists—from tips for using your product to installation or training videos. You may be surprised to learn what content has already been developed but is not being used.

On the flip side, if you are working solo, you may reach out to vendors or other associates and ask if they would be interested in providing content suitable to both of your audiences that can be shared. Inviting someone to contribute a guest post to your company blog is also a commonly used approach to accessing more quality content when you are stretched for time or ideas.

GOING MOBILE

Speaking of utilizing resources you already have available, as a salesperson one of your best tools is your smartphone or tablet. When you are out of the office or traveling, these devices can turn a (parked!) car or a coffee shop into a remote office where you can make calls, check your email, send sales proposals, and more. You can just as easily use your phone to manage your social media efforts.

Most social networks and social media tools have mobile apps, or applications that allow you to access your networks. You can also choose to allow the apps to ping your phone with real-time updates. (If you are not familiar with the term *ping*, it simply means to send a message or contact you via phone or email.) Implementing mobile apps is a simple, low- or no-cost option for helping you make the most of your time on social media. It lets you respond faster to questions, comments, or invitations to connect, and extends the amount of time you can give to social selling by picking up an extra ten or fifteen minutes between sales appointments, or while waiting to board an airplane, or waiting in line for lunch.

It's amazing how much extra time you can find for social media with some advanced planning—time that will allow you to identify helpful resources and put some of the tools you already have available to work for you!

―

Equally important to making time for social media is the need to find financial resources to support your efforts. While some parts of social media are free, many others require a minimal investment. Having a defined budget is a way to maximize your resources and make sure you are spending your dollars wisely. In the next chapter, I show you how to put together a budget that supports your social selling goals.

CHAPTER 9

FREE AND NOT QUITE FREE

Determining Your Budget

Social media is free—for the most part. The fact that it costs nothing to participate has undeniably helped fuel the rapid growth of social networks, making it easy and affordable for people to congregate, network, and share. The zero-participation cost has encouraged a wider audience, from all corners of the world, to tweet, post, Like, connect, pin, and +1. If all of this is true, then why do you need a social media budget and how much is it going to cost you?

RECOGNIZING THE COST OF "FREE" AND INVESTING IN YOUR SUCCESS

When it comes to social selling there are lots of opportunities for you to find and engage with potential customers without having to spend a dime. But even "free" comes with a price tag. That's because the no-cost version of social selling means that much of what you are doing relies on a manual process, which ultimately costs you in time and money. It takes more than a few minutes to sort through all the social networks where you may be active and then search, read, comment, post, and share. Without any short cuts or time savers, it also takes longer to identify worthwhile opportunities—it's just you, scrolling through every social network feed and every group discussion to find anything relevant.

Instead, by using—and paying for—a few social media tools, or more advanced versions of free tools, you not only better manage your time but you have more of it to focus on activities that cannot be automated (like selling!). Think of it in terms of a chef with a dull knife. What happens when she uses a lesser-quality knife or the blade of her knife is not quite as sharp? It takes longer to slice and dice the food, and the cuts aren't as clean or even as they should be (an important attribute that speaks to a chef's knife skills). Technically, the chef is still able to do her job, but not as well as she could have. Investing in a set of high-quality knives that are kept sharp is a must for any chef. Investing in social media tools is very similar.

Of course, a social media budget is about more than tools. It also includes investing in social media ads, contests, and community sponsorships to make yourself more visible and interesting when you are prospecting or selling through social media—that is, become someone others will want to pay attention to. A reasonable budget combined with a solid social media strategy can give you a leg up over your competition in the world of social selling.

DECIDING HOW MUCH TO SPEND TO RAMP UP YOUR SELLING GAME

You have to be smart about budgeting for social media; it's easy to be dazzled by the latest, greatest tool or ad campaign—but that doesn't make it the right investment for you. Having worked for many small businesses, and having been self-employed, I am a big believer in cautious spending and using free or low-cost options first, before jumping into products that cost several thousands of dollars (or more!). You may work for a company that already invests in some of the big-ticket social media tools, and those tools are paid for out of the organization's corporate marketing or IT budget. If you are lucky enough to be in this situation, then as a salesperson, your *personal* budget may not have to bear the cost of investing in the more advanced social media tools. (By the way, as a salesperson or marketer, there may be some tools, activities, and events that you are able to expense through your company instead of paying out of pocket and absorbing the cost yourself. But depending on the company, some or all social media tools may not be eligible for reimbursement by a salesperson; so always check the corporate policy for what qualifies as an approved expense.)

Whether you are talking about a salesperson's personal expenses, a departmental budget, or a budget of an entire corporation, it's important to understand and plan for the costs involved in helping make *you* successful in social selling.

So, what are the spending expectations when it comes to social media budgets? Exactly how much should you spend?

Some research indicates that the amount of a company's social media budget should coincide with its level of digital "maturity." A survey commissioned by the Altimer Group, a digital consulting firm, indicates that the more active and advanced your social media acumen, the greater your budget might need to be.[1] That makes sense. If you're already familiar with what works and what doesn't, and you actively use social media and have validated its benefits for you, then you probably need more money to support everything you are doing. But, let's say you are the average company using social media. How much should you invest?

As of early 2012, a survey of marketing executives indicated that companies were spending approximately 7 percent of their total budgets on social media.[2] Using this data point as a guideline, if you have a marketing budget of $50,000, then less than $5,000 is likely to be designated for social media. However, those numbers are rapidly growing. And in the next five years, these executives say they plan on nearly tripling the amount of their social media budgets, increasing it to almost 20 percent of the total marketing budget.

Which companies are spending the most? B2C companies (led by product companies, but including B2B service-focused companies, too) are spending the most on social media. And, B2B product companies are most likely going to have the most growth in their social media budgets. Christine Moorman, the director of The CMO Survey (where this data was found), explained the findings this way:

> Given the role that social media can play in acquiring and retaining customers, I think it is perfectly logical that B2B-Product companies are amping up their investments in this area. The advantage B2B companies have is that they often know who all their potential customers are. This means engaging with them using social media tools is easy and content can be customized. I would guess that B2B-Service companies have the same opportunities.[3]

Follow-up studies in 2013 seemed to confirm the expectations for growth in social media budgets. They indicated that organizations have already jumped from spending 7 percent to approximately 10 percent of their marketing budget on social media, with B2B product and B2C product companies accounting for the highest spending levels.[4] Looks like organizations are well on their way to meeting or exceeding that 20 percent social media spend predicted for 2017!

Some larger B2C companies, like Coca-Cola, have paved the way for not only investing heavily in social media, but also developing a specific spending formula to ensure they consider all possible opportunities. The company had been very open about this strategy; you can probably do an online search on the Internet and find lots of details about their social media spending habits. During a public forum via Twitter in 2013, Coca-Cola executive Wendy Clark explained the formula: "Coca-Cola puts together a 70–20–10 budget, which is 70 percent goes to what you know; 20 percent to trying something new; and 10 percent is for spend on the total unknown." In another tweeted response, she noted, "70/20/10 is a now/new/next model to ensure we're innovating in our marketing investment."[5] This type of strategy helps the company make a majority of safe bets, going with proven social media opportunities but also ensuring they spend some on the new opportunities that pop up.

In your social media budget, you may want to use a similar strategy to how the allotted money is divided. You may also want to detail specific costs or items that should be included in your budget. The remainder of this chapter will detail where money is typically allocated for social media–related efforts. Not all sections will apply to you. If you are part of a smaller business, for instance, you may not have any dedicated staff resources budgeted. It's also possible that money isn't set aside in your budget specifically for social media but rather is absorbed as part of a general marketing line item in the budget. Even so, this information provides guidance on what you should start considering as part of your social media spend. As an individual salesperson, you may want to convince your company to invest in social media training, but you may also want to commit a small percentage of your personal budget to some tools and resources. The potential return on investment should materialize in the form of more leads, shorter buying cycles, and increased sales. That's money well spent in my book!

SUPPORT COSTS

In planning a social media budget, support functions, also known as soft costs, are the expenses usually dedicated to people resources and ongoing educational fees. Even if you don't have a social media team on staff, you are still likely to spend money for training and education—and those costs can add up quickly. In Sonoma County, California, social media training is provided to many of the county's employees. In 2011, the county government dedicated $24,000 for a series of social media training classes. In 2013, they voted to increase the budget by $56,000 for additional training. The county's total social media budget now sits at $80,000.[6] Again, your training costs may not be as high as Sonoma County's, but setting aside money for social media education is important.

As a salesperson or marketer, there are lots of affordable opportunities, including social media conferences that cost only a few hundred dollars to attend, such as the annual New Media Expo (NMX)—one of the longest running conferences focused on social media. The Social Media Marketing World conference, sponsored by *Social Media Examiner*, is a popular online magazine dedicated to social media. If you cannot make it to a live event, many conferences offer virtual conference passes for significantly less (usually under $100), which includes access to live or recorded conference sessions that can be viewed from your desktop.

In addition to training, here is a snapshot of some of the items that typically fall under support costs:

> ➤ **Internal resources:** This includes staff dedicated to social media strategy or monitoring and related positions, such as community managers. It may also include positions such as lead-generation and marketing specialists, who assist with finding social media conversations for the sales team to engage in and enriching inbound leads to be passed to sales.

> ➤ **External resources:** It's not always easy or practical to manage social media efforts yourself. You may want to budget external resources to contract with an agency for additional support or to create and run social media campaigns. The types of agencies you might hire include boutique (small, specialized agencies), traditional advertising agencies, public relations (PR) agencies, social media firms, or independent social media consultants. You may think only large companies would have an expense such as this and that it would be used to pay to outsource the daily management of your social media accounts. It's actually very common for small companies or solo sales and marketing practitioners to spend a few hundred (or few thousand dollars) to hire an outside agency to put together and run a one-time or short-term social media campaign that could be used as a source of lead generation, for example.

> ➤ **Training and education:** As mentioned previously, it's important to not only get initial training on social media platforms and topics, but ongoing education to keep up with the fast-changing trends in social media and social selling. While

there are many free webinars, there are also low-cost virtual events; affordable on-site events and live conferences; and mid- to high-cost investments for in-house training. You may also want to invest in books (like this one!) and other training material that would be budgeted for under this category.

➤ **Membership fees:** There are some organizations and member-based associations that require annual membership fees to participate. These organizations can also be a great resource for and provide access to additional training, books, and conferences. Membership fees can range from under $50 to $3,000 or more, but can also provide good networking opportunities as well as ongoing education. The Word of Mouth Marketing Association (WOMMA) is a good example of this type of organization. MarketingProfs is an online organization that offers a paid "Pro" membership for more access to articles, training, and virtual events focused on online marketing and social media, particularly for those in B2B sales and marketing.

PROGRAM COSTS

Whereas support costs are aligned with expenses benefitting your internal resources, program costs are usually costs associated with your external, customer-facing initiatives. This is the part of your budget that would include money for ads on social media networks. It's where traditional advertising or online marketing is needed to support your social selling efforts. While you can certainly get "free" exposure and engagement from much of your interactions in social networks such as Facebook and Twitter, social media marketing includes some paid advertising and sponsorships to increase and accelerate your reach (or audience exposure) in social media.

Fortunately, ads on many social networks are often inexpensive—and can cost less than a hundred dollars. Of course, you can also spend thousands of dollars on social media ad campaigns and sponsorship programs. Because these costs can quickly escalate, it's advisable to budget for these items and plan not only how much you can spend, but where you should spend on a monthly or quarterly basis. Here are the areas where you might invest in program costs:

> **Online community sponsorships:** These are sometimes called *pay-to-play* opportunities. This refers to the practice of requiring vendors (or companies and brands) to pay for sponsorships in order to engage with users of highly targeted communities. Unlike paid advertising, sponsorships allow your company to be the sole financial supporter of a particular section of the community's website.
>
> For example, Spiceworks is a popular online community made up of millions of IT users. It allows technology vendors to have a company or brand page, but it also has sections of its site based around popular technology topics, where members can share tips and information and have questions answered about technology products and services. This is a great opportunity for a B2B tech salesperson to find and engage with prospective customers. Companies that are paid community sponsors not only get to have their brand exposed to users, but also get increased levels of access to the community members. For online communities that have large, active member bases, paid vendor sponsorships are very common. The cost of sponsorships often correlates with the strength of the community and number of users, but can be many thousands of dollars per quarter.

> **Media/Ads:** As in traditional advertising and PR, in social media you can often differentiate between *owned media*, *paid media*, and *earned media*. Owned media is advertising you place on your own websites, blogs, and social media accounts. Paid media refers to those advertising opportunities that you spend money to get, for example an ad on Facebook or an ad in a magazine. Earned media is free exposure you get online from news articles and mentions that either occur organically (you don't control) or as a result of your work reaching out to bloggers and other online reporters to get

them to do a story about you or your company. You want to have all of these types of media, but you will need to budget money for both owned media (the cost of creating on-site ads) and paid media (the cost of creating your ads and paying for them to appear on social media sites).

According to a report by Vizu, a digital media agency owned by Nielsen, paid social media ads are on the rise, with 66 percent of companies saying they now use it to support other online advertising campaigns.[7] You might place a paid ad on LinkedIn or Facebook. You might also pay Twitter to have some of your tweets appear more often and in conjunction with certain popular Twitter discussions. These social media advertising opportunities are often called sponsored tweets, or sponsored posts, and they simply ensure that your social media posts or conversations get more exposure.

The advantage of social media ads is that they offer the unique opportunity for the viewers of your ad to immediately engage on your social networks and can be valuable lead sources.

➤ **Social contests:** Similar to paid media, there are costs specific to setting up and running contests on social media. The contests are often used both for brand awareness and for lead generation. You might need to pay for apps (social media applications) that help you set up and manage a contest on Facebook. The benefit of these apps is that they often charge a relatively low fee on a month-to-month basis, with no contract (which means you can cancel at any time). This makes it both affordable and easy to run a social media contest. Remember, as part of your budget you also want to include the expense for prizes! You will probably also want to budget some money for paid social media advertising to promote your contest.

➤ **Influencer programs:** Your social media influencers are often popular bloggers who write about products or trends related to your business or industry. While it's possible to get earned media or free exposure from bloggers, getting their attention may also require a little bit of budget (or a whole lot of budget, in some cases!). It can be as simple as budgeting for product samples or demo equipment being sent to an influential blogger that writes about your market space.[8] Or, it could be as expensive as a large conference you orchestrate to bring in multiple bloggers and media professionals for coverage on your company. Part of your budget for influencer programs may even include the cost of online tools that help you identify who the influencers are in your industry.

TOOLS AND TECHNOLOGY

The importance of social media tools was discussed in Chapter 7, and we talked about some of the tools you might need to use. As a reminder, I want to mention that many of the most popular social media tools are free. To get more functionality or additional benefit from these tools, however, usually means paying a fee to upgrade the tool to a "Pro" version.

Sometimes, social media tools are available to individual users without cost, but then require businesses to pay for accounts that provide access to multiple users. That means it may require paying a small monthly fee for your entire sales or marketing team to use the same tool. In most cases, I have found that the paid versions of social media tools can range from as little as $5.00 per month to $99.00 per month. There are also tools that cost several hundred dollars (or more) per month, particularly with more complex tools, such as social media plug-ins for your CRM applications. I'll explain this in more detail, below, and I'll review some of the other categories of tools that you may find worth the investment:

> ➤ **Monitoring and tracking:** Any tool that helps you keep track of your social media conversations or brand or production mentions, or that makes it easier for you to post comments and engage with others, is considered a worthwhile monitoring tool. HootSuite and Mention are good examples of tools that offer both free versions with basic functionality enabled and paid versions that give you greater flexibility.

➢ **Social CRM:** Having a good Customer Relationship Management (CRM) application to track valuable prospect and customer data and trends is critical for most sales, marketing, and customer service teams. As social media's role in the sales process and customer support process has increased, many CRMs now offer some type of compatible social media plug-in that gives you an integrated view of your prospects' social activity. Radian6 is a social media tracking platform that was bought by and integrated into Salesforce.com (the CRM component). As I mentioned, having a view into the social activity of your prospects and customers from your CRM is valuable, so expect to pay several thousand dollars (on a quarterly or annual basis) for the additional license or plug-in module to grant you access to the information.

➢ **Video:** Any type of visual content is important to the social selling process, but video is increasingly an influential type of content to use and share across social networks. The only downside is that it does require some equipment (even if that's the ability to capture video from your smart phone) and it is helpful to use a third party to host your video online because the video files take up so much space and can bog down your website. As part of your social media budget, plan for the expense of making and hosting videos. It's typically a small cost that comes with a big social media payoff.

RESOURCES

When it comes to your social media budget, there are also some items that do not fit as neatly into one of the other budget categories. In general, these are expenses you are likely to encounter when planning your social media budget that help support any of your social networking activities. There are two categories that you are likely to use on a regular basis:

➢ **Content development:** As discussed in Chapter 6, content is a critical component in your social selling strategy. But it's difficult for an entire marketing department to keep the content machine fed—and it's even more challenging for a salesperson to tackle this endeavor by him- or herself. There are, however, many resources available to help you create content that can be used across all your social networks and blogs (as a reminder, these sources are also mentioned in Chapter 6).

What is most important to know about outsourcing content development is that it does cost money. Although you can often get a 300-word blog post written for less than a hundred dollars, or a white paper written for less than a thousand dollars, if you pay for content on a regular basis you will see that it can add up to big dollars. To protect your budget, set a monthly or quarterly amount that you can spend and have a firm understanding of how much content that will buy you. Otherwise, you may find that content production sucks up most of your money and leaves very little for the other social media components in your budget.

➤ **Account upgrades:** Similar to paying for social CRM integration, it's important to set aside money to pay for Premium account status on social media networks, such as LinkedIn. Paying a small, monthly fee for a premium or upgraded account means you get access to advanced features or access that can be extremely beneficial to the social selling process and reaching out to prospective customers. In Chapter 11, I discuss in detail how you can use an upgraded LinkedIn account to increase your selling opportunities.

There may be other categories of expenses that you may want to include in your social media budget, but this solid list will get you started in planning how to spend your money wisely.

⌒

Equally important to budgeting how much and where you invest in social media is to create a strategic plan. The next chapter shows you how to bring together the elements of time management and budgeting to form a solid plan.

CHAPTER 10

DEVELOPING YOUR SOCIAL SELLING STRATEGY

The Components for a Realistic Social Media Sales Plan

While it's possible to make progress in social selling, and perhaps even generate a few decent leads, even if only occasionally reaching out to prospects through social networks, without a *defined strategy* it will be difficult to repeat or maintain any successes you may have achieved. High-performing salespeople will tell you that their days are well planned and the techniques used for prospecting are consistent with best practices and based on proven sales methodologies. The same can be said for achieving sustainable results in social selling. You need a plan to follow, and a strategy to guide your actions.

Developing your social selling strategy for a social media sales plan ensures consistency and focus in your social prospecting. There is no shortcut to social selling; it takes time and patience to build online relationships that turn into sales. Without a plan in place, you may eventually question the effectiveness of social media networking, get discouraged, and possibly give up. An organized approach using an articulated social media strategy ensures you have a daily game plan for the online sales process.

A STRATEGY FOR YOU AND YOUR COMPANY

There are at least three types of social media strategies, and it's important to understand the differences among them. The first is all about you. Its objectives usually focus on your professional goals, such as building a personal brand to support career growth. It involves using social networks to make you more visible, noteworthy, and valuable to other future employers (or recruiters). Another common goal is positioning yourself as a social media influencer for your company. For instance, an industry analyst or a reporter would want to build her personal brand on social media, to help support and further the goals of her employer, as well as her own. Ultimately, she becomes an individual influencer in her industry, and her influence reflects positively on her organization.

Having a personal social media strategy also lends itself to your objectives as a salesperson. As you build credibility in your personal social media profiles (on Twitter, LinkedIn, and others), that same credibility extends to your reputation as a trusted, reliable expert in your field. Keep in mind, as a salesperson, you may represent the company or brand for which you currently work, but you (not the company) are the one in front of prospects and customers communicating solutions, making promises, and solving problems. Your *personal social media profile*, not the company's profile, is what you use to find and engage with prospects and customers. You are the face of the company—online and offline.

This brings us to a second and related type of social media strategy. It is the strategy that is most relevant to you today. It builds on your personal strategy, but takes that a step further because it's focused on developing a social selling plan. However, this type of strategy can be developed for an individual salesperson (or marketer) as easily as it can for an entire sales organization. A social selling strategy is completely focused on social prospecting.

The third type of social media strategy is for your organization and is centered on the company or the business brand. The goals and objectives of an organizational strategy are typically pretty far-reaching, and permeate numerous areas of the company. Social selling is most likely only one goal within that strategy. The organization's plan may also include goals for maintaining exceptional social customer service, assisting the Human Resources team in its recruiting efforts, and utilizing social media to support and further the company's search engine optimization (SEO) strategy. There can be other goals as well, but these are some of the most common. As for the stewards of this approach, your company's marketing communications team, dedicated social media team (depending on how big the company is), or other collective group of employees may own the social media strategy.

There are five primary steps involved in creating a solid (social selling) strategy:

1. Establish goals and objectives.

2. Set the rules of engagement.

3. Conduct research.

4. Know your assets and get organized.

5. Develop an outreach schedule.

Whether you are creating a strategy for an entire organization or developing a social selling strategy for yourself and your sales team, these same five steps will apply. Let's take a closer look at each of the steps involved.

ESTABLISHING YOUR GOALS AND OBJECTIVES

For any sales effort to be worthwhile, it needs to show results tied to meaningful metrics. In sales, those metrics are typically associated with *revenue* (money you are actually banking from winning deals and making sales) and *pipeline* (the dollar value of potential revenue based on sales forecasts), and your goals are to hit targeted values for those metrics each quarter. There are also other specific sales and marketing metrics that serve as signals to indicate whether or not you are on track to make your pipeline and revenue numbers. These signals might be particular objectives to ensure you achieve your ultimate money goal. Your goal, for instance, may be to have $75,000 in pipeline for the quarter. One of your objectives supporting that pipeline goal might be to generate 300 new leads. The goals and objectives you establish for your social selling strategy work the same way.

Your social *goals* may be directly or indirectly associated with amount of pipeline or revenue. Your *objectives* then become the actions that support or feed your goals, which in this example are revenue-related. You may be wondering if your goals should always include pipeline and revenue targets associated with a particular social network. After all, how else are you going to know if that network is worth the effort? Any time you can tie specific metrics to money goals, it helps provide a better picture of your return on investment for social media.

Unfortunately, tracking pipeline that's tied to a specific social platform can be tricky. Sometimes you can associate specific social media ad campaigns to a single social network, like Facebook, to track influence on pipeline. Or you may be able to associate a specific individual as a lead from LinkedIn, for instance, and tie her actions and buying behaviors into your revenue goals. But at times you may need to set goals that are only indirectly associated with revenue and pipeline. For example, you might consider setting goals that are tied to obtaining a certain number of new leads from social prospecting, or that show an increased percentage of white paper downloads or webinar registrations that originate from social media campaigns. Ultimately, choose goals that you can track and tie them to real dollars whenever feasible.

SETTING THE RULES OF ENGAGEMENT

The *rules of engagement* set up the parameters for how you will handle the various stages of your social selling efforts and how you will measure your progress. This step is particularly important if you are implementing a social selling strategy across a larger sales organization or as part of a cross-team effort between sales and marketing because it also addresses who is responsible for handling each area of your social selling plan. Here are the parameters you want to address:

> ➤ **Decide how you will track and measure progress:** Once your goals and objectives are established, you want to agree on how to determine success. Will you track progress on a monthly or quarterly basis? Which indicators will decide if you continue to dedicate resources to social selling? For B2B sales, it may take more time to build leads or pipeline from social selling than it does for B2C sales. Will you commit to a six-month window, for instance, before you measure progress, or will determination be based solely on meeting your objectives and goals for the year? How important is increasing Facebook fans or Twitter followers to your progress? Many organizations use this type of measurement as a simple, straightforward way to prove to executives that your social media efforts are improving.
>
>   If you are considering this as a way to track success, I will caution you that increasing your number of followers, fans, and connections rarely correlates directly to social sales (or revenue, as mentioned earlier). A better indicator, or signal, may be the number of *engaged* followers you have, and the number of times content is shared, comments are made, or conversations are started. As discussed in previous chapters, social selling is about having *positive interactions* that help build relationships and eventually lead to purchases; tracking interactions may be a better indicator of your progress.
>
> ➤ **Determine roles and responsibility:** Divide and conquer is perhaps the best way to think of managing your social selling efforts across a sales team or across several teams within your organization. You may have certain salespeople who are responsible for or have ownership of specific social networks. Janice handles activities in LinkedIn and Robert

manages Twitter, for example. Or you may want each individual salesperson to be active in multiple social media sites. So Janice and Robert are each active in Twitter, LinkedIn, and Google +.

Another consideration is whether to divide up responsibilities by actions instead of by social networks. Perhaps your sales and marketing teams are working together, in which case you may want marketing to handle all content development actions, and also help monitor for opportunities where sales can engage. If you recall, this is similar to the strategy my organization has used where a marketing specialist may identify and start conversations with potential prospects and then transfer the conversation, and the lead, to sales when it gets to a certain stage or when it seems most appropriate. This is the equivalent of a warm transfer, or handing off a lead that is already primed for a more in-depth sales interaction. In this step of your social selling strategy, another decision you need to make is choosing not only who is responsible for monitoring online comments, but also deciding who will monitor your overall success based on the parameters you set.

➤ **Choose your tools:** In Chapter 7, I introduced several types of tools you can use for everything from monitoring social networks for brand mentions to assisting with content development. As part of your official strategy, you must decide which tools to invest in and use, and confirm that everyone understands how to use them. This is particularly important if you decide to integrate some of the more complex social selling tools that are typically more expensive. These types of tools may also get integrated into your CRM software (Salesforce, for example, or SugarCRM), or your customer nurturing systems (such as programs like Eloqua or Marketo, which manage your customer emails). The implementation of these tools or the approval of the budget for these tools may stretch beyond your sales and marketing teams, so it will be important to get corporate buy-in to use them.

Along these lines, there are also some social networks, like LinkedIn, that have additional social selling tools you can purchase that provide your sales team with enhanced views of prospect activity or increased access to prospects. Again, these types of tools are somewhat more expensive but they often integrate with your CRM software. Planning which tools you want to invest in and deciding who has access to them is an important part of your overall strategy.

CONDUCTING YOUR RESEARCH

The next step in your social selling strategy requires a bit of due diligence. The research you conduct will help you determine where you are most likely to make headway in your social selling efforts. Proper research also helps to narrow down the social networks that may prove to be most lucrative for you. As a salesperson, this is similar to the type of offline customer research that you would do to gather information about who your target customers are and where you need to spend time to reach them. For this step, you want to put effort into the following:

> ➤ **Research where your target audience is most active:** If you are in B2C, you may find your potential customers are most active on Facebook, or that they regularly read and comment on certain blogs. For B2B sales, your prospects may be active on both Twitter and LinkedIn, along with certain industry communities or forums. Once you find out where your prospects are, you can put together a plan for interacting with them.

> ➤ **Review your history of engagement and take note of where you've been successful**: This type of information provides a good baseline for where to start interacting. If you or your company have already spent time on social media, review those sites where you have had the most luck interacting with prospects and customers. Look back at previous

interactions you have had on social media and note which types of information that you tweeted, posted, or shared got the most feedback or interactions. Your track record may quickly improve once you have a cohesive plan in place that ensures you are consistently active and are offering quality content that your social prospects have indicated they want to receive.

➤ **Build a list of your influencers:** Social selling is based on the concept of being, well, *social*. And, just like in the offline world, there are some people who have mastered the ability to socialize and network. Those people are your go-to contacts for introductions to prospective customers or vendors. They always seem to be in the know. In the world of social media, these networking gurus are called "influencers," and they usually have a large online network of fans, followers, and connections that actively engage with and respond to them. You want to identify the influencers in your industry so that you can be part of their circle. Engaging with and getting to know influencers is a good way to gain visibility with your potential prospects, or at least find out where they are and what matters to them

By the way, it's not only *external influencers* who are important. You also want to identify *internal influencers*, or those people within your organization who are already active in social media and participate in online communities and groups that are part of your industry. It should be easy to start connecting with your internal influencers and then expand from there to the external influencers you have identified.

➤ **Identify your keywords:** Similar to building a list of your influencers, you also want to create a list of keywords, which are specific words and terms that are used in your industry or by your customers. Keywords can be product names or categories of products. They can even be the names of your competitors, names of celebrities, or geographical locations that are particularly of interest to your customers. They can also be terms commonly associated with your products, such as particular features or benefits.

Once you create a list of the most important or most often used keywords or phrases, you can identify these as words that you want to track in social media. When those words appear, it is an indicator that there may be a conversation occurring that is relevant to you. Social monitoring tools can help automate the tracking of these key terms, or you can conduct manual searches within social networks to find potential conversations based around these keywords.

KNOWING YOUR ASSETS AND GETTING ORGANIZED

As you become more active in social media, you will increasingly see the wisdom in the declaration, "Content is king!" As discussed in Chapter 6, content is the linchpin of your social selling efforts. Quality content is used as a conversation starter. It's used as a proof point or educational opportunity in response to online conversations. Content is the carrot that you can easily offer your fans, followers, and connections when asking them to get to know you, and can help build their trust in you as an influencer and subject-matter authority.

As a salesperson, you probably already use a great deal of content—such as company brochures, product collateral, and Power-Point presentations—in your offline sales efforts. Those same pieces of content are used online. But social media conversations move fast, so it's important for you to know the content you have available, understand when it is most appropriate to use it, and have a way to deliver it electronically through links you can include in your posts via social media. Basically, this part of your social selling strategy requires some advance prepping and organization, and you want to take the following preliminary actions:

- ➤ **Inventory your content**: Know every piece of content you have available and take time to make it accessible through online links that can be easily posted to social media. Using a spreadsheet is a great way to keep track of your content, along with short explanations of how it is best used and active links so that it can be accessed online.

> **Map your content:** In that same spreadsheet, map (or associate) your individual pieces of content to specific products, prospect buying stages, customer needs, or common sales objections. If you take time to identify which pieces of content address which concerns, it makes it quick and easy for you to pull the best content for use in response to online conversations or questions. Don't forget to include a mix of content types, such as articles, brochures, videos, and slide presentations. You want to make sure that not all the content is focused entirely on your company or products as well. Some of the content should be vendor-neutral, and all of it should be quality material that is interesting or helpful.

> **Update your social media profiles regularly:** As part of knowing your assets, you also want to have available a standard description of you or your company that you can use on all your social media profiles. As you have probably noticed, every social network (and many communities and forums) provides the opportunity for you to create a profile that then shows up on your social media account and is visible to others. This is your elevator pitch, or your quick introduction to the social media world. It is a very brief summary, sometimes a couple of sentences or less, of who you are and why you are interesting. It's the introduction that potential prospects will see, and it will help them decide if they want to interact with you. It's helpful to use some of those important keywords and phrases that you already identified in your social selling strategy as being important. By using some of these words in your social media profiles, it helps you be found on LinkedIn, Twitter, or Google+ when someone searches for those related terms.

DEVELOPING AN OUTREACH SCHEDULE

The final part of developing a useful social selling strategy is to create a schedule of social media posts that will start conversations. The easiest way to do this is to set up a calendar that details when, what, and where you will post content or conversation starters. Conversation starters are short statements or questions that you post online; examples include (but are not limited to) interesting facts, company news and announcements, and polls (where you pose a question and provide a choice of answers).

The goal of posting content and conversation starters is to entice people to interact with you and share your information. This provides visibility to your prospective prospects and begins building relationships. Using the calendar, you may want to map or plan certain posts to coincide with other company events or promotions.

The important part of an outreach schedule is that it helps you budget time to devote to social selling. You may want to commit to a particular schedule based on a formula I use—it's a 3/2/3/1 strategy for posting, sharing, and interacting. My weekly schedule equates to posting *three* pieces of fresh content that is informative or educational; starting conversations with or interacting with *two* new influencers; sharing *three* links (that other people have posted) within each social media platform where I'm active; and commenting on at least *one* group thread, article, or blog.

This formula works well for me, but you can create any type of schedule and combination of activities that fits your social selling goals. I update this schedule each week, and note it on my social media calendar. As mentioned in Chapter 8, you can also keep a separate spreadsheet of prescheduled posts. Tweets or Facebook updates that you schedule ahead of time should be used to support—but not replace—real-time comments that are part of your outreach efforts.

Outreach posts are used to actively engage people (for example, "What's your favorite social media tool?"), while prescheduled posts may not typically ask for or encourage direct feedback ("Check out this list of top 5 social media posts at www.blogpost.com"). But any type of post may end up triggering a response from someone and that's why you can't use prescheduled posts and expect to completely ignore them—you must always watch for and respond to interactions. I suggest keeping your prescheduled posts in a separate spreadsheet because some social media tools, like HootSuite, allow you to bulk upload, or import a large number of prescheduled posts at one time. And even if you don't keep separate spreadsheets, you should at least note prescheduled posts as part of your main social media calendar.

INTEGRATE ONLINE AND OFFLINE SALES EFFORTS, THEN REPEAT

Although these five steps will help you create a solid strategy to boost your social selling efforts, there are a couple of other factors to consider. In particular, it's worth mentioning that your strategy shouldn't operate in a vacuum. As both social media and the way businesses use it have evolved, I often hear marketing and sales executives lament, "It's changed; social media doesn't work the same anymore. It's hard to have big success right out of the gate." For larger brands that invested heavily in social media very early, this thinking may be true. It probably is harder to stand out from the crowd with viral, one-hit wonders that take the social media world by storm. But that's because more businesses are figuring out that social media is part of the business landscape now and you really have to have a presence there.

Speaking of not operating in a vacuum . . . don't keep your social media goals to yourself. Share your strategy with your peers and across teams within your organization. Unlike traditional sales, where there tends to be a competitive nature that is exclusive rather than inclusive, you can be more effective in social media when you have more people within your team or company involved and working toward the same goals. The more educated everyone in your company is about social media and the more they understand the benefits of being socially active, the better chance you have of accelerating your social selling success.

In addition to introducing your social strategy to other people in your organization, your social media or social selling strategy should be integrated with your other sales and marketing efforts, both online and off. Once you build a relationship through social sales and convert that interaction into a lead, that lead shouldn't float out in the social media landscape indefinitely but instead be brought into your other sales processes and nurtured, as you would leads from other sources. That's not to say you pluck or scrape an unsuspecting prospect out of a social media channel and force her or him into one of your other sales buckets. After the lead is nourished in social media, a warm transfer into other nurturing programs is encouraged.

One last critical to-do item that goes along with your social selling strategy is the review process. After you have met your initial priorities, schedule time to analyze your results, review your progress, and make adjustments based on what did or did not work. Then repeat the process—over and over again.

Now that you know the basics of creating an effective social selling strategy, it's time to introduce you to the specific social media platforms where you will put much of your strategy to work. The next few chapters show you how to make the most of your time in social networks such as LinkedIn, Twitter, Facebook, Google+, YouTube, and others.

CHAPTER 11

LINKEDIN

Turning Connections into Sales

As a sales professional, how big is your most extensive network of contacts? You may be used to having a rolodex (digital or otherwise) filled with many dozens of customers, vendors, prospects, and other contacts. But what if you could expand that network into the hundreds—or beyond? Social networking allows you to grow your network bigger and faster than any traditional method, and LinkedIn is leading the way for professionals worldwide.

Unlike other social media sites, LinkedIn came out of the gate targeting professionals, and establishing itself as a site for furthering your career as opposed to sharing personal updates with friends and family. Once you are signed up as a member, LinkedIn gives you the ability to create a professional profile largely centered on your career. Similar to a resume, your work history, skills, education, and other credentials are all prominent components of your online profile, making it a rich database for job hunters and human resources (HR) recruiters alike. This helped create its reputation as a job search site early on. But it quickly became clear that this professional networking site was much more than a digital resume repository, and was equally valuable to sales and marketing professionals as it was to HR recruiters.

EXPANDING BEYOND A DIGITAL RESUME

The growth in LinkedIn's extensive membership base is undeniably helping fuel its role in the social selling process. Since its official launch in 2003, LinkedIn has expanded to more than 200 million members globally. Seventy-four million of those members are in the United States, while nearly 64 percent of its total member base is from other countries. The expansion rate doesn't show any signs of slowing down. According to usage statistics from LinkedIn, approximately two members join every second—that's nearly 173,000 new member profiles created each day.[1] The seemingly endless stream of new, active members helps make it an appealing lead source.

LinkedIn's layers of easily accessible data about its members, such as where they work, who they know, and how to reach them, also supports the social selling process. And just for good measure, it provides you with tools (both free and paid) to help you search for, connect to, and interact with both customers and potential prospects, even those that are the most difficult to reach using other traditional methods—such as phone calls and emails. It shouldn't be a surprise that so many adept salespersons quickly realized its potential; and to LinkedIn's credit, the site has been fast to respond, moving the site well beyond a place to manage your digital resume. According to Koka Sexton, the global senior social marketing manager for LinkedIn:

> LinkedIn is already being used by a very large number of sales people and that number is going to grow a lot over the rest of the (upcoming) years. We know that when sales people think "social" they think about LinkedIn and we want to create an environment so that sales professionals can leverage our social network to be more productive.[2]

You may have even heard LinkedIn referred to as the replacement for cold calling, but it's so much more than that. If used to its fullest capabilities, it could possibly become your number one prospecting tool, particularly for B2B sales. Unlike Facebook and other social networking sites that lend themselves to B2C marketing, LinkedIn has always been known for its emphasis on *professional* networking versus *social* networking. Businesses have seemingly upheld this view, reinforcing it as a valid social media site for professional purposes. It is this recognition of LinkedIn's value as a sales tool that separates the social selling pros from the amateurs and the dabblers. According to Sexton, social selling high achievers use LinkedIn as their *primary sales tool*. "High achievers always use LinkedIn to identify potential contacts," he says. "They are connected to over 50 percent of their customers and they leverage those connections to get introductions into new accounts."[3]

How do you become a high achiever and turn connections into sales? It starts with a few basic rules, a handful of LinkedIn tools and strategies, and a serious commitment of your time.

SOCIAL MEDIA FIRST IMPRESSIONS START WITH YOUR PROFILE

The foundation of a successful LinkedIn experience starts with the *profile*, or public LinkedIn page, that you create on the site. Although your profile is more than just an online version of your professional vitae, there are many shared attributes when it comes to leveraging it to reach prospective customers. Showing your job history, especially your current position, is actually helpful in the social selling process. First, it provides an immediate association with the company you represent, and second, your experience (if described properly) reinforces your expertise in a particular area. Remember, a great deal of the social selling process is about establishing your credibility and building a relationship so that you can guide prospects through the buying decision. If you are connecting with prospects and customers via LinkedIn, you want to demonstrate why you are the best person to help them find a solution in the industry you represent.

But your job history is only the beginning. There are five key areas, as shown in Figure 11–1, that are critical to complete as you begin constructing a LinkedIn profile. These core areas, along with several other sections (which I describe below), come together to form an influential profile that allows you to connect with and sell into your targeted audience. In addition, LinkedIn allows you to include images, video, presentations, and other documents that add visual interest to certain areas of your profile. This is a good opportunity to include company brochures, product videos, or sales presentations that not only make your profile stand out, but immediately provide visual representations of your work—or your company's products and services. You also have the flexibility to rearrange the order in which some information appears in your profile sections. But let's start by taking a closer look at the five key profile components (including those that allow you to attach images and documents):

1. **Photo:** Your professional picture appears at the very top of your profile page and is used as the visual icon that shows up

FIGURE 11–1

Your LinkedIn profile has five key areas.

next to each and every action you take on the site. For example, if you post a comment anywhere on the site, your photo shows up next to it. One of the most common mistakes inexperienced LinkedIn users make is not including a photo, and that mistake could mean fewer people see your profile. According to data from LinkedIn career expert, Nicole Williams, people are more likely (up to seven times more likely!, believe it or not) to look at your profile if a photo is included with it.[4]

When choosing a photo, select one that looks professional and preferably is a head shot, or a photo that clearly shows your face. I also think it's preferable to smile in your photo so that your picture is more inviting or likeable. Using pictures that are off-putting, blurry, or unprofessional are almost as bad as having no picture at all! Keep in mind that LinkedIn is a social network geared toward professionals, and your picture serves as your first impression. While that photo of you at the beach may be a fun shot for your personal Facebook page, it does not belong on LinkedIn. Your photo should help reinforce or build confidence in you as an expert, not distract from your professional qualifications.

2. **Overview:** This section appears at the top of your profile page, next to your photo, and it includes your *Name*; a *Headline* (which can be as simple as your job title or position, or it can be a short sentence or list of keywords that highlight your responsibilities or areas of expertise); your *Location* (where you are geographically based), and the *Industry* in which you work. Think of this section as being similar to your business card. Along with your photo, it is the information that is most visible to others and is usually seen first by other LinkedIn members.

   It is also one of the sections of your profile that has the least flexibility. You can change your picture, of course, but it must always reside at the top of the page—and there's no option to add images or documents to the overview. This information, however, is searchable both within LinkedIn as well as in search engines such as Google. It's possible to change the privacy settings to control what information is public and whether it is viewable by search engines—but when it comes to using LinkedIn for professional purposes, especially as part of the social selling process, you should always make your profile visible to the public and to search engines.

3. **Contact information:** This information is also visible in the top section of your page (and you do not have the option to move it around). It includes your email address and up to three websites related to you or your company. When adding your website, instead of showing only the URL or address (such as www.mycompanyname.com) and linking to the company's home page, use a descriptive sentence or call to action in its place (such as "Get a Free Guide to Social Selling") and link to a specific page that provides an offer for those coming from LinkedIn. The call to action makes it more likely that someone viewing your profile will click the link, helping transition a potential lead from LinkedIn to your company website.

4. **Activity:** Almost anytime you do something in LinkedIn— whether it's making a new connection, endorsing one of your existing connections, or sharing an article—it becomes immediately visible to others who are connected to you. These actions are documented as activities and appear toward the top part of your profile page (so it is seen by anyone who views your profile); they also show up in weekly activity summaries that are sent from LinkedIn to all of your connections. Like the overview section, you cannot reorder where the activity section shows up on your page. It always remains toward the top of your profile. Because this information is readily visible, it's yet another reason to stay active, so that both your connections and other people viewing your profile see that you are involved and active. This is a great reason to share industry or company-specific articles or presentations as well, since they appear on your profile.

5. **Background:** There are several important pieces of information that make up this section, including a *Summary*, or short description of your capabilities; an outline of your career *Experience* that shows current and past positions (this part most closely resembles a paper resume); and a *Skills and Expertise* list that allows you to include specific keywords associated with your professional capabilities, such as "lead generation" or "online marketing." This is an ideal spot to incorporate phrases that are important within your industry, or keywords that your prospects might use to search for information related to your products or services.

   The background section is your chance to shine! It provides you the opportunity to rearrange the order that your information appears and allows you to add lots of eye-catching visuals and engaging presentations and videos in the Summary and Skills and Expertise areas. You don't even have to list your work experience in any type of chronological order, if you prefer. It's up to you to choose what information is highlighted—and where it appears.

Now that you understand the basic information that's included in your LinkedIn profile, there are several other helpful areas or descriptions that can be added to your profile. Using these optional sections, you are able to provide a more complete picture of who you are. Not only does this provide more reasons for people to connect with you, but it also reinforces your knowledge and expertise in a particular field. Some of the more important profile add-ons, as I refer to them, include the following:

➤ **Recommendations:** Any time a customer, vendor, coworker, or boss (past or present) provides a public testimonial on your behalf, it's called a "recommendation." These testimonials are visible on your public profile page. As you might expect, having glowing recommendations show up to those viewing your profile is a great boost for your credibility as a salesperson. Even better, you don't have to wait for people to recommend you. Instead, you are able (and encouraged!) to send requests for recommendations to those in your network. Figure 11–2 shows how easy it is to send a request for a recommendation to one of your LinkedIn connections. Even if it's been a while since you've worked with someone, it's worthwhile to revisit past employers and customers and suggest that they write a brief recommendation for you

➤ **Endorsements:** This is a relatively new feature for LinkedIn. As the name implies, it provides a way for your connections to "endorse" you for a particular skill set—usually, these skills are pulled directly from your *Skills and Expertise* section, but people may choose to endorse you for a skill not even included in your profile. While recommendations require a more extensive process and provide detailed descriptions of the work you did, endorsements can be completed with one simple click on a link. You may even receive endorsements from people you have never worked with directly. For those reasons, the validity and value of endorsements are still being debated, particularly by HR recruiters.

For now, I think endorsements can still be valuable in the social selling process because they do provide a quick overview of how people categorize your capabilities. Plus, LinkedIn keeps a public tally, visible next to each skill, of how many times you are endorsed for a particular skill. If you have been endorsed 118 times for being a *Public Speaker*, people viewing your profile for the first time are more likely to believe you must be pretty good at that skill! Why not use this public validation of your skills to your advantage?

Additionally, when people endorse you for a skill, it's a good excuse to reach out to them and potentially renew an old connection. You can also thank the person for the endorsement, and if it's someone you have worked with, ask him or her to expand upon the endorsement and write a recommendation for you. On the flip side, if you are looking for a subtle way to get on the radar of one of your connections,

FIGURE 11-2

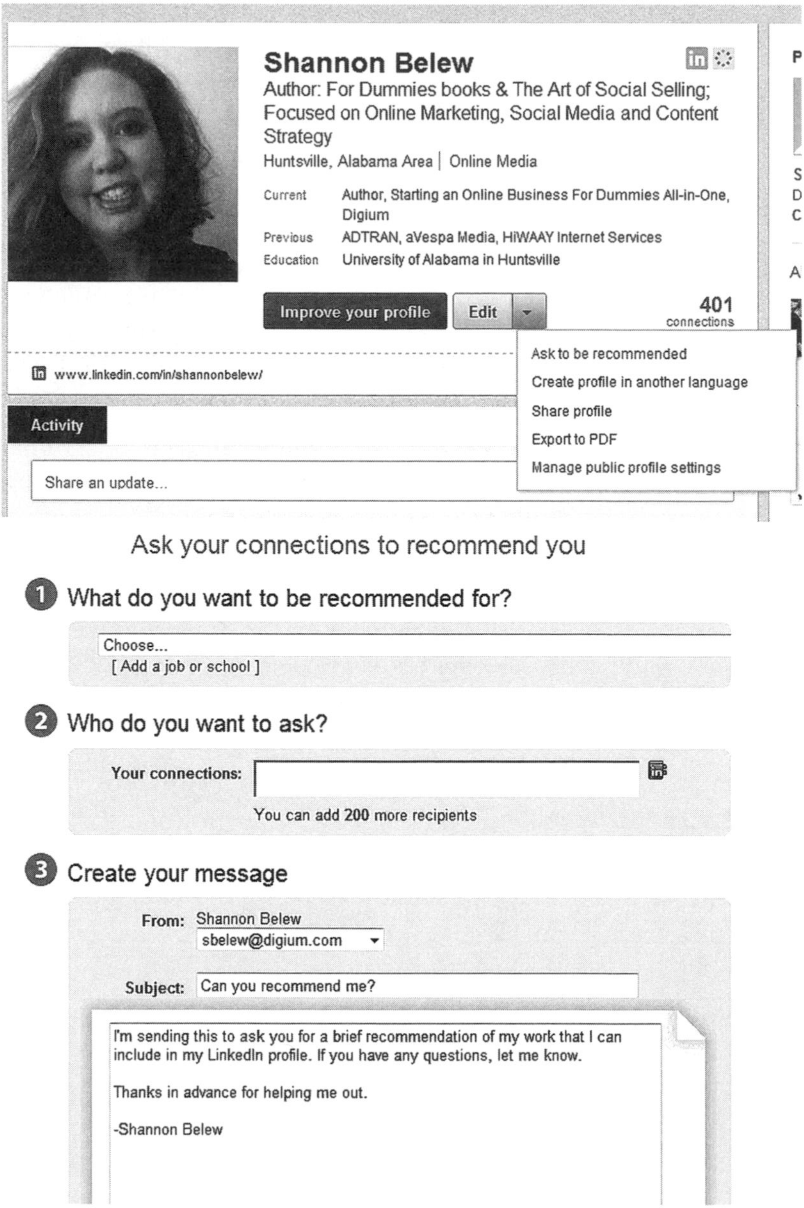

Ask your connections to recommend you

1 What do you want to be recommended for?

> Choose...
> [Add a job or school]

2 Who do you want to ask?

> Your connections: [   ]
>
> You can add **200** more recipients

3 Create your message

> From: Shannon Belew
>   sbelew@digium.com   ▼
>
> Subject: Can you recommend me?
>
> I'm sending this to ask you for a brief recommendation of my work that I can
> include in my LinkedIn profile. If you have any questions, let me know.
>
> Thanks in advance for helping me out.
>
> -Shannon Belew

LinkedIn profile is designed to make it easy to request a LinkedIn Recommendation.

you may want to endorse that person! (But only do so if you truly have reason to know that she or he is good at the skill for which you are endorsing her or him.)

➤ **Education:** Showing any degrees you have earned, or making visible the time you spent at a college or university, is often less about your knowledge in a particular area (unless your degree ties closely to the product or service you are selling) and more about a shared experience that provides another reason for someone to connect with you or trust you. The fact that you spent time on a particular college campus is also a great nugget to start a conversation online or on the phone. "I see you and I both attended the University of Kansas . . ." Even if you didn't graduate, it's still worthwhile including the time you spent at the school because it places you in the general network for that university so you have access to connect with anyone else who attended. This is a powerful connecting tool!

➤ **Projects:** Particularly if you are in some type of service-based sales, such as an IT consultant, describing current projects is a good way to demonstrate the type of work you or your company is doing (or can do) for customers. Any type of project or research is helpful to include in this section. For instance, if you are putting together a webinar or writing a white paper on a topic of interest to your prospects, mentioning it as a project is a good way to promote that information to interested prospects and get inquiries about it before it is even ready to launch!

➤ **Interests:** Similar to "projects," this section falls under the Additional Information section of your profile. Most people treat interests the same on LinkedIn as you would on your resume—the spot where you provide additional color to your activities and hobbies outside of work (cycling, rock climbing, etc.). But in your LinkedIn profile, *Interests* is the place to reinforce the professional skills or expertise you have in two or three short sentences. It's the opportunity to once again use strategic keywords that are searchable in and outside of LinkedIn, which makes it a valuable component to helping you get found online for what you do best!

➢ **Other profile sections:** While this is not an all-inclusive list of additional sections that LinkedIn lets you include in your profile, these are some of the more helpful to the social selling process. All of these are self-explanatory, but I want to point out that each one provides you with another opportunity to describe or note something that could be potentially interesting or helpful to prospects or customers viewing your profile.

- Certifications

- Patents

- Organizations

- Honors and awards

- Languages

Whether it is an optional section or one of the five core sections that make up your profile, as you complete each one, keep the following in mind. It may be tempting to use descriptions similar to what you would use on a resume—short, bullet-point style phrases that focus on key accomplishments or goals. Instead, think of your profile in terms of *how you want your customers to see you* rather than how you might want employers to see you. Use descriptions and keywords that matter most to prospects in your industry. Write sentences that illustrate how you have helped customers, as opposed to how you helped the company for which you work. Use your profile to make a good first impression—and to *sell yourself as an expert who can help people identify and solve their problems as a consumer* (B2C) *or a business* (B2B) as they relate to the types of solutions or services your company provides.

EXPANDING YOUR CONNECTIONS

Once your LinkedIn profile is completed and fine-tuned, you are ready to start building your online network. You may already have started this process and know that it's not difficult to ask for a *connection*, which is how LinkedIn describes the relationship between its members. Instead of followers or fans, you make connections on LinkedIn. There are, however, some basic guidelines to consider when attempting to make connections; and there is a strategy you can use to more effectively and efficiently grow your network.

First, exactly how many connections do you need? That depends on how you are using the networking site. Consider the conclusions from Steve W. Martin, who interviewed top IT salespeople about how they used LinkedIn in the sales process.[5] He labeled the most active users *"enthusiasts"* and noted that, on average, each enthusiast had over 700 connections—and more than 85 percent used it to "engage prospective customers during the sales process." Not surprising, nearly half (40 percent) of the enthusiasts confirmed they had generated revenue as a result of their connections and activities on LinkedIn. It's difficult to say with certainty that more connections lead to more social selling success, or that 700 is the magic number for connections that generate revenue. But other research and informal data I have seen in the last few years seems to show similar patterns, namely that the more active LinkedIn users tend to have more connections.

One reason that a greater number of connections may equate to more success is due to the way LinkedIn connections are structured. Using a degree-of-separation theory about the power of your extended social network, not only do you have first-degree connections, but also second- and third-degree connections that are based on association. First-degree connections represent the people you actually know and to whom you have the most direct connection. As LinkedIn founder Reid Hoffman explains: "Your friends know people you don't know. These friends of friends are your second-degree connections. And those friends of friends have friends of their own— those friends of friends of friends are your third-degree connections."[6]

The takeaway is that there should always be one person in the middle, or someone who knows both you and the person in that second or third degree, and who can make the introduction to the person to whom you want to connect.

Technically, everyone and anyone on LinkedIn is a potential connection, but there are many reasons to be strategic when growing your online network. For starters, LinkedIn imposes some restrictions and guidelines for connecting. When you send an invitation to connect with someone, LinkedIn wants to understand how you know the person and asks you to select whether or not you have an existing relationship (such as a coworker, friend, classmate, or someone you've done business with). If you don't know the person in one of these ways, then you'll be asked to provide an email address of the person before LinkedIn lets you continue. What happens if you send requests to people you don't really know? If the person responds to a request saying they don't know you, then LinkedIn may penalize you. According to a LinkedIn policy, they could require you to provide an email address for some or all of your future connection requests. And, if you send too many invitations to connect with people who don't respond to your requests at all, or who mark your connection invites as spam because they don't know you, then it could raise a red flag in LinkedIn's system. This may result in having your account temporarily restricted or suspended, making it inaccessible to you for a certain period of time.

Similarly, if you search through too many profile pages in a single day, LinkedIn may label it as excessive activity and associate it with a robot or a spammer. As a result, you may receive a restricted action message that temporarily limits your page views within LinkedIn. Because you can be penalized for being too active on LinkedIn or for being too aggressive in connecting to people, it's important to think of building your connections in phases, and over a period of days and weeks, making connections in small batches at a time. Don't worry—your patience and methodical approach will pay off! I suggest building your contacts in the following layers:

- ➤ **Friends and professional associates:** Start with people who know you best and are most likely to respond to your requests to connect without hesitation. Connecting with professional associates as you are just starting to build your network is a good way to quickly broaden the reach of your small but growing list of connections.

➤ **Past and current coworkers and bosses:** Adding people you work with is a great way to ensure your connection requests are accepted. It's also helpful in gaining access to second- and third-degree connections that may come in handy to you later.

➤ **Vendors or strategic partners:** Similar to coworkers, connecting with those who do business with you can open doors to new connections that you may not know personally but will become part of your extended network. This is mutually beneficial to you and your vendors, so it's very likely that they will respond to your invitations to connect.

➤ **Customers or clients:** Connecting with customers may seem odd at first, but it is beneficial for both of you. Customers are able to receive updates in your feed that may be helpful to their business or the use of your products or services. Inviting customers into your network is especially important for you because it allows you to ask for a recommendation on LinkedIn. It also lets you see their updates and provides insight into changes in their business or employment (which can impact your current and future sales relationship). And, of course, it exposes you to others in their network—connections that could become prospective customers.

➤ **Influencers:** There are people you will interact with online, or through social media, or during conferences—people who are high achievers or who have lots of influence. Think in terms of speakers at events or on webinars, authors, sales leaders, and other influencers in your industry. These are people you may not know well or may not ever meet in person but for some reason your paths have crossed. Many of these influencers actively encourage people to connect with them.

Take them up on that offer, as it's a good way to quickly broaden your connections (particularly those second- and third-degree connections) and get exposure to a very large network.

➤ **Prospective customers:** This type of connection can be a bit trickier and is why I suggest saving it for last, after you've already begun building a strong, extensive network. Once you have a broad network of first-, second-, and third-degree connections, it makes it easier to find people and activities you have in common so that you can reach out to prospects and start building a mutually beneficial relationship.

As you are expanding your list of connections and sending out invitations to connect, there are a few best practices that are considered musts if you are going to find success on LinkedIn. These include:

➤ **Always customize the standard LinkedIn invitation to connect message:** LinkedIn does an amazing job automating processes and making it as simple and frictionless as possible for you to make the most from your time on LinkedIn. One of these efficiency shortcuts it offers is an automated message that shows up when you choose to send someone an invitation to connect. The message says: "I would like to add you to my professional network on LinkedIn." While this message is rather innocuous, it's almost considered sinful to use the message as-is. Instead, craft a concise message that explains how you know the person or why it's important for her to connect with you.

➤ **Include a call to action in your message:** The ultimate goal of a LinkedIn invitation is to connect with the person, of course. But don't stop there. Give that person one more memorable nugget of information about you or provide an incentive for him or her to take action. For example, suggest a group that you belong to that may be of interest to them, too.

Or, provide a link to an article you found on LinkedIn that might be helpful or interesting.

> ➤ **Send invitations to connect sooner rather than later:** When you first meet someone, particularly if it's at an industry tradeshow, networking event, or business meeting, send an invitation to connect on LinkedIn as soon as possible. It helps make sure your invite is accepted, since they are more likely to still remember you. After hours or days have gone by, it's easy to forget how you know someone.

With the need to be so strategic in the way you connect and given the limitations and penalties LinkedIn puts on you, it may seem that LinkedIn is making it hard to expand your horizons. In actuality, they are trying to preserve the value of the overall network and ultimately the quality of the relationships being built. To do this, they have to minimize low-quality connections and keep what might be considered spam at a minimum. Not to worry! LinkedIn even provides you with tools to make it possible to meet people outside your network and expand your connections, using the following two tools:

> ➤ **Introductions:** The idea of *introductions* is a fantastic, free tool for opening doors to new prospects, even at the highest executive level, or to someone you may not otherwise have been able to reach. LinkedIn provides the introduction feature as a way for you to grow your network using people you already know. As long as your intended connection is either a second- or third-degree connection, you can be introduced by one of your first-degree connections. In essence, it occurs the same way you use introductions offline. You want to meet with the CEO of Company X, but you don't know her. However, your old college roommate plays golf with her on occasion, so you ask for an introduction. The same thing happens within LinkedIn, but the introduction happens virtually.

> ➤ **InMail:** Should someone be completely outside your network or you don't have the right person to help make an introduction, LinkedIn offers InMail. Similar to email, these are private messages that you send directly to the person via

LinkedIn, but you don't have access to all of their profile information. InMail isn't free, either. As a basic member with a free account, you can purchase a certain number of InMails. If you have a Pro or upgraded account, then you receive a certain number of InMails as part of your Pro membership. Since you have no common connection with the person, it puts a lot of pressure on you to create a message that will elicit a response. The best approach for InMail messages is to be quick and to the point of why you are getting in touch with the person and be clear about why it's beneficial for them to connect with you or respond to your message.

PAID VERSUS "ORGANIC" OPPORTUNITIES FOR SOCIAL SELLING

Most social networking sites offer a multitude of ways to interact with people you know, and increasingly the sites are trying to help you engage with people you don't know—or expand your reach to a larger audience. In part, this is to help you get more value from networks like LinkedIn, especially when using it as a medium to reach potential customers. Of course, social networks are also trying to support their own business model by monetizing some features and services. LinkedIn, a public company, is no exception and offers a couple of paid engagement opportunities of which you can take advantage.

Ads and sponsorships are two of the biggest components of paid opportunities, but I also include any prospecting tools and upgraded memberships that incur additional charges as part of the non-organic (paid) category. LinkedIn offers all of these and I view the paid components as being equally important to the social selling process as organic opportunities; the two often go hand in hand in order for a salesperson to be most effective. Not only do fee-based options typically provide a more direct route for lead generation through social media channels, but they help create brand awareness. The awareness, or having your company visible in LinkedIn through ads, for example, can make it easier for you to then connect and engage with a prospect if she or he already has an idea of who the company is. This is especially true if your company isn't a well-known brand. Here are the paid opportunities that may be helpful to you when prospecting within LinkedIn:

- ➤ **Ads:** Just like Facebook and Twitter, LinkedIn lets you buy ads that are displayed on the personal profile pages. The ads are similar to those you would find on any website. Placing LinkedIn ads is a great way for you as a salesperson or for your brand to target your prospects using such barometers as industry, company size, geographic location, position type, and more—and have your ad shown to persons meeting those criteria. LinkedIn ads are also very affordable—you can spend less than $100 for an effective ad on LinkedIn compared to having to spend many thousands of dollars for a similar ad on other websites. (Of course, there are larger advertising opportunities available if you have a really big budget; otherwise you can use the basic ad program to build and manage your own ads.) Because you can easily target specific subsets of LinkedIn members, I typically use ads on LinkedIn to promote webinars or special events, or to promote offers for white papers and other content used for lead generation. Using LinkedIn ads not only allows you to generate direct leads in this way, but it helps raise the visibility of your brand to support your organic (non-paid) efforts. In other words, someone may be more willing to connect with you if they have recently seen an ad for your company and recognize the name.

- ➤ **Premium Memberships:** As an individual user, you can upgrade your profile to a premium account, which gives you access to more features and functionality. Depending on which account upgrade you choose, you get more search results, can use additional InMail messages and introductions, can see who has viewed your profile and the complete profiles of others, and gain access to tools like Profile Organizer, which lets you store and organize important member profiles (very helpful when maintaining lists of prospects and customers, for instance). Premium accounts are also nice because you can pay monthly fees and cancel or downgrade at anytime. Suppose you are getting ready for a trade show or special event and want to have greater access to reach prospective customers and research and follow up those attendees afterward? You can upgrade your personal account for the months surrounding the event and then downgrade to a free or less expensive premium account later. *Saved Alerts* is another benefit of having a premium account. It allows you to save searches for types of profiles and then notifies you when any new profiles are created that fit your criteria. This is a smart way to track prospects new to LinkedIn who match your target criteria.

➤ **Sales Navigator:** This tool was designed specifically with social selling in mind—it's the premium of the premium accounts! Sales Navigator gives you greater access and insight into people and companies that you are trying to sell into or make a connection, including sending you sales alerts, building your pipeline, and managing your leads by creating and saving lists of your prospects. Once you have Sales Navigator, you can also connect directly in Salesforce (the CRM tool) and use TeamLink, a function that lets you see who your coworkers are connected to (and vice versa) so that you can find common connections. Sales Navigator is a more expensive commitment than other lower-level, premium accounts, but you get a great deal of access to prospects in return.

Of course, you don't have to spend a lot of money on LinkedIn upgrades to find social selling success. There are other ways to reach and engage with prospects through organic (no-cost) activities. Again, paid opportunities often support the organic opportunities, but you can achieve success in LinkedIn with minimal or no expenditures. Growing your network with connections and asking for recommendations is at the root of organic activity, but here are some other ways you can take advantage of LinkedIn—for free!

➤ **Group participation:** LinkedIn provides you the opportunity to interact with people outside of your profile page and in what are referred to as *groups*. These are conversation threads, similar to forums or mini-communities, based on a shared interest or topic, or even based on an event or product. You can join up to fifty groups on LinkedIn at any given time and interact as often as you like. You can also start your own group, but I wouldn't recommend this until you've familiarized yourself with other groups and what's expected from them—and only if you have plenty of time to keep up with managing the group. Personally, I think a better use of your time is to join and actively participate in other groups that already have a large or very engaged group of members who fit your target audience.

   Since you are limited to how many groups you can join, and because you want to select ones that are most active, get to know more about a group before you join. LinkedIn includes information about the group that is accessible from the public view of the group's main page. The information, called *Group Statistics*, located in a box toward the bottom of the page, as shown in Figure 11–3, allows you to see such facts as how many participants a group has, how active the group is (the number of recent discussions), where the majority of the group's members are located, and what seniority most members have. Staying active in multiple groups is a tactic top sales professionals use to find and engage with leads. In fact, the "high achievers," as referenced by LinkedIn's Koka Sexton, are members in thirty or more groups and contribute to them at least two times a week. Examples of some types of "contributions" you can make include:

FIGURE 11-3

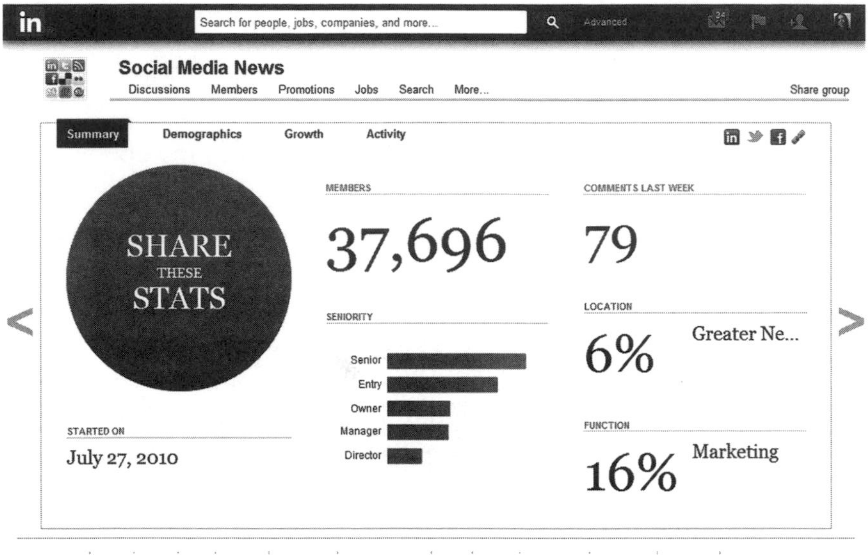

Before joining a group, check out its statistics to see how active it is.

- Posting your own content to the group.

- Sharing links to other people's comments.

- Asking a question or starting a conversation by asking for feedback on a news item.

- Posting a poll to elicit easy participation and feedback from group members.

An extra benefit of participating in groups is that it provides you with another legitimate reason to extend an invitation to connect when building your network. Even though you may not know the person well, you can still send an invite to connect because you share membership in one or more groups.

➢ **Follow LinkedIn Today's influencers:** LinkedIn has expanded the amount and types of news and articles that are shared and promoted within the networking site. LinkedIn Today is the name of the company's social news page that consists of "channels" of content segmented by topic. It includes articles written by top "influencers," or contributors, who are experts in certain subjects. You can determine which channels are most important to you and have the most recent articles show up in the updates section of your profile page. You can also follow any of the top influencers as a way to stay informed of the latest trends. Commenting on and sharing these influencer articles is a simple way to not only keep up with industry news but to also provide value to your connections by sharing the information.

➤ **Follow companies:** Even if you cannot connect with certain prospects or you're having a difficult time identifying certain contacts within a company you have on your prospect list, you can still follow the company's page on LinkedIn. This simple action helps you keep in touch with what's happening within the company, learn more about the company's needs and how you may be able to assist them, and could even give you a reason to contact them outside of LinkedIn if you see an update that could be used as a conversation starter.

You don't have to participate in or utilize all of these organic activities within LinkedIn. These are examples of the various ways you can remain visible in LinkedIn, reach prospective customers, and expand your network of connections. If you can't consistently keep up with all of these areas, don't stress about it. Pick one or two of the easiest or least time-consuming activities and start there. But remember, as with networking offline, the more time and effort you put into smart, strategic networking on LinkedIn, the more of a return you are likely to see—especially for B2B prospecting.

In the next chapter, we will look at Twitter, another social networking platform that lets you connect with potentially thousands of friends, prospects, and influencers—in less than 140 characters!

CHAPTER 12

TWITTER

Social Selling in 140 Characters or Less

Even if you have never used Twitter, you most likely have spotted the iconic blue cartoon bird that represents the site. The symbol for the social networking platform shows up frequently on websites, email signatures, and even on television shows. The bird is used as a reminder and a call to action, asking you to flock to Twitter and share your thoughts. Technically referred to as a "microblogging" site, Twitter provides users the ability to publish updates, similar to a blog post, but much shorter. An update, called a *tweet*, is restricted to a maximum of 140 characters (including spaces and symbols), or the same length as this sentence.

Figure 12–1 shows you what a typical tweet looks like, in an example taken from my personal Twitter feed, found at www.Twitter-.com/ShannonBelew. (Your Twitter *handle* is displayed by putting the @ symbol in front of whatever name you choose. My Twitter handle is @ShannonBelew.) It may seem challenging to construct short *and* meaningful messages, but more than 400 million tweets are sent

FIGURE 12-1

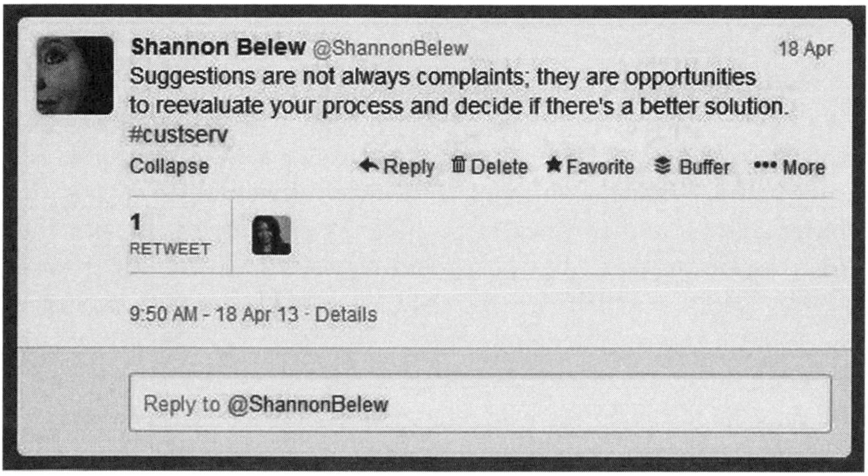

A tweet may be short, but it can still say plenty.

daily—and they are influencing a lot of people worldwide, including both B2C and B2B buyers.[1]

INFLUENTIAL TWEETS

There are always skeptics who view the 140-character microposts that show up on Twitter as unimportant and filled only with personal status updates and rants. However, Twitter's ability to disseminate information quickly to the masses is increasingly being recognized for its influence on matters from politics to the stock market, and everything in between. In fact, Twitter was widely credited by the media and world political leaders for its role in helping protestors respond to a repressive government in Tunisia in 2011 (and later in other countries), taking its place as a leading platform to aid social activism.

The platform is equally persuasive in the entertainment world, partly as a result of its ability to integrate new and traditional media. As testament to this, a Nielsen Twitter TV Rating was established in 2012 to help measure how much social engagement occurs on Twitter when focused around particular television programs. The measurement, or rating, was warranted because there is often so much real-time chatter happening on Twitter about a TV program as it is being aired. What if you happen to have a product or service that shares a target audience with a popular TV show or live event? Then this type of interactive or participatory viewing behavior through Twitter could provide you with easy, no-cost access to hundreds of thousands of prospective customers.

Gaining access to actively engaged consumers is certainly one of the reasons the business world has taken note of Twitter's growing influence. Even the stock market has officially recognized it as a credible, influential source. The Securities and Exchange Commission announced in early 2013 that it would allow public companies to make disclosures of key corporate information on Twitter and other social media sites. Not long after the announcement, the world saw exactly how much power Twitter has on the stock market when a fake tweet about a bomb at the White House turned into a few moments of market panic. The hoax "caused the Dow to drop 140 points and wiped $136 billion from the S&P 500."[2]

Following events such as this, even the skeptics are finding it increasingly hard to argue about the social networking site's level of persuasion in everything from stocks and bonds to pop culture to business. The same wide-reaching influence is also what makes Twitter so appealing for use in social selling.

TWITTER BASICS FOR BUSINESS

Usage updates from the social networking site indicate there are more than 200 million registered, active users on Twitter, and the numbers continue to grow. Already available in 20 languages, the real-time flow of tweets worldwide means that information spreads at a lightning-fast speed to a vast number of people. Even if you don't have millions of followers in your network, your tweets can still be seen far and wide thanks to Twitter's multiplier effect that allows one tweet to be seen and resent by any number of people. Before discussing the details of how to reach all those prospective customers, there are a few basics you need to understand, especially if you're not familiar with Twitter.

To begin, when you become a registered user, you choose a Twitter *handle*, which is displayed each time you tweet. It uses the @ symbol in front of whatever name you choose. You can change your handle at any time and it can be completely different from the name associated with the account. For example, Jane Smith may be on your account but your Twitter handle is @B2Bexpert or @salesguru. In my case, I used my actual name for my handle, so it looks like this: @ShannonBelew. In addition to selecting a Twitter handle, you also have a home page that displays your feed of tweets, and from which you have access to various features and account controls. Your *feed*, or Twitter stream, is made up of tweets published from everyone that you follow. Each time someone you follow posts an update, it shows up in your feed. As you might expect, the more people you follow, the more active your stream of tweets.

Any time you see a tweet of particular interest, you have the opportunity to engage with the person that sent it by doing one of the following:

> ➤ **Favorite:** This is the equivalent of a Like, and it uses a star symbol which shows up to others, including the person who sent the tweet, as having been marked as a favorite. I often use this as a way to bookmark a tweet that contains an interesting article or statistic, or that needs follow-up at a later time. I also use it to acknowledge a final comment to bring a Twitter conversation to a close, following an exchange of tweets.

> ➤ **Retweet:** Represented by the shortened symbol "RT," this option means you are simply sharing the tweet with others in your network, and within the network of anyone else mentioned in the original tweet. The RT is responsible for that

multiplier effect I mentioned earlier. You may only have 300 followers, but each person mentioned in your tweet may have several hundred followers. That means your RT is now potentially seen by tens of thousands of people instead of only the 300 in your network.

➤ **Reply:** You can respond to or make a comment directly back to the person who first sent the tweet. A reply shows up in the public stream, like a retweet, but it doesn't repeat the contents of the first tweet. Your reply will also go to everyone mentioned in the tweet, unless you manually remove their names, or Twitter handles.

Keep in mind that each time you engage with someone else's tweet, whether yours is a reply or a retweet, your handle is attached to that tweet for all to see. This is another reason your exposure is increased. If a potential customer sends a tweet asking a question and you answer it, your response is spread well outside your network.

Another basic but important element of tweeting is the use of the *hashtag*, which is represented by the pound symbol (#). Using a hashtag is a way to draw attention to an important phrase or keyword, or to help make sure that term can be more easily tracked and searched. Hashtags can also be used to call attention to certain live events, like tradeshows. So an annual technology healthcare tradeshow may use the hashtag #MedIT2013 to draw attention to the show before, during, or after it! In almost every industry, there are common terms or abbreviations and these are used as hashtags on Twitter. Knowing these industry-specific hashtags is a great way for you to find conversations related to your business, whether used by peers or customers. For instance, in my industry VoIP (#VoIP) and Unified Communications (#UC) are common hashtags that are often used, so I search for conversations using those hashtags. As you may have guessed, a single hashtag can potentially represent multiple topics, so you have to use common sense to make sure the tweet is indeed relevant to your business.

In addition to these basic but most-used functions of Twitter, any time a particular tweet appeals to you, there are also options to *embed* a particular tweet on your website, or to *email* a tweet (it will be sent from the email address you have associated with your account). Emailing comes in handy for sending yourself a copy of a tweet to refer to later; or for sending a particular tweet to someone in your customer support team or sales team. And you can do all of this without having to leave the platform!

Remember that unless your account is locked or made private (which it never should be, for social selling purposes), your tweets will almost always be public. Should you ever want to send a private tweet, there's a Twitter function for that, too! You can use the *Direct Message* (DM) function to contact anyone who follows you. Simply put "DM" in front of your follower's Twitter handle and it will send a message only to that person. As you engage with potential customers and the conversation or relationship progresses, using the DM function is a great way to start moving the conversation off Twitter. You can, for example, DM your phone number or a link to a product demo to encourage the next level of engagement for the sales process. As always, use this function with discretion. Twitter users are sensitive to random or inappropriate DMs and often get mad if you blast automated DMs to everyone in your network—it's the equivalent of email spam. It's also considered a no-no to make a blatant sales pitch using DM before there is enough of a relationship or cause to warrant it.

THE ADVANTAGES OF USING TWITTER FOR YOUR BUSINESS

As you can see, even with some of the cautionary tales, the ability to interact with prospective prospects on Twitter is substantial. Add that to the number of people potentially being exposed to your messages and the ability for those messages to be shared outside your network, and you have a big advantage when trying to reach and influence your target audience. In fact, you will quickly discover that is one of the great advantages of this social networking site. It lets you follow and interact directly with other Twitter users without having to be accepted as a "friend" or without agreeing to be "connected." Unlike Facebook and LinkedIn, for example, Twitter is a very open platform, which makes it easy to engage with people you may not know on a personal level; and this open network is what has fostered the widespread flow of public information.

The Twitter platform offers other advantages, too—especially when it comes to what you are able to tweet. Whereas you may initially view the requirement of 140-character tweets as severely limiting, they can actually be expanded to include more than just static text. You are also able to attach images and videos that can be viewed within Twitter, as you see in Figure 12–2. Plus, you can always include links to other websites or articles to access more in-depth information. (Be sure to use an abbreviated URL, as discussed in Chapter 7, so that you use fewer characters when including external links in your tweets.) Expanding your tweets in this way makes it easy to attach product photos and how-to videos, or to use links to drive prospects back to your website or a landing page that contains special offers—although it's best to use pure promotional tweets sparingly. As I mention over and again (and probably can't say often enough!), you want to *balance how much you talk about your company,* especially if it comes across as a sales pitch, by sending information that *educates or entertains* versus *sells.* A 1:10 or 1:5 ratio is often recommended. I prefer the latter and send only one promotional type of tweet for every five non-promotional tweets.

Beyond the ability to send lots of engaging content, another reason Twitter is attractive to businesses as part of the social selling process is that it has made it possible to identify and follow *trending topics,* the most popular information being discussed on the social media platform at any given moment, as seen in real-time. A list of trending topics is always viewable directly from your Twitter home page, appearing in the sidebar next to your feed of tweets. The topics are typically identified and tracked by the use of the hashtag symbol (#Trends). However, you may have some names or terms that are used in such mass quantities that they don't require having the hashtag symbol next to the trending word or phrase. You can also adjust

FIGURE 12-2

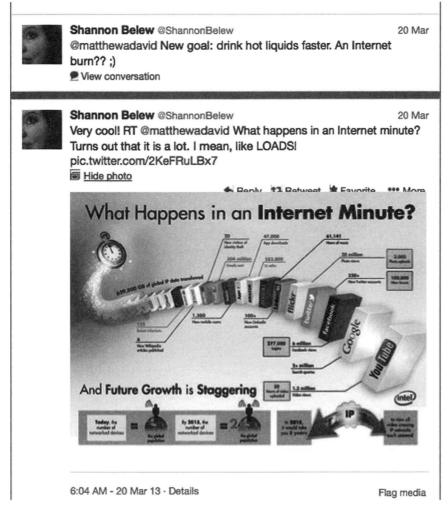

| | Shannon Belew @ShannonBelew | 20 Mar |

Shannon Belew @ShannonBelew   20 Mar
@matthewadavid New goal: drink hot liquids faster. An Internet
burn?? ;)
💬 View conversation

Shannon Belew @ShannonBelew   20 Mar
Very cool! RT @matthewadavid What happens in an Internet minute?
Turns out that it is a lot. I mean, like LOADS!
pic.twitter.com/2KeFRuLBx7
📷 Hide photo

6:04 AM - 20 Mar 13 · Details   Flag media

Tweets can include photos, videos, and links to more information.

your profile settings for trending topics so that you see all global topics, or you see topics based only in a certain geographic region (country). You can also choose to have Twitter tailor trending topics to you.
It tries to line up with your interests, followers, and keywords that

most often occur in your feed. The tailored trends are my preference because it further automates information and users that I am most likely to want to see.

However you set your topics, if you happen to have a business tie-in to an issue or keyword that is trending, you can join in the conversation and immediately get exposure to people participating in a large, active discussion thread. For example, if you sell designer sunglasses and a trending topic is "summer," then this is an opportunity to enter the discussion stream. Participating in the conversation is a matter of coming up with a message that pertains to the topic and then adding the trending topic (with a hashtag) to the end of your tweet. In the example of the trending topic #summer, you might want to create a tweet that says: *It's almost #summer! How many pairs of sunglasses do you use each season? Take the poll!*" Then you could add a link back to a poll on your website where visitors could vote on how many pairs of sunglasses they like to have during the summer.

Another example of a tweet you could use would be something like this: *"How would you complete this sentence? 'I wear my sunglasses at _____.' #summer"*—and notice that the trending topic with the hashtag is placed at the end of the sentence to make sure the tweet gets associated with the popular topic. You could include a hashtag within a sentence, but it's cleaner to place it at the end. And it's recommended that you use no more than two hashtags with one tweet. You can also work it into the sentence, as in the first example. The goal is to include the trending topic, with or without the hashtag, somewhere in your tweet so it gets fed into the trending stream of tweets.

That said, there is a big caution flag I want to raise when discussing this opportunity. There is a big difference between joining a conversation about a trending topic because you truly have something relevant or applicable to say and randomly jumping into a trending topic only because you want to try to get your name in front of a lot of people. Before sending out the first tweet in response to a trending topic, it's highly advisable that you do a little research. Check out the

Twitter stream and see exactly what people are talking about in relation to the popular topic. In our example, the *#summer* might be in
response to the death of Summer Sanders, a one-time popular kids'
show host on Nickelodeon television. If that were the case, you
wouldn't want to post lighthearted or frivolous tweets about #sum-
mer and sunglasses because you would be considered insensitive and
rude! Every so often, brands make the mistake of jumping in on a
trending topic only to later discover it had a negative connotation,
was political, or otherwise volatile. Always make your tweets appropriate to the conversation.

It's not only in trending topics that you will want to engage prospective customers; there are lots of existing conversations happening on Twitter that are focused on a customer's need or desire.
People—and businesses—are constantly tweeting about their problems and seeking solutions. You can search Twitter for keywords or
hashtags used in conversations that may relate to the products or
services your company offers. As discussed in Chapter 7, you can also
use social media tools that automatically track certain keywords so
that you can more easily identify conversations in which you might
want to comment or respond. Twitter also has a built-in search function that allows you to do basic or advanced searches. The advanced
tool allows you to search for specific phrases (an exact match) or
individual keywords. You can even search by language, location,
user, and sentiment (positive or negative comments, for example).
Searching for negative sentiments associated with industry keywords
or names of your competitors, for instance, is a smart way to identify
tweets by potential prospects who may be unhappy with an existing
product or service and in need of an alternate solution. It's advantageous to use monitoring tools that reduce the risk of missing important opportunities to respond and engage.

It's important to point out that some of the same benefits of Twitter can also become negatives for businesses that are trying to have
positive, timely interactions with customers and prospects. Consider
the speed and quantity of tweets. Twitter acts as a continually updat-
ing feed of posts or tweets. The volume of data passing through the
site can be overwhelming, especially if you follow lots of people or

Twitter accounts. You could potentially have dozens of tweets appear in your feed in a matter of one or two seconds. Having so much information flowing so quickly through Twitter means that it can be easy for your tweet to go unnoticed (or for you to miss an important tweet). That's why, as part of your Twitter strategy, it's critical that you post or tweet frequently—but strategically—so you have a better chance of being seen.

It's important to carefully consider your approach to the frequency of your tweets, because you can also tweet *too much*. For example, if you have followers on Twitter who don't have a large network, you may be only one of twenty-seven people filling their stream of tweets. If you're tweeting fifteen times in a single hour, you are likely going to swamp that person's Twitter stream, which is more than a bit obnoxious. Even if one of your followers is following *many* people, your constant flurries of less-than-meaningful tweets are not going to be received well—and the person may decide to *un*follow you! The best guideline is to make sure you are sending interesting, helpful information that people want to receive; and that you are interacting with people as part of a natural online conversation. If you take this approach, you will end up posting tweets. It's a balancing act.

Oh, there's one more important piece of information when discussing how often you tweet. Twitter itself imposes some limits on the number of tweets you can send—100 per hour or 1,000 per day. If you exceed these limits, your account will be temporarily frozen for a short period of time—this is referred to as being put in *Twitter Jail*! (And, of course, if you were to send 1,000 tweets in a single day—or a hundred in an hour—you sure wouldn't have time to make any sales!)

The fact that so many people can potentially see tweets about your brand has created a bit of a sore spot for customer support, too. Some businesses see Twitter only as a place where customers publicly complain and try to force a company to resolve problems without going through traditional customer service channels. To add salt to the wound, these complaints are visible to both prospective customers and competitors. As mentioned previously, while this can be a strategic advantage to you if searching for your competition's unhappy customers, this level of exposure can also put you in a more vulnerable position if the unhappy customer belongs to you! As discussed in Chapter 2, this is one reason it's important to have your customer support team in agreement on how to handle social service issues. Because the conversations are open for everyone to see, it's either a great opportunity to show prospects how you treat customers and take care of a problem, or it becomes a reason for prospective customers to seek out your competition.

EQUAL OPPORTUNITIES FOR B2C AND B2B PROSPECTING

Considering the social selling process, one of the important things that sets Twitter apart from other social media platforms is your ability to use it to reach out to prospects in both the B2C and B2B markets. Unlike LinkedIn, which tends to favor the B2B market, or Facebook, which is better known for reaching out to the B2C market, Twitter is a platform that has managed to successfully target a mix of both B2B and B2C audiences! That's not to say that this capability is exclusive to Twitter, but it happens to do a better job at it.

The Grilled Cheese Truck (@grlldcheesetruk), a consumer-focused food company in California, uses Twitter to identify and reach out to customers on a daily basis. A restaurant on wheels, the company tweets updates on where its food truck is stationed throughout the day, and broadcasts information about specials and new menu items. With more than 60,000 followers, the Grilled Cheese Truck uses Twitter's real-time stream to reach hungry patrons at the height of lunch (and dinner) time. Putting the full power of Twitter to use, it further entices customers by sending tweets laden with pictures of their food and locale. With Twitter, you do have the opportunity to target people based on geographic location. One way of doing this is by using a hashtag for a specific city (or other location or landmark). This approach makes it easier for the food truck to reach customers based on location.

Other B2C companies have found Twitter just as appealing. The Greek yogurt company Chobani (@Chobani) used Twitter to help celebrate its five-year anniversary. Chobani created a paper birthday hat that people could print and cut out. The company asked customers to wear the paper hat and take a picture of themselves celebrating with Chobani yogurt and post it to Twitter, along with the hashtag #ItsCHObirthday, for a chance to win a year's supply of yogurt. This is another example of how to use a specific hashtag to promote a campaign and to track when a tweet from a customer is used. Having the hashtag and the picture of the product appear in the tweet meant that Chobani's followers could also potentially see its tweet about how great its yogurt is. This is a great example of using Twitter to encourage existing customers to talk about your product for you, and promoting it to a wider base of prospective customers—their own friends.

Although I've highlighted two food product companies, the potential to sell and market via Twitter is just as great for any other type of B2C company; and I've personally seen great examples of customer engagement from brands such as Sharpie (@sharpie), Volkswagen USA (@VW), and even smaller brands such as Dormify (@dormify), which sells products for college dormitories. In all cases, these brands do a fantastic job of tweeting interesting and helpful content, as well as using a mixture of fun contests, campaigns, and images or video to engage their target audience.

If you are targeting a B2B customer, it may be tempting to think it's just not as easy to find and interact with this type of customer on Twitter. However, NeedTagger, a company offering a social selling tool by the same name, spent more than a year studying B2B opportunities available on Twitter.[3] Specifically, NeedTagger looked for tweets that contained "commercially-relevant intent" or business needs. In their report, the company defined a commercially relevant tweet as being one that "an average sales, customer support, or marketing professional would classify the tweet and the person as worthy of further monitoring or worthy of taking some sort of action such as: following, retweeting, sending an outreach message, etc."

Based on this definition, NeedTagger's research indicates that up to 5 percent of tweets meet this commercial criterion. While that may seem like a low percentage, let's look back at Twitter's published usage figures and do some math. Twitter reports approximately 400 million tweets are sent daily. Five percent of 400 million is 20 million! Okay, of course you can't engage in that many commercially relevant tweets in a single day. Even so, consider the number of opportunities that NeedTagger exposed during their research period. In a single month (March 2013), NeedTagger reported identifying 200 million opportunities that potentially warranted some type of engagement or interaction. They also identified industry-specific opportunities available in an average month. For instance, legal issues had more than 240,000 opportunities that month, whereas insurance had just over 10,000 opportunities.

Being in the telecom industry, I follow lots of technology companies on Twitter. Many of them do a great job using Twitter to identify prospective leads and keep customers informed. For technology companies, in particular, Twitter is a good platform to use for finding companies or people who have problems that your products can solve. For technology sales purposes, Twitter is also a logical place to promote company webinars, invite people to product demonstrations, and share informative content and industry news. In fact, having the right content, as discussed in Chapter 6, is critical when tweeting—and content helps you stand out in that crowd of 400 million tweets each day.

Esri, a geographic information systems mapping company, is a good example of how a B2B-focused company with a seemingly bland or highly complex product offering can use Twitter as part of its social selling strategy. The company, which does geospatial mapping, tweets images of maps that show what the company does and explains how its products can be used in various situations. It also tweets product update messages, instructional tips, and offers its Twitter followers the opportunity to be first to test new products. In an effort to show the innovative ways businesses use the social platform, Twitter promoted a case study discussing how Esri published an interactive map of Japan in the days following the 2011 earthquake. By using Twitter to engage with people from around the world, Esri racked up more than 500,000 page views to their interactive map and caught the attention of national and international media who were also covering the story. The ability to use unique, informative content in response to a trending topic helped draw more attention to the company's capabilities. Any time a tweet was shared or mentioned, it should also have presented a perfect opportunity for a salesperson to engage in the conversation and explain their products.

BEST PRACTICES AND TIPS

Whether you are selling into the B2C or B2B market, Twitter provides a way to engage with an almost unlimited number of prospective customers—if you have the right mix of useful, entertaining, and company-specific content. Here is a list of best practices and tips to make your social selling experience more successful on Twitter.

> ➤ **Optimize your profile:** When other users visit the public version of your home page or look at your handle, they see a Twitter profile, as Figure 12–3 shows. This is your opportunity to immediately tell a user who you are and what you are about. Your Twitter bio is also searchable, on and off Twitter, so it is critical to use keywords that a prospective customer might use when trying to find the type of products or services you offer. A good Twitter profile should contain a memorable, easy-to-see photo of yourself, a description about what you do, and a link to your website. You can include a direct phone number or email address in your profile description as well.

> ➤ **Background image:** Your public profile page can also contain a background image that appears around your feed. Use this as a chance to show images of your products or other descriptive photos that further illustrate who you are and how you can help someone who chooses to follow you.

➤ **Communicate:** Twitter is a community of very active, engaged users. One of the best things you can do is start conversations with other users, and *thank* users who engage with you. Any time someone mentions you in a tweet, retweets you, or follows you—publicly thank them for doing so. The more you communicate and highlight others, the more people will want to connect with and follow you.

➤ **Follow and follow back:** Not only should you actively look for and follow Twitter users of interest, but you also want to follow back those who connect with you. This is the best way to start building your reach and potential exposure to a wider network.

➤ **Get involved:** In addition to starting and engaging in Twitter conversations, you can step up your activity level by participating in a Twitter Chat. These are regularly scheduled group conversation threads that are based on a particular industry, topic, or interest. It's like a virtual meeting to discuss a shared topic of interest, but it happens publicly on Twitter. To find a Twitter Chat to join, simply search for hashtags of topics that apply to your industry or for "chats." As you build your own following, you may decide to host your own Twitter Chat! The secret to Twitter Chats is to actively participate in the conversations to be seen. This is a terrific way to meet new people on Twitter—people that are interested in topics related to your business.

➤ **Build Lists:** Twitter has a unique feature that allows you to create "lists" that you keep on your home page. These lists can be open and viewable to the public, or private and viewable only by you. A list is helpful for segmenting a group of Twitter users based on a certain attribute. You can then go to the list to quickly see tweets from anyone in that list. You may have a private list made up of your competitors or prospective customers, or you may want to create a list that is made up of analysts or influential tweeters within your industry.

FIGURE 12-3

Your public Twitter profile lets users get to know you, quickly.

Ultimately, the best way to use Twitter as part of your social selling strategy is to participate! Twitter is a superactive social network and you will gain the most from it by being engaged. Tweet interesting content and tweet often. Because Twitter is less formal than LinkedIn, it's also a good platform in which you can have some fun—within reason.

Of course, LinkedIn and Twitter aren't the only social networks that provide a way to reach prospective customers. In the next chapter, you can see how to use other powerful social media platforms like Google+, Pinterest, and more.

CHAPTER 13

FACEBOOK, GOOGLE+, AND ONLINE COMMUNITIES

Targeting Your Social Customer Base

Given the amount of media attention that both Twitter and LinkedIn receive, you might think they were the only social networking sites that matter to your business, or to your prospective customers. But when it comes to consumer preferences, you may be surprised to discover which social media entities carry the most weight when it comes to buying behaviors. According to research from Technorati Media, Facebook and blogs are most likely to influence a consumer's purchase, with retail (shopping) sites and brand sites considered to be the most influential.[1] Consumers consider blogs, which are also part of the social networking landscape, to be among the top five *most influential and trustworthy* of all online resources.

It's not only about trust—size and popularity matter to consumers, too. And that's where Facebook and Google+ really shine. Not only are they the largest of the social media sites, but consumers rank them as two of the top three *most popular of all platforms* to use, with

YouTube rounding out the list. As you might expect, being able to find and engage with your prospects on any of these sites can go a long way in helping to keep your sales pipeline fed.

From the sheer number of active users to wielding influence over buyers, there are lots of reasons that make Facebook, Google+, blogs, and other online communities beneficial to your social selling strategy. This chapter takes a closer look at each of these platforms, along with the specific steps you can take to further your prospecting goals.

USING YOUR PERSONAL FACEBOOK ACCOUNT

Given it was one of the very first social networking sites, and is still the largest by far, you may wonder why Facebook is lumped in with other social media instead of getting its own chapter. When it comes to social selling, there are some factors that make it potentially less appealing than sites such as LinkedIn or Twitter. The most notable of these is that selling through Facebook is better achieved with a brand leading the effort, rather than an individual. That's because the social media site is designed to connect you to friends and family—and not to strangers. Brand pages, however, were developed to allow companies to connect with a much wider network of fans, even if there's no other type of personal relationship. This means that you really need to use your company page to be most effective, although as a salesperson or marketer you can still use your personal Facebook profile to assist and further the social goals of the brand.

While much of the activity on Facebook will revolve around your company page, there are some ways in which you can still use your personal page as part of your social selling strategy. These include:

> ➤ **"Like" other company pages:** You may want to Like industry-related pages, competitors' pages, and customers' (or prospective customers') pages. This allows updates to potentially show up in your personal newsfeed so you can

keep up with the latest information from these organizations, which may be useful to you in the sales process.

➤ **Become a friend or subscriber:** When appropriate, you may also want to use your personal Facebook account to become friends with vendors, customers, and others. Or, you may want to subscribe to (or follow) personal pages of industry analysts and journalists. These are other ways to stay connected to important or influential contacts. You can use connections through social networks like Facebook to glean helpful information that may even point to certain triggers in the buying process.

➤ **Comment and get noticed:** By actively posting comments or replies to updates from other brands' pages (including those in your industry or of your customers), and by sharing others' posts on your own Facebook page, you remain more visible. Keep in mind that Facebook updates and their comment threads can potentially show up in the news streams of many fans or followers, as well as their friends' newsfeeds, casting a wide net of exposure when you comment and share updates.

➤ **Update your "About" section:** Make sure your personal Facebook profile indicates your current professional position and where you work. It doesn't do a lot of good to get exposure in other people's feeds if they aren't able to tell where you work or what you do. When you share or comment on an update in Facebook and it shows up on someone's newsfeed, the reader is able to hover over your name or profile picture to learn more about you. A small pop-up box appears, like the one shown in Figure 13–1. Whatever information is the first to appear in the About section of your personal profile will also show up in this pop-up box. For instance, if you only complete the sections about what college you attended or where you live, then one of those items will appear next to your name, instead of details about where you work.

FIGURE 13-1

Information from the About section of your Facebook page is visible in newsfeeds.

In the About section of your profile, the Work and Education information will show up first, so keep this updated with your current position and company name, as well as your company website address. While Facebook is centered on lots of personal information, this is the place where you can tout professional information that will be potentially seen by many others, especially those who may be in need of your product or service.

➤ **Share company updates:** One way to help your company get more organic exposure in Facebook is to share and comment on updates made on your company page. For clarification, "share" is an option you have on a Facebook post allowing you to repost it on your own timeline (or Facebook page), a friend's timeline, or in a group, on another Facebook page you manage, or even in a private message sent via Facebook. The more people within an organization who can share updates, the more likely this information is to show up organically in others' newsfeeds. Even if you are not an admin for your company Facebook page, you can still be very active on the page and help increase its ability to be seen by others. (An "admin" is someone specifically authorized to own a Facebook page and make changes to it; but usually anyone can share or comment or Like a post that appears on the company page.)

When using your personal Facebook page as part of your professional initiatives, there are a couple of important points to keep in mind. First, remember that Facebook was the platform designed to highlight and share your life with friends and family, and that your page is likely to be filled with very personal information and photos and typically promotes a much more casual tone and lighthearted exchange of conversation (such as, "Wow! I guess what happens in Vegas doesn't always stay in Vegas! LOL!"), especially when compared to a site like LinkedIn. Because of the more informal approach of Facebook, it is critical to do the following when using your personal profile in your professional networking efforts:

➤ Use privacy settings to control what information and pictures are visible to the public.

➤ Choose to use profile pictures that are somewhat less formal but are not lewd or offensive and that show you clearly (avoid using profile pictures of your family pets, children, or other icons or images that do not include you—this is not the place for the dramatic sunset on the beach).

➤ Use a more casual tone when interacting, but steer clear of using offensive language or slang.

➤ Avoid making derogatory or potentially inflammatory comments, especially about your work—or your competitors.

➤ Share positive, helpful public updates, as they typically receive better feedback and engagement, and are more likely to be shared.

Also, when using Facebook for social selling purposes, it is more difficult for your brand to get high levels of engagement through organic (non-paid) interactions. Paid advertising is often the way you gain your biggest reach on Facebook—and that, too, must be coordinated from your company's page by a page administrator (which you may or may not be for your company).

Though advertising costs are considerably less on this platform than other traditional mediums and can help you target your prospects, it still requires a steady expenditure of your marketing funds. This isn't to say that you cannot achieve low- or no-cost results on Facebook, it's just harder, especially from your viewpoint as an individual salesperson.

USING A COMPANY FACEBOOK PAGE TO TURN FANS INTO CUSTOMERS

Facebook has been one of the first social media sites to aggressively offer businesses the opportunity to monetize the social experience, banking on its ability to provide highly targeted access to its expansive number of monthly active users (over 750 million of them at last count).[2] That makes it a natural place for you to reach prospects, especially if you are selling into the B2C market, where there seems to have been the most documented success. For example, Aria Resort and Casino of Las Vegas has seen a tremendous response to their social selling efforts on Facebook.[3] The company uses a strategy that combines both organic and paid efforts to convert fans into paying customers.

Here's their story. On an ongoing basis, Aria posts frequent updates to their Facebook page in an effort to connect with their fans. But as part of a specific social campaign, they also began posting updates about a special Facebook offer for a $110 credit to their casino and VIP access to a club. Aria then paid to promote, or "boost," one of the posts that described the offer. Boosting a post in Facebook is as simple as checking a box and setting a budget, as shown in Figure 13–2. A post that you boost ensures you get more exposure in the feeds on your fans' pages and in the feeds of the friends of your fans.

FIGURE 13-2

Gain more visibility in newsfeeds by promoting a status update on your brand page.

The budget is a matter of how much you want to spend to promote or "boost" a particular post. Facebook will automatically put a default maximum budget amount, but you can change it to reflect the maximum amount you want to spend. When you put in a maximum amount, Facebook will show you an estimate of how many people will see your post for that amount of money. For example, a maximum amount of $30 may mean that between 1,500 and 3,500 people see your post. Facebook will continue to promote your post until all of your budget is used or until you manually stop the effort.

This type of investment for a social campaign is important for a couple of reasons. Facebook uses an algorithm to determine when and how a brand's update should be displayed in a fan's newsfeed—so just because you post an update it doesn't mean every one of your fans will see it. Paying to promote the post is more of a guarantee that your update is seen.

Keep in mind that Facebook says 40 percent of its users' time is spent within their newsfeeds. And they estimate that a user is 40 to 150 times more likely to engage with content from a brand if it appears in the fan's newsfeed versus seen directly on the brand's page. The moral of this story is that the more of your updates that show up in newsfeeds, the more likely you are to get results. For Aria, their decision to expand their organic efforts and pay for Facebook advertising to increase their ability to appear in fans' newsfeeds netted them a return on investment of 485 percent and an increase of 25,000 new fans on the brand's page.

When considering your own goals in social selling through Facebook, what results in equal success? For Aria, they obviously had an offer or limited-time deal that they wanted fans to purchase as part of a specific promotional campaign. But you may not always have a product or offer, or that strategy might be better suited for a B2C brand and not a B2B brand. As you think about your objectives, remember that the foundation of successful social selling is based on your ability to *build relationships with prospective customers* and *have positive interactions over time*—interactions that build trust and eventually help transition that prospect to a customer. Doing this on Facebook begins by increasing your number of fans.

Building the fan base of your brand page is easy to measure and a simple way to show your progress in social media. It also helps increase your reach into the social network. Facebook statistics indicate that a brand with 500,000 Likes (or fans) has the potential exposure to an additional 40 million friends of fans. Additionally,

Facebook stats show that 51 percent of users are more likely to make a purchase from a brand after Liking their page.

While Aria, with its increased number of fans and offers purchased, is an example of the fantastic results you can achieve with a B2C audience, don't rule out the potential to achieve similar results with B2B customers on Facebook. After all, even though you are selling to businesses, you are ultimately interacting with individual decision makers, many of whom are on this platform!

One of the best examples of a company successfully using Facebook to reach its B2B audience is American Express Open, which targeted their credit cards to small business owners. The company launched a brilliant campaign on Facebook, called Small Business Saturday, that was designed to get consumers to support small businesses by shopping at their local businesses, particularly on one designated Saturday (on the Thanksgiving weekend, following Black Friday). American Express offered downloadable marketing materials to businesses to help them promote the "shop local" campaign in their city and provided similar social sharing icons for consumers to share with their friends on Facebook so they could support the cause and help spread the message.

In its third year of the campaign (in the fall of 2012), American Express reported that consumers spent $5.5 billion with small businesses on Small Business Saturday and that general public awareness of the campaign hit an all-time high of 67 percent.[4] The American Express Small Business Saturday Facebook page also boasts over 32 million Likes—and continues growing, daily. The annual campaign targets the average consumer (or customer of small businesses)—many of which are on Facebook; and it targets the many small business owners (direct customers of American Express) who are also on Facebook. The social selling campaign works for many reasons:

➤ It provides a cause that appeals to a wide audience.

➤ It offers something helpful to its prospects—in this case it is the free marketing materials that small businesses can print out and use to promote the event.

➤ It provides social sharing buttons, icons, and other virtual promotional material that makes it easy for Facebook users to share with their friends.

➤ It encourages fan engagement with regular updates or Facebook posts that are helpful, entertaining, and inspiring.

➤ It integrates online social strategies with offline marketing efforts.

Although you may not reach the levels of American Express, there are a number of basic elements that you can use when developing any social selling campaign. In fact, Facebook encourages you to follow five basic steps to find success for your business:

1. **Build your business page:** Get the most from your page by completing all areas of the page and the About section, and using your logo and memorable images for the cover photo. (This is, of course, separate from your personal Facebook page.)

   If you are a marketer, your team is likely responsible for creating and maintaining your organization's business page. As a manager or "admin" of the Facebook page, your goals should include keeping the page updated with interesting and helpful information.

   And if you are a salesperson, you're probably not going to have much (or any!) involvement with creating or managing a business page. If you are an independent salesperson, however, or work with a very small organization with limited marketing resources, you may need to spearhead the effort to start and maintain the company's Facebook page.

2. **Connect with people:** In addition to encouraging existing customers to Like your page, you can use inexpensive Facebook ads to target prospective customers and grow your fan base.

3. **Engage your audience:** Increase brand awareness and loyalty by interacting with fans on your page and by posting quality content frequently. Use contests, polls, open-ended questions, and video and pictures to encourage positive interactions. As a point of interest, the use of photos in your updates usually get 100 percent more engagement and the use of videos get 120 percent more engagement.

4. **Influence friends of fans:** To increase your exposure to prospective customers, encourage existing fans to share your content on their personal page by Liking, commenting on, or sharing your page updates. You can also use paid advertising, including:

   • Placing ads that appear in the sidebar of fans' personal profiles.

   • Promoting your posts to increase visibility in newsfeeds.

   • Creating an offer with a promotional code or link that can be redeemed within Facebook or through your website that allows fans to share with their friends when they redeem the offer.

   According to Facebook statistics, 80 percent of people are more likely to "try new things" if friends suggest it on social media.

5. **Measure progress:** Facebook offers built-in tools for your brand page. Ads Manager lets you measure the results of ad campaigns and expenditures, and Page Insights provides detailed information about the number of your page Likes, the demographics of your fans, and which page updates get the most interaction and engagement from your fans.

Following these five steps is a good guideline for creating your overall Facebook social selling strategy or for developing specific social campaigns using both organic and paid initiatives. And even though these actions are specific to your brand's page, remember that you can use your personal profile to comment on and share updates as a way to help increase the reach or exposure your brand has on Facebook.

GOOGLE+: TURNING CIRCLES INTO OPPORTUNITIES

While Facebook is recognized as an established, viable social networking site, that's not necessarily the case with its fast-rising competitor. In fact, all bets are still on the table when it comes to the role Google+ has in social selling, as well as in social media in general. Even considering that it is still not clear how much you get from Facebook without paying to play, there is equal if not greater uncertainty about whether there is any type of value gained through Google+. Some skeptics already view the search engine giant's attempt to create a viable social networking hub as a failed experiment. Others simply think it's just a social networking shell made up of numerous but inactive users spawned by some level of early adopter excitement that never caught on. Now for the good news: For as many naysayers that exist, there are easily twice as many proponents (myself included) who see Google+ as having significant potential for connecting with prospects and customers, particularly for companies providing technology-related solutions in the B2B market.

One reason for the support of Google+ is the sheer number of users. As of early 2013, Google+ had amassed 359 million active users, according to GlobalWebIndex, an Internet analytics company.[5] While that number is just more than half of Facebook's claim of over 750 million active monthly users, it still lets Google+ glide past Twitter and lay claim to the title of the number two social networking site.

Another benefit to Google+, especially when compared to Facebook and LinkedIn, is the ability for you to connect to people you don't already know and to interact with them simply based on common interests. Instead of friends or fans, Google+ is based on "circles" that allow you to connect with lots of other users and then classify them in these virtual networking circles structured around how you know them (coworkers, friends, customers, prospects, influencers, and so on). As you might expect, the ability to openly connect with potentially millions of contacts and then segment those connections for further, targeted engagement are real benefits in the world of social selling.

A third, somewhat controversial but extremely advantageous benefit of the social networking site is its influence in Google's search engine results. Some think because Google wants you to adopt and use its social network (over others), it is rewarding you by integrating more of your social activity on Google+ into general search results. In other words, the more you participate on Google+, the more likely it is that you or your brand is going to show up in response to search queries on Google. Given that Google currently dominates the search engine market, if your social media activity ranks higher in search results and makes it easier for prospective customers to find you, that benefit alone, many industry experts say, could make it worth the investment of your time.

So, is Google+ right for you? As part of creating your social selling strategy, and as discussed in Chapter 10, it's implausible to think you can successfully participate in all of the top social networking sites. Instead, you are better off targeting a few sites—those places where you know your prospects are spending their time and where you are most likely to see results. Google+ is one of the social media platforms where your target audience may not be all that engaged, yet. So, you may not end up spending a lot of time there. But Google+ is still a good place for you to establish a presence, both personally and for your brand, for all the reasons I mentioned.

The easiest way to get started is by setting up a profile. Similar to other social networking profiles, a Google+ profile, like the example shown in Figure 13–3, lets you use images and text to provide details about you and your business. Having a profile in Google+ for you or your business ensures that no one else can use your name (or your company's name) within the social networking site. For instance, I have a profile for "Shannon Belew" and one for the "Art of Social Selling." That means no one else can use either of those names.

FIGURE 13-3

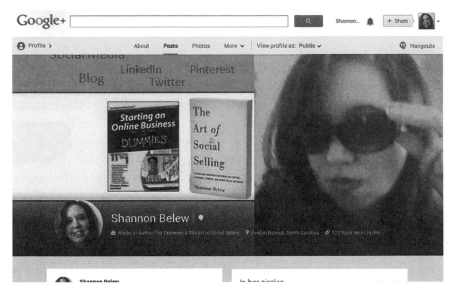

Use images and text to make the cover of your Google+ profile more inviting.

Another advantage of having a Google+ profile is that you can connect your Google+ profile to your website and other social media profiles, increasing your exposure to prospective customers and helping your content be seen by a wider audience. One way of increasing exposure is through the use of the "g+ share" button and the "+1" designation (the Google equivalent of a Like). For any content that you post, someone else can validate it as useful or liked simply by clicking the button to share it on their Google+ profile. When others see the content, they can click the "+1" icon to like and share the content from within Google+. As you might expect, the +1 is an increasingly important designation since it increases the visibility and reach of a piece of content. Of course, the use of Google+ may potentially help you show up in Google search engine results for related keyword searches. If you are a local business (as opposed to a national brand), getting the improved search result rankings may also make it easier for local prospective customers to find you or your business.

Although Google+ has grown tremendously since it first launched in 2011, both Google and the site's registered users are still deciding all the best possible ways to maximize the social experience. As the site continues to evolve, there are still very specific ways you can incorporate Google+ into your social selling strategy, including the following:

➤ **Expand your circles:** Find people you know on Google+ and invite them to connect. This includes everyone from coworkers and friends to prospects and strategic partners. Google+ has a feature that makes it easy to find contacts from your email database who already have Google+ profiles.

➤ **Find influencers:** Because it is easy to connect with strangers, use this opportunity to find and follow industry analysts, journalists, and other influential people in your industry.

➤ **Engage:** Post updates to your profile and comment "+1," and share updates from others in your circles.

➤ **Give +1:** Outside of Google+ you can still give (or get) +1 on content found on blogs and other websites; this is another way to create positive interactions with others, get noticed, and help build your social reputation in and outside of Google+.

➤ **Participate in communities:** A relatively new feature in Google+, communities are like forums or LinkedIn groups, which are formed around certain topics or interests. Joining a community that is focused on some type of event or topic specific to your industry is an easy way to identify and meet other Google+ members, as well as potential prospects. If you have the time to stay active enough, you can even start your own community!

➤ **Participate in "Hangouts":** Google+ created the ability to hold or join a virtual discussion or a video broadcast in a format referred to as a Google+ Hangout. You can use it as you would a webinar, or you can have a small online meeting via video for up to ten people. And when you stream a live Hangout event, you have the added advantage of having it appear on Google+, your website, and YouTube. Plus, a recorded version automatically posts to YouTube at the end. Hosting or participating in a Hangout is a great way to connect with prospects or influencers and progress into a higher level of engagement within the sales cycle.

➤ **Take advantage of "Google Authorship":** When you have a Google+ profile, you can establish what's referred to as "Google Authorship." Basically, this is a feature of Google that allows you to enter information about blogs and websites where you post articles, and then Google attaches your author bio and photo to the articles you publish. The benefit of this is that it is another way to help you show up in Google search results. In addition, your photo is included, which makes the link to your content even more visible. It's another way to establish yourself as a credible resource in your field of expertise and make it easier to find you and your published articles.

SPREADING YOUR MESSAGE ON BLOGS AND ONLINE COMMUNITIES

The ability to connect with a highly targeted audience based on similar interests is not unique to Google+. There are actually lots of other community gathering spots where you can find and reach out to your existing and prospective customers. You may not think of blogs, forums, and other community-centric sites as social media sites, but they often prove to be important components of any social selling strategy. Blogs and communities are important because:

> Active, engaged users congregate there.

> It's easy to identify your specific customer base and prospects.

> Users are openly looking for solutions to problems and for product recommendations.

> Loyal customers can be found participating and providing unsolicited testimonials.

> They are often less crowded, so it's easier for your voice to be heard (or comments to be seen).

> Participating means goodwill for your brand (when addressing support issues/concerns).

> Contributing helps establish you as an expert or helpful resource.

What's the difference between each of these online entities? Blogs are basically websites that contain frequent posts (articles, photos, short quips) by one or more contributors or authors, and the information is often based on a particular topic or theme. They can be incredibly helpful to any social prospecting strategy, as blogs are considered the third most influential online resource for consumers looking to make a purchase, according to Technorati Media.[6] It's highly likely that your company already maintains a blog as part of its corporate website. You may even have a blog that you use for either personal or professional reasons. Whether you are contributing content to one of your blogs or you are interacting with and commenting on other blogs, these activities really pay off—especially when you make a habit of consistent and frequent participation. Here are some specific actions you can take to include blogs in your social selling activities:

> Identify public blogs where your customers and target prospects congregate.

> Follow the blogs or add them to your RSS feed so that you are notified when new content is published.

➤ Comment on articles and respond to other contributors' comments when appropriate.

➤ When commenting, try to avoid making a sales pitch and instead offer to provide advice, but be upfront that you are a salesperson or represent a particular company.

➤ Provide links to additional resources when responding to comments or questions, if the blog permits it.

➤ Contribute articles or guest posts for other blogs, when possible.

➤ If your company has a blog on its website, offer to contribute articles at least once a month.

➤ Always include a byline (recognition that you are the author of the article) with contact information.

➤ When possible, include an About the Author section at the end of the article with a couple of sentences about you (tie this in to your Google+ Authorship, as discussed earlier).

➤ Use your social media profiles, like your Twitter handle, and ask readers to follow you (readers may not want or be ready to contact you but they are often willing to follow you on social media).

To make the most of the above activities and stay on track, it's helpful to make them part of your daily routine. Participating for thirty minutes every day is often plenty of time to dedicate to blogging, especially if you schedule it during your less busy times—early in the morning, during lunch, or between sales calls. Contributing articles can take a little extra time. As a salesperson, if you are not comfortable writing an article for a blog, you can sometimes partner with someone in marketing and ask them to ghost-write the post for you, which means they write the article but let you take credit publicly as the author. This is standard practice, so don't hesitate to ask about it!

Like blogs, online communities and forums provide a home base for people who share a specific cause or interest. Communities provide a mix of information—such as articles specific to the community topic or helpful resources for problem solving around the community topic—or you can solicit advice from other community members. Inbound.org is an example of an online community specifically for inbound marketers. It is filled with articles, tools, and helpful advice about inbound marketing. The site also highlights its most influential members, which is a trait common to other online communities, as well. And even though it's a niche topic, this particular community averages about 45,000 visits per month!

Though you might think bigger is better when it comes to online communities, it's not always the largest or most popular sites that are necessarily the most effective. According to the *2013 Digital Influencer Report*, 54 percent of consumers thought that "the smaller the community, the greater the influence."[7] Perhaps this viewpoint relates back to the issue of trust. Often, smaller online communities allow for more interaction among their members. There is also more opportunity for top influencers to build their credibility and become well known among community members; this intimacy breeds trust and authority.

As a salesperson who is active in a forum, group, or other community, you have the ability to be seen as a go-to resource for information and to become a trusted influencer, provided you contribute and engage frequently. Online community members are typically very active, and they are protective of the community. Active members don't always appreciate the occasional drop-in commenter, especially one who is obviously there to try and sell something. However, they are typically very supportive of and willing to listen to other community members who are:

- ➤ Frequent participants.
- ➤ Providers of interesting and helpful information or comments.
- ➤ Respectful of other members and their comments.
- ➤ Sincere and willing to help.

You often find that an online community has its own distinct "personality." Once you understand this personality, it becomes easier to contribute and engage. In my industry, there are lots of technology-based online communities that are centered on a specific type of technology or user profile (IT professional or small business executive, for instance). One example of a community that I've found particularly exciting in the B2B technology space is Spiceworks. The growing online community is made up of primarily IT professionals and is divided into smaller sets of niche technology topics, which makes it easy to engage with members who share a very specific interest. (In my case, that happens to be an interest in Voice over IP (VoIP) technologies, Unified Communications solutions, and the Asterisk Open Source telephony platform. By the way, those are all industry terms and products related to a more generic term— business phone systems!) While the community has specific guidelines on how you, as a salesperson or a company, can promote your products, it's a great site for interacting with both existing customers and prospects. It's also a great way for both salesperson and marketers to discover firsthand what types of problems members are trying to solve and how they have used various (and sometimes competing) technologies within their organizations.

But to be successful in Spiceworks and communities like it, you have to participate on a regular basis and build the trust of other members that you have interesting and helpful information to contribute. Because Spiceworks is made up of IT professionals, the community does have a very specific personality based on its savvy, technical users. As a contributor, you often have to be sure that the information you contribute is high level and technically specific when discussing a particular product or solution.

Whether you are selling into a B2B technology market or a C2C clothing market, there's an online community filled with your target customers who are receptive to you interacting with them—on their terms.

Many of the activities that are recommended for you to do for blogs also apply to online communities. However, here are some additional actions you can take to make the most of participating in online communities:

- Create a profile (or register) on each online community and, when possible, tie your profile back to one or more of your other social media profiles (such as Google+).

- Respond to comments and questions quickly (unlike blogs, the conversation in communities often flows at a very rapid pace and the sooner you engage, the better).

- Use the on-site search function to find specific conversations about your products, services, or industry-specific terms.

- Contribute often with meaningful comments. (Many online communities reward or highlight the most active or helpful members; this is a good way to be seen by prospective customers and establish your credibility.)

- Thank other members for their comments or questions. (This simple form of recognition goes a long way in tight-knit communities.)

- Start a conversation thread by posting interesting questions or useful polls; these are likely to elicit responses—and lead to your ultimate goal: positive interactions.

- Share current industry news and other interesting updates as a way to get other members engaged in a conversation.

- Respond to customer concerns and negative comments (You may run across complaints from existing customers or negative comments from competitors. Don't ignore these comments; address them and try to move the conversation offline to email or customer support, when feasible.)

- Consider sponsoring an online community. (Some communities allow brands to sponsor certain sections or topics within the community, which is a good way to make your brand

more visible to community members; sponsorship can sometimes provide additional community privileges specific to the
lead gen or sales process.)

➤   Participate in off-site community events. (Online communities typically offer small, offline networking events in various
cities. This is a fantastic way to extend the online relationships you've already made and meet potential new prospects.)

———

The truth of the matter is there are hundreds of thousands of online
communities, blogs, and forums where you can participate—and
there are lots of options for how you participate. But you might also
want to make time for a few other social networks. In the next chapter, you will learn how to take advantage of some visually based
social media sites, including YouTube and Pinterest—both of which
continue to grow at phenomenal rates.

CHAPTER 14

THE RISE OF VISUAL CONTENT AND ITS INFLUENCE ON SALES

YouTube, Pinterest, Infographics, and More

A picture may be worth a thousand words, but in social media the use of visual content is priceless. Photos, videos, graphics, charts, animated GIFs (moving graphics), and more are all voraciously shared and consumed across social networking sites and blogs every minute of every day. There are entire social media platforms based almost exclusively on imagery, from YouTube and Instagram to Pinterest and SlideShare. Whether you are focused on B2C or B2B sales, including visual content in your social selling strategy is a necessity if you want to increase the likelihood of your message being seen, understood, and redistributed. Deciding what types of media or images you should use is only part of the equation. You also need to understand which social media platforms are most conducive for using visual content to reach your prospective customers.

VISUAL CONTENT THAT HELPS CONVEY
YOUR MESSAGE

There's no doubt that sharing videos and images resonates with online consumers. Each month, people watch more than 4 billion hours of video on YouTube alone![1] Maybe it's because visuals offer a way to quickly and succinctly tell a story (if done well). Or perhaps visual content is successful in social media because it appeals to different types of learning styles. It is generally accepted that visual learners make up approximately 30 percent of the population and auditory learners account for around 25 percent.[2] While visual learners do use text, they prefer the inclusion of graphics and charts to help them better understand concepts; and those labeled as being auditory learn best by listening. It's no wonder videos are so effective, given their appeal to both of these learning preferences!

There's a proven history that images sell as well. As any marketer will quickly point out, the use of imagery has been a staple in advertising since long before anyone ever heard of the Internet. It seems only natural that we would continue using this successful methodology to get our point across online, especially when you consider the limitations often placed on the amount of text you can use for posts, tweets, and text messages. In addition, visual content, whether a video or a still photo, also has a reputation for going viral, quickly spreading to the masses through social sharing.

One of my favorite examples of a brand capitalizing on the viral nature of imagery is Oreo's social success during the 2013 Super Bowl. When the lights went out during the nationally televised football championship, Oreo's social media team quickly created a picture of a single Oreo cookie that was slightly illuminated in an otherwise dark "lights out" background. The caption on the image read: "You can still dunk in the dark." The team sent out a tweet that simply said, "Lights out? No problem." They then attached the picture of the Oreo sitting in darkness. In a matter of minutes, it had been retweeted 15,000 times and the same image posted on Facebook received 20,000 Likes.[3]

Granted, not every company, let alone an individual salesperson, has access to a team of graphic artists and videographers who can produce a never-ending stream of clever images. But it's actually pretty simple to create visual content. Chances are you already do it frequently. One thing I know about both sales and marketing professionals is that they tend to be really proficient at creating everything from simple charts and graphs to intricate PowerPoint presentations and eye-catching videos—all of which you can use in the social selling process. Here are six types of visual content that are commonly used in social media:

1. **Video:** The nice part about using video in social selling is that it doesn't have to be an expensive commercial production. You can just as easily create an effective video with the camera from your smartphone. Videos are well suited for product demonstrations, for sales presentations about your company or services, and for offering quick tips or information that benefit your prospective customer. A general rule of thumb is that they should be no longer than two minutes; otherwise you risk losing the attention of the viewer. Videos are easily shared across almost all of the social media platforms. In fact, when you include a video in a social media post it is three times more likely to get linked to (or shared) than a text-only post.[4]

2. **Photos:** From products to people, snapping a quick photo with your phone is an easy, yet powerful way to communicate your message online. On average, there are more than 300 million photos uploaded to Facebook daily as well as at least 40 million photos uploaded to Instagram.[5] While there are plenty of personal photos uploaded, businesses frequently post photos and customers are typically willing to take and share pictures of products and places they love.

3. **Graphics:** Included in this category is everything from bar charts and pie charts to illustrations and animated images. Although you may not have a large inventory of art to choose from, it's not difficult to create simple images. You can also

access stock images (images and photos licensed for public use) from fee-based sites like iStock.com or use free images from clipart programs. Images, charts, and graphs can be pulled from existing sales and marketing presentations.

4. **Infographics:** Infographics, which visually convey particular data points, have become a popular way to display and share information. Research from Bit Rebels, an online news outlet, showed that infographics used on Twitter received 832 percent more retweets than tweets that only contained text or images.[6] LinkedIn status updates with infographics were shared 629 percent more often than those without. Most likely, you have seen an infographic, like the one in Figure 14–1, shared on a blog or online news site. It's typically a long image that includes lots of graphic elements and illustrations combined with short text descriptions. If you have a lot of information to get across, or if it's data that may otherwise be complicated or boring, you can use infographics to convey the key facts through engaging graphics. There are lots of online services, like Visual.ly, that will develop infographics for a fee and some do-it-yourself applications, like Piktochart .com, that guide you through the process of creating simple infographics.

5. **PowerPoint presentations:** If you have ever given a presentation to customers or peers, you have likely used PowerPoint as a way to visually support your sales pitch or speech. This popular application lets you import graphics, photos, and videos to accompany text, quotes, bulleted lists, and other short bits of information and then compile it into a structured presentation format. For most B2B sales professionals, PowerPoint presentations are a standard (and much accepted) part of your toolkit. In addition to realizing that PowerPoint presentations are useful pieces of visual content to share on social media, you can use the application as a tool to help you create other graphics—even infographics! I have close to zero graphic illustration skills, but I find it convenient to use PowerPoint to create a

FIGURE 14-1

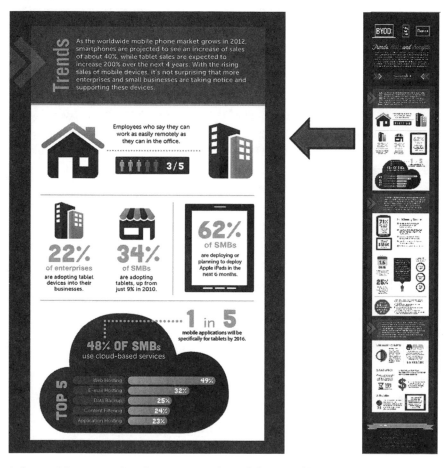

Infographics are a visual representation of data, making it easy to digest, like this one from Digium, Inc.

graphic for use in social media. Options include using a single slide as your image or creating a graphic within a single Power-Point slide, then using your computer to take a snapshot of only that graphic, and, finally, saving it as a single image such as a .jpg or .png file. It's that easy! PowerPoint presentations may also be reformatted as SlideShare presentations, which is a social sharing platform owned by LinkedIn. I'll explain more about SlideShare later in this chapter. For now, just know that if you are comfortable using PowerPoint, then you will have no problem developing engaging visual content.

6. **eBooks:** You are probably familiar with ebooks and have likely downloaded them from a website to learn about a particular topic, or have used them as a way to share information with your own prospects and customers. Of course, published books (like this one!) can be downloaded in a digital format and are also considered ebooks. But, in the context of social selling, think of the electronic books commonly used by sales and marketing as finely tuned PowerPoint presentations or as a grown-up version of children's picture books with clear calls to action included. The most effective ebooks focus on explaining or highlighting a single concept or topic and are filled with images paired with minimal amounts of explanatory text. These image-packed digital books are effective pieces of visual content to use as part of your sales process.

INCORPORATING VISUAL CONTENT INTO YOUR SALES PROCESS

Show, don't tell. That's the general idea behind the use of images in your sales messages. Particularly when bringing visual content into the social selling process, think about what it is you want your prospect or customer to take away from the image or video. Are you showing your prospect how to solve a problem? Are you illustrating how your product or service can make their lives easier or help them achieve a goal? Are you using the content to reinforce your expertise and demonstrate the capabilities of your company? Consider the specific purpose of your sales process. It is often one of the following:

➢ **Instructional:** Takes a how-to approach.

➢ **Informative:** Uses facts to educate.

> **Persuasive:** Often touts a benefit by using either logic or emotion.

> **Entertaining:** While fun, its purpose is often to create brand awareness.

Using visual content reinforces or supports the messages you are verbally sharing with prospects and customers. It also gives you new and more memorable ways to present that information.

Once you decide on the message and how you want to deliver it, you next want to think about what you want your prospect to do once they see your content. Usually, you want to create content that prompts your prospect to act in one of the following ways:

> **Share the content** with others.

> **Respond to a call to action** that brings the prospect back to your website or landing page.

> **Complete a form or provide contact information** as part of lead generation.

> **Take a specific step in the sales process**; for example, request a sales demo or product samples.

> **Initiate contact** with you or provide a reason to start the sales conversation.

> **Make a purchase**; this is most likely to occur with B2C rather than B2B.

Obviously, to elicit these types of responses you need to make it clear what action is expected. If you create an infographic and your goal is to get people to share it so that it reaches a larger base of potential prospects, be upfront about it. Add a message at the bottom of the infographic (or on the blog where you might first post the content) that asks people to repost the infographic on their blogs or to share it on their social media networks. If you create a how-to video for your product, include a call to action within the video that gives the viewer a clear next step to take. You can embed a visual call to action anywhere within the video, such as a link to a landing page to request a personal demo or a phone number to call for more information. Visual calls to action are helpful because you can place them throughout the video (or at the end) and can easily change them to suit a new campaign; changing a verbal call to action is more complicated and expensive because you must re-record those parts of the video.

Incorporating visual content into your online sales process is really no different from the traditional offline sales process. You always want to provide an initial reason for the prospect to engage with you, followed by prompting a need or desire to move forward in the buying process, and finally providing a clear next step on their path to purchasing from you.

SHARING VISUAL CONTENT USING APPS

Once you know what types of visual content you want to use and have decided how you want prospects to interact with or use your content, there's still one piece of the equation remaining. You must choose where you want to distribute the content. After all, having a fantastic piece of visual content does you little good if no one actually sees it!

One of the first places to share visual content is across your social media networks—Facebook, Twitter, Google+, LinkedIn, and your blog. Keep in mind that certain pieces of your content may be more appropriate to share on one platform than others. A funny video that's meant to encourage sharing may be great for Facebook but may not be as well received on LinkedIn (try a SlideShare presentation for these professionals).

There are also applications that provide another way to create visual content or are even specific to a particular social network. Here are a few of the most popular apps:

> **Vine:** Twitter introduced this app, which is best explained as a miniature video. Vine allows you to use an iPhone, iPod, or

iPad to create a six-second continuously looping video or to edit video segments together (think stop-motion–style video). Vines can be shared on Twitter or Facebook, or embedded just about anywhere on the Web that you want to put them! You might not immediately think of Vines as being useful in the social selling process but several brands have been quick to illustrate the advantages of a Vine video. Lowes Home Improvement is one of my favorite examples of a brand getting creative with Vine. They created a series of videos easily found using the hash tag #LowesFixInSix (a nod to the six-second limit). The videos provide (very) quick home improvement tips that have been extremely popular with its target customers—not to mention that they have received plenty of comments and shares across social media. I especially like this app because this style of video is fitting for almost any salesperson to emulate. Whether you are selling into the B2C or B2B market, you can create six seconds' worth of product or service tips for your prospect.

➤ **Instagram:** Considered both an app and a platform, Instagram lets you apply a filter to any photo or video you take on your smart device and then lets you share it on the Instagram platform. You can also just as easily post it to Facebook (which now owns Instagram), Twitter, or Tumblr (one of the blog platforms). Instagram introduced videos to their app in 2013, to compete with the ever-popular Vine videos. Unlike Vine, Instagram videos can run fifteen seconds. In general, I like to think of Instagram as an accessory for your photos because the filters change their look. You might create a retro look, a black and white version, or simply soften the edges of the photo. You can use similar filters (and editing options) to change the look of videos, too.

Instagram is a popular application and has lots of photos and videos that get commented on, Liked, and retweeted. According to the company, there are more than 100 million active users, and every day approximately 40 million photos are posted to Instagram.[7] Instagram's videos also seem to be surging in popularity, with some reports indicating they are outpacing the use of Vine videos. But, it's really too early to say for certain which video app will pull ahead as a clear winner (at least at the time of writing this)—so stay tuned!

No matter which video app becomes a front-runner, Instagram is clearly a fun and easy way to share pictures and videos of your products or offer a behind-the-scenes look at a trade show or other event. Keep in mind, however, that the current average user of Instagram tends to be younger. Approximately 28 percent are between eighteen and twenty-nine years old, while only 14 percent are between the ages of thirty and forty-nine, according to Pew Research.[8] While Instagram is equally suitable for both B2C and B2B, the age difference in users may skew whether or not you reach your target prospect.

➤ **Snapchat:** Speaking of a young audience, Snapchat is a private photo-sharing app most used by teenagers and best known for sending self-portraits (also called "selfies"). The appeal of this photocentric app is that it allows you to snap a photo with the phone on your camera and send it to other users. However, the pictures aren't permanent; you can view images for less than ten seconds (depending on the setting you choose) before they disappear—unless you choose to archive them.

Why bother mentioning this app? If your target happens to be younger customers in the B2C market, you have a built-in audience that's eager to share through social media. According to Snapchat data, more than 200 million photos are sent each day![9] That may be why some brands have ventured into Snapchat territory by using it for contests. Since photos can be saved, brands ask customers to snap pictures of themselves using their products and then post the Snapchat photos to the brand's blog (or other site).

SOCIAL SHARING PLATFORMS MADE FOR PROMOTING VISUAL CONTENT

Apps aren't the only way to spread your visual message. Both B2C and B2B sales and marketing teams have found plenty of success using social media platforms that were designed completely around the promotion of images and videos, including YouTube, Pinterest, and SlideShare. Before diving into each of these platforms, I want to point out another huge benefit that comes with using visual content—getting a boost from the search engines! Photos, videos, infographics, and other images that are used on these and other social networks are easily searchable and found by the top search engines like Google.

As you think about the challenge of reaching a larger pool of prospects, it's important to understand that visual content (which you can post on all of these channels) is very likely to rank well in search engine results. As potential customers are looking for answers to their problems, your how-to videos and infographics may very well show up at the top of search results. This is yet another reason to designate time for creating and sharing visual content. Now, let's take a look at some of the specific social media platforms that can give your visual content—and your social selling strategy—a boost.

PUTTING YOUR VIDEOS ON YOUTUBE

Home to many of the most viral videos that ever crossed social media (and traditional media) channels, YouTube is the recipient of more than one billion unique visitors each month. While there, visitors end up consuming four billion hours of video. That stat is made possible because each minute that passes means another seventy-two hours' worth of video is uploaded to YouTube.[10] That's a lot of video!

Using YouTube effectively means rereading the information I shared earlier in this chapter about the best practices for videos. In a nutshell, you want to create videos that have a purpose, aren't too long, and that can be shared across all your social networks for maximum exposure. Remember, video has been proven to be many times more engaging on Facebook, alone, than other types of posts! But it's recommended that you create a branded channel for your videos so that you can upload business videos and create playlists (of multiple videos) for your prospects to find online and see. It's a snap to create a public YouTube channel in the name of your business—especially if you have a Google + account for your business. Even without the Google + presence, it takes only a few minutes to sign on to YouTube and follow the simple instructions to "create a new channel." Think of your company's channel as a website for your business that's located within YouTube. That means all your videos are captured in one place, making finding them easier for your prospects and customers.

You can further increase the opportunity for your videos to be found by optimizing them. Did I mention that search engine giant Google owns YouTube? Just as with Google +, when you put content into YouTube, Google wants to help the right people find it, since the video becomes one of their properties. But you have to help Google get your content out there by being specific about who you want to target and using words with your video that your prospects are most likely to search for the video content. While YouTube is a visual platform, it still uses text to help with search results. Take time to note the important keywords mentioned in your video—and then use them in the title of the video and the description that goes with it. For maximum benefit, you can repeat the keywords, or tags, by listing the most important individual words or phrases in the tags section (it appears under the description section) when uploading a new video. As with any Web page or non-visual content, tags or keywords help search engines find your content. You can help boost search results even more if you attach a script or, rather, translate the video into a text-only document and attach it with the file.

Many sales professionals (and marketers, too) are reluctant to make YouTube videos because it seems too difficult or expensive. Naturally, you want videos to be professional, with a clear message, good sound, and no blurry images. But you really *do not need a professional video production service* to create usable, good-quality videos. Here are some simple types of videos that work well with social selling and that can be created using an average video recorder, flip camera, or the video camera on your smart device.

- ➢ **Product demonstrations:** A brief visual illustration of how to properly use your product, or an overview of interesting or unique ways to use it.

- ➢ **Presentations:** A video recorded at a trade show or special event.

- ➢ **Customer testimonial:** A video of the customer talking about their experience with you.

- ➢ **Customer success stories:** A video that discusses a particular case study and reviews the solution that your company provided; this is an easy way to do a customer testimonial if the customer is not available for a video interview.

- ➢ **Interviews with a product manager or other company employees:** A video discussing specific product features or other soon-to-be-released products are often popular. Or, you can use employee-focused videos to provide a behind-the-scenes look at a particular product or part of the company.

- ➢ **How-to or "quick tip":** These are very effective videos if they are indirectly related to your specific product or service so as to avoid coming across as a sales pitch.

- ➢ **Interviews with a vendor:** These videos help provide credibility about doing business with you.

- ➢ **User-generated video content:** YouTube is the ideal venue to showcase videos that existing customers or prospects submit to you as part of a contest or as a way to feature their business by showing how they use your product. Customers are usually eager to help spread the videos that they produced across their own social networks.

> ➤ **Quick trend update:** Videos of yourself or another colleague discussing industry trends or other current event–style news that may be of interest to your prospects.

> ➤ **Q&A video:** A video of an existing customer or employee asking a common question about your product or service, after which you provide the answer. We discussed this at greater length in Chapter 6.

> ➤ **Press release announcement:** A video used to share important company news.

> ➤ **Short clips of company events:** Videos offering a look at what goes on inside your company. This is a surprisingly popular way to engage prospects and help put a personality with your business. Unlike the interviews with company employees or videos that focus on a product, this type of video offers a more personalized (or humanized) view of your company and might include videos of milestone celebrations, company picnics, employee birthday celebrations, and more.

The list can go on and on, but hopefully this is enough to get your creative juices flowing. You are also welcome to include training videos or other support-related videos, but keep in mind that these are less likely to be useful in the prospecting process. It's great to have them as part of your brand's channel for use by existing customers, but as a salesperson, your time is best spent on the videos that are of interest to and shared by prospective customers.

Staples, the office supply store, is a good example of a company using YouTube well to target B2B consumers. Their YouTube channel features a mix of video types, from informational to entertaining, and even includes some videos that tout special offers or discounts. Staples' channel has more than 1,400 subscribers and has had nearly 400,000 views of videos. I like that Staples puts social sharing buttons in the sidebar of their YouTube channel to encourage users to engage with them on other social media channels. As always, social selling is dependent upon information being shared across channels, so anytime you have the opportunity to promote sharing, it can only help you in the end.

PINNING YOUR VISUAL CONTENT TO PINTEREST

While YouTube is a channel equally suitable to B2B and B2C sales, Pinterest is a visual content platform that skews heavily toward a specific demographic within the B2C market—women. According to Pew Research, 15 percent of all Internet users are on Pinterest, and "women are about five times as likely to be on the site as men." This statistic applies specifically to adults over the age of 18 and the report notes that no other social media site listed in the research showed as large of a usage gap based on gender.[11] Of course, Pinterest users also tend to be older, have some level of college education, and earn more money. Nearly 40 percent of users are between the ages of eighteen and forty-nine, and 41 percent of users have household incomes that exceed $50,000 annually. If this describes your target customer, then Pinterest is the place for you!

Before explaining how you can find and engage these prospective customers, let's make sure you understand exactly how people use Pinterest. It's essentially a social media platform based almost exclusively on sharing images. The site uses the concept of "pinning," or saving images found on the Internet, to a personal "board," or account. You can then share those images with other Pinterest users.

Like other social networking platforms, Pinterest works because it allows you to Like, share, or comment on others' images; repin them to your own boards; or share or post those images to your other social networks (like Facebook).

You can also follow other users' boards. It may sound confusing but think of a Pinterest board as a virtual board where you tack images you like and organize multiple boards by topic or type of interest. For example, you might have a Pinterest board called "Fast Cars," and then anytime you find an image of a sports car you like, you save, or "pin," the image to your Fast Cars board.

Retailers and online magazines have found that users are eager to pin and share images of clothes, food, recipes, home décor, gardens, exotic locations, and other similar types of photos. By adding a "Pin It" button to your website pages, specifically those with photos, users can click the button to pin the image to their preferred board.

Pinterest has recently started partnering with some of its more active brands to offer additional features to assist with engagement and (ultimately) sales. For instance, the brands can include expanded information with each image so that users don't have to leave Pinterest to get more information about an image. Depending on the brand and image, you might see additional product details or descriptions, pricing information, or informational content (such as a recipe or directions to a store). If the expanded features work well for these initial brands, it's possible that the features would be rolled out to smaller companies in many different categories.

For these types of consumer-based brands, Pinterest has already proven to be effective, particularly in:

> ➤ Building awareness.

> ➤ Showcasing products.

> ➤ Driving traffic back to a website or product page.

> ➤ Promoting contests.

> ➤ Sharing videos.

For the most part, B2C brands tend to enjoy a wider audience on Pinterest. But is Pinterest really *only* for B2C brands? Who is having the most success? Unmetric, a company specializing in benchmarking social media, released data showing the top brands on Pinterest.[12] Based purely on the number of followers, the brands making the list include L.L. Bean, Nordstrom, and Lowe's (all B2C). Top brands based on number of comments posted to their Pinterest images include Purex, HTC Mobile, and Mashable (a popular online news site for technology, social media, and current events). Although Mashable is not a pure B2B brand, it does have an audience largely made up of businesses and tech users, so it's particularly interesting to see it on the list. It also serves as an indicator that Pinterest is not exclusively of use to consumer-based brands.

Like the benefits to B2C brands, Pinterest offers businesses an opportunity to build brand awareness, increase exposure and sharing of visual content, showcase products and services, build leads, and drive Web traffic. But I consider one of the biggest boosts you can hope to get from Pinterest in the B2B space as being related to that last benefit—*driving Web traffic and search results*, That's because Pinterest is a high-traffic social network site, and search engines (like Google) now index or include information found on Pinterest when returning search results.

Search engines are also placing more value on social activity (referred to as "social signals"), and the fact that your content gets pinned, shared, or commented on in Pinterest can help boost how much value search engines place on your content. If you are a B2B salesperson or marketer, you should start posting images that link back to the following content:

- ➤ Infographics
- ➤ Books, white papers, and other collateral
- ➤ Product images
- ➤ Videos
- ➤ Webinars
- ➤ Blog posts
- ➤ Customer case studies
- ➤ Job postings
- ➤ Press releases
- ➤ Event invitations

When posting content (or the image representing the content), be sure to include a description that uses important keywords and a link back to landing pages or product pages. When posting B2B content to Pinterest, it's critical that you include a strong, eye-catching image to represent the content. Obviously, the more interesting your image, the more likely it is to be noticed and shared!

As a B2B salesperson, if you want to spend time on Pinterest, the best place to start is creating a personal or business account and then posting to your Pinterest boards the same content you use in other places as another way to build reach and exposure for your brand. Don't forget to complete your profile or the About section of your Pinterest account, and use keywords to describe what it is you do (again, this is helpful when it comes to search engine results). This is also a great place to insert a call to action that will direct Pinterest users to your website.

As a B2B marketer, I use my personal Pinterest account in these same ways—to gain exposure and (hopefully) increase visibility in search, or how easily I show up in search engine results. My primary objective with Pinterest is setting up boards, as you see in Figure 14–2, that are primarily focused on business-related topics specific to social selling, online marketing, and tech trends (but include boards about all subjects that I write about and areas where I look for followers to engage with me). I use Pinterest specifically to share blog posts and drive traffic back to my website.

I also follow other companies of interest to me, such as Marketo, a provider of marketing automation software to the B2B market. Marketo uses Pinterest for everything from promoting events and trade shows to sharing presentations and providing information about working for the company. While they are still building followers and engagement, they do a good job of organizing visual content that both prospects and customers will find useful. Again, these are basic ways to get started using Pinterest. Then you can decide whether or not you are getting enough return on investment for your time.

Whether you are focused on B2B or B2C, here are some other simple but popular ways to get started posting and to engage fans, prospects, and customers on Pinterest:

FIGURE 14–2

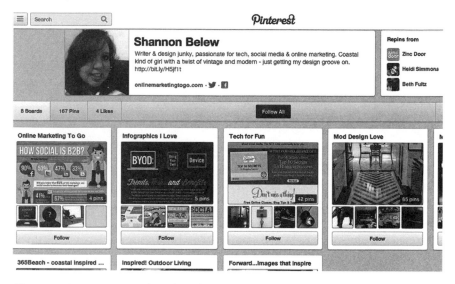

Pinterest lets you organize visual content and share it with its users.

> ➤ Create theme-specific boards for your Pinterest account (it's not unusual to have a dozen or more different boards).

> ➤ Create special occasion or holiday-themed boards.

> ➤ Post a variety of photos and graphics (both product and non-product images).

> ➤ Create a customer board that showcases your customers or pictures of how your customers use your products.

> ➤ Encourage customers to create their own Pinterest "wish list" board of your products they want.

> ➤ Start a Pinterest contest. (For example, ask customers to repin a product image from your website and then select a random winner from all those who have pinned an image from your site, or use the customer board described above, and randomly select a winner).

- ➤ Create an "Events" board that promotes upcoming special events, exclusive sales and offers, trade shows, and more.

- ➤ Share and repin content from businesses that complement your product or service.

In each of these suggestions, the goal is to post visual content that gets the attention of your prospects and customers and encourages them to share it with others.

SHARING TOP-PERFORMING PRESENTATIONS ON SLIDESHARE

Billed as the world's largest network for sharing presentations, Slide-Share (now owned by LinkedIn) attracts nearly 52 million monthly visitors with approximately 159 million page views across the site—making it one of the top 150 sites on the Web today.[13] That's a lot of traffic being driven to a site that hosts your content! Unlike the other popular visual content platforms, SlideShare is really tilted in favor of B2B consumers, with lots of professionals turning to the platform for information sharing. According to data from SlideShare, business owners use SlideShare five times more than Facebook, Twitter, You-Tube, and LinkedIn.[14]

What can you do with SlideShare? In addition to uploading your PowerPoint or other sales presentations, LinkedIn supports just about any type of document, PDF, or webinar. The sales-friendly nature of SlideShare makes it one of my favorite social selling platforms. You are able to upload presentations to your blog or website, add audio files to it to create webinars or sales presentations, and share your presentations on other social media platforms like LinkedIn.

To get even more out of SlideShare you can upgrade to a "pro" account (starting at around $20 per month); a pro account gives you access to more features—or a greater number of the free features. These features include being able to embed videos (including You-Tube videos), collect leads from within each presentation, access information on when and how people view your presentation, and even get use of a dedicated conference line for Web-based meetings. The lead collection is particularly useful and you can add the call to action or prompt for the lead form at any point in the presentation, even making it mandatory. Plus, if the viewer is already a registered user of SlideShare, the lead form auto-populates, making it super convenient for your prospect.

For the B2B sales professional, SlideShare is a useful platform because it's easy and it builds upon your capability with sales presentations. I point to the simplicity because you can take almost any piece of existing content and upload it to SlideShare, instantly creating a brand new piece of visual content. The built-in social sharing buttons also make it easy for viewers to share the content within their social media channels—including LinkedIn, Pinterest, Twitter, and many others. Here are a few ways to extend your reach with SlideShare:

➢ Use video and audio files to increase viewer engagement.

➢ Post each SlideShare presentation to LinkedIn (it's currently an underused asset within LinkedIn but it's a platform that LinkedIn seems to want to vigorously promote for its members).

➢ Share your presentations across as many of your other social media channels as possible (not just LinkedIn!).

➢ Create as many SlideShare presentations as you can because quantity does appear to help increase the views you receive.

➢ Add relevant keywords throughout your presentation to increase the likelihood of getting picked up by search engines.

➢ Increase the chances of having your presentation featured on SlideShare's home page by creating interesting covers and meaningful headlines for your presentation—and by posting each new presentation in the morning so that it collects views all day long (the more views it gets, the more likely Slide-Share will feature it on the home page).

> ➤ Make presentations even more useful by including embedded links to your website.

> ➤ Send each SlideShare presentation to your offline or existing prospects because it's more likely to be shared than a standard PDF or other file.

> ➤ Create a branded or company channel on SlideShare (easy to do with your pro account) so that your presentations are found in one place, allowing prospects to easily access additional information.

SlideShare, along with the other platforms and applications discussed in this chapter, provide plenty of opportunities for you to find and interact with prospective customers. As always, it's up to you to determine which social networks are the best match for the products and services you represent and which sites make the most sense to be included in your social selling strategy.

When considering where and how to engage with your prospects, another factor that is growing in importance is *mobility*, that is, the use of smartphones and tablets to access digital information. As users are increasingly turning to their mobile devices to view information and interact on social networking sites, that means you have to understand how to respond to the challenges and opportunities that mobility presents for the social selling process. The next chapter provides an overview of mobile commerce and what it means to the B2B and B2C sales process.

CHAPTER 15

SOCIAL SELLING TRENDS

Harnessing the Growth of Mobile Sales

When was the last time you checked your email on your smartphone? How long has it been since you used your mobile phone to send a text, look up directions, or check out online reviews of a new restaurant? How many times have you watched a video or downloaded a book on your iPad or other tablet? More than likely you do most, if not all of these activities, on a daily basis. That's because your mobile device stopped being *just* a phone a long time ago.

Consider that smartphone adoption has now exceeded 50 percent market penetration in the United States, with more than 125 million devices currently in use, and that tablet use is headed in the same direction with well over 50 million devices in use.[1] The number of devices is only part of the story, though. Of particular interest is how consumers are using those mobile devices, and how that use impacts the social selling process. Let's take a closer look at why now is the time to factor mobile into your sales strategy.

THE INFLUENCE OF MOBILE DEVICES BY
THE NUMBERS

Whether you are a salesperson or marketer, you have probably realized that your prospects are most likely going to engage with you or your brand via a mobile device at multiple points during the sales process. In fact, prospects may discover your brand for the first time through some type of mobile touchpoint, whether that be via mobile search or through content shared in social media, for instance. And whether you sell B2C or B2B, you may even be able to use mobile devices to prompt a sale by targeting prospects by location and offering immediate coupons or discount offers. A constantly increasing number of people are using mobile devices (rather than their desktop or laptop computers) to get online for everything from networking to shopping.

A 2013 study by The Media Behavior Institute indicated that nearly 44 percent of total weekly time spent online was done through a mobile phone, while 17 percent of time was via a tablet, and the report indicates that both of those numbers are expected to continue to rise.[2] The report also reveals that email, social networking, and entertainment were among the top online activities conducted via a mobile device in the first quarter of 2013. Research from comScore indicates similar trends, finding that in the single month of December 2012, social networking via mobile devices accounted for 55 percent of time spent online![3] The question remains whether or not all (or even some) of this mobile activity and social networking is adding up to real dollars for brands. The short answer is yes!

For starters, let's take a look at buying trends from the daily deals website, Groupon. In 2011, only 14 percent of its deals were purchased via a mobile device. By the start of 2013, that percentage had more than tripled to 45 percent of transactions being completed via mobile, according to an annual Internet trends report.[4] The same report showed that the social networking site Facebook credits the explosive mobile usage with driving similar upward trends in both number of users and amount of ad revenue generated. In the first quarter of 2013, Facebook saw traffic from 751 million mobile active users, or 68 percent of active users. That category of mobile users has maintained double-digit growth for at least eight consecutive quarters. Similarly, ad revenue for Facebook hit $1,245 million in the first part of 2013, with 30 percent coming from mobile—more than double the percentage from just nine months earlier, when the data was first available.[5]

For other companies, the influence of mobile devices still looks to be in its infancy. For example, analysts estimate that for Amazon, the Internet retail giant, only eight percent of sales (not including downloads to its electronic book reader, the Kindle) come from mobile devices. In comparison, the same resource looked at mobile influence for the following sites: Google gets as much as 25 percent of its search queries from mobile; LinkedIn receives on average from 15 to 20 percent of its page views from mobile; and Walgreens says that 40 percent of its prescription refills are derived from mobile devices.[6]

Though some industry experts consider these numbers to be low for mobile-based sales, researchers seem to agree that mobile commerce, or m-commerce, is only going to continue to grow. Internet trend tracker eMarketer anticipated that mobile transactions will account for 15 percent of all online retail sales in 2013, adding up to a whopping $39 billion; and that by 2017, they expect three-fourths of "digital buyers" to make at least one purchase via a mobile device.[7] While this is a good sampling of the impact of mobile on various established brands, what does the rise of mobile commerce and the growing number of buyer interactions from mobile devices mean for you?

MOBILE COMMERCE IN ACTION

First, I must be clear that mobile commerce and mobile marketing are not new. Both have been around for a while and marketers, along with various technology companies, have already had lots of experience trying to figure out how best to reach consumers via mobile devices, and then how to engage them and get them to convert to customers. In a survey of its small business users, the online company Web.com found that 69 percent of respondents considered mobile marketing "crucial" for growing business in the next five years, and that 36 percent already had success in using mobile marketing to attract local customers.[8]

I'm always curious to see exactly how companies like those surveyed are using mobile to market and sell, so not long ago I couldn't help but take note while shopping in a clothing store with my daughter when a sales associate offered a paper coupon, of sorts. The in-store "coupon" contained instructions for sending a text message from my mobile phone to a special phone number, and in return I received a code for an immediate 20 percent discount on anything purchased in the store that day. (Using text messaging in this way is typically referred to as *SMS marketing.*) Once I used the code, my phone number was captured by the retailer so it could continue marketing to me long after I walked out of the store. And ever since that day, I receive weekly text-based alerts on my phone for "happy hour" discounts or other "exclusive" specials. (Of course, consumers can opt out of receiving these text messages at any time, just as you can opt out of receiving emails from companies.) Another example of mobile marketing came to my attention after the end of a meal at a popular sushi restaurant. When the waitress delivered the bill, it also included a small card with a *QR code*, a printed image that is scannable via your cell phone. The scanned QR code revealed an online customer satisfaction survey, along with a discounted offer for my next meal.

You've probably experienced mobile marketing in action as well. Perhaps you have been encouraged to use your smartphone to "check in" at a restaurant or special event via a location-based social networking site like FourSquare. You can even be rewarded by earning special badges from your frequent social check-ins. This activity can be shared with friends in your other social networks to show that you are frequenting certain stores, restaurants, or events. It's also used by the social networking site to make recommendations to others. Similarly, perhaps you have used a mobile device to search for a review of a restaurant on a site like Yelp.com, which then instantly influenced your decision on where to eat that day.

The power of mobile devices doesn't stop at marketing. Using a smartphone to accept or make payments is another growing trend. You may be familiar with a product called Square (or similar products), which allows you to easily add a small device to your mobile phone via the USB port, after which you can literally swipe credit and debit cards for payment. Talk about enabling a true mobile salesforce! In fact, the Girl Scouts of America has started allowing some of its troops to use this payment method during its annual Girl Scout cookie drive. What happens if a customer doesn't have a few dollars in cash for a box of cookies? No worries; they simply have their debit or credit card swiped on a Girl Scout's (or troop leader's) cell phone. If you haven't purchased cookies this way, chances are you have used mobile payments in other ways.

Starbucks makes it easy for customers to pay for their morning ritual cup of coffee using nothing more than a mobile phone. After downloading an app to your phone, and transferring money to this new virtual wallet, you can then use what is the equivalent of a customer loyalty card that's stored on your smartphone. Simply flash your phone to the barista and use the app to pay for your coffee. It's quick and easy, and Starbucks uses the data it collects on your purchases to better market to you, sending you rewards and special offers. The idea of using your mobile device to accept or make payments had already added up to nearly $13 billion in 2012, and the mobile payment industry is expected to see $90 billion in sales by 2017, according to Forrester Research.[9]

SOCIAL SELLING AND PREPARING FOR MOBILE SALES

While all of the above are great examples of mobile marketing in action, and certainly demonstrate the power of mobile payments for grabbing sales on the go, you may be wondering how you, as a salesperson, can capitalize on the mobile sales trend.

To start, I think it's important to think of mobile as more of a team sport. As I mentioned, mobile marketing isn't completely new, though it continues to change and grow into unexplored territories on a daily basis. Nonetheless, it has matured to the point that there are lots of components to making it work, including everything from choosing the best technology or application to enable mobile sales to developing and implementing a complete mobile marketing campaign or strategy. Most organizations leave these types of details up to their marketing and Web development teams.

One critical key to mobile sales and marketing is ensuring that your website is enabled for mobile viewing. If you have ever visited a site that's not set up for a mobile format, then you know how your user experience is diminished. It's often difficult to read the text, the information on any given Web page doesn't properly fit on the screen of your mobile device, it's difficult to navigate the site and find the information you need, and sometimes there are pop-up ads or other images that can't be minimized or that don't work at all. From a customer perspective, this type of experience is frustrating and often results in leaving the site quickly.

Making a website ready for mobile is usually referred to as making it "responsive," which means the site can detect the type of mobile device or desktop being used to view it and then adapt or change how it is displayed so it is optimum for that particular device. This isn't necessarily a hard thing to do (if you use WordPress as a blog, it's often the matter of checking a box to ready your site for mobile viewing), but usually this task is left to your company's Web team or IT department to handle.

That's not to say that as an independent sales professional or small business that you should not or cannot do any of these things for yourself. Yes, you can explore and implement mobile marketing on your own. However, you will need a different book, one dedicated solely to that topic! (Hmmm, maybe soon! Follow me on Twitter @ShannonBelew to find out.)

My purpose in introducing you to mobile sales in this book is, first and foremost, to make you aware of the trend and its importance in helping drive revenue. I also want you to see how mobile sales and marketing increasingly goes hand in hand with social media. As discussed earlier in this chapter, more people are using their mobile devices to access and use social networking sites, so it's to be expected that mobile marketing would be executed through social networking channels. Finally, it's crucial to understand that when you communicate with your prospects, there is a very high probability that they are accessing your information while on a smartphone or tablet. And just as your company website needs to be set up to be viewed on a mobile device, the same rules of viewing should be applied to all your content, emails, and promotional offers.

Here are a few of the ways that you, as a salesperson, can be prepared for mobile:

> ➤ Make sure your content and especially emails are easily viewable on mobile devices.

> ➤ Include key contact information near the top of mobile Web pages or any content that you send prospects so that phone numbers and email address (or other pertinent facts) are easily seen and accessed from a mobile device.

> ➤ Use third-party platforms, like SlideShare, for your sales presentations and documents so that they are readily accessible by clicking a link (or URL) to view them, instead of requiring that the information be downloaded or opened (which isn't always easy from a smartphone).

> ➤ Incorporate audio in the presentations and content you send to prospects so there is another option for receiving your information via mobile devices that doesn't require the prospect to stop and read or look at your content.

> ➤ Make sure any calls to action that are included in your emails and content are clearly visible and simple to respond to from a mobile device.

> ➤ Include social media sharing icons or buttons on all your information so that prospects can share on their networks from their mobile devices.

As you can see, a big part of using mobility in your social selling process is ensuring that your content is easy to access and view from both smartphones and tablets, and providing multiple options for prospects to consume your company's messages over mobile devices.

—

Now that you have an idea of how mobile is being incorporated into the sales process, in the final chapter of the book you get a glimpse at several companies (both B2C and B2B) who have found success with social selling.

CHAPTER 16

CASE STUDIES

Social Success Stories for B2C and B2B

It's easier to write (or read!) about all the things you must do to find success with your social selling strategy than to actually do them. But there are plenty of others who have already tested the waters and learned what worked and didn't work for them. I chose three companies to speak with that I have personally interacted with online to find out how they have used social selling to drive traffic, increase sales, and encourage engagement—and in each case found they have done it well. The results of my interviews with their owners follow.

Company: Caron's Beach House, a specialty online retailer
Target Market: B2C

By the time Caron White officially opened her online store specializing in coastal home décor in March 2010, she had already had a presence on social media since September of the previous year.[1] Long before she had even a single product to sell, she had created a Facebook page for her business and immediately began sharing coastal and beach-related posts and pictures. "Starting the business page before our online store launch was part of a long-term strategy to have a built-in, engaged audience when we did open the site," White explained. Today, the store has more than 7,050 Likes and White, who manages all of her own social media, posts an average of three to five times per day, every day. The vast majority of the posts include photos as well as text, which help boost social interactions.

But White's social media goals extend well beyond the number of Likes or comments she receives, and her strategy includes using a mix of social networking sites and blogs for distribution and engagement.

First, let's look at her top four objectives as they relate to social selling:

1. Producing product sales.

2. Attracting potential customers.

3. Engaging customers.

4. Building an in-house email list.

The key to meeting these four key social selling goals is sharing *a lot of content* and having a great many *positive social interactions* with her online target audience. White's content, which consists of most anything related to the coastal lifestyle, includes original blog posts, articles, coastal news, decorating ideas, and beach-style recipes. But photos definitely rank as the top type of content to share, and she uses them in practically every post.

That brings us to the second part of her plan—distribution to spur customer engagement. Currently, Caron's Beach House has three separate blogs and all have content that can be shared between them. Updates are then pushed out to the various social media sites, including networked blogs, Twitter, Facebook, StumbleUpon, Kaboodle, Tumbler, Pinterest, and LinkedIn. So far, all of the content and opportunities to engage are paying off—especially on Pinterest, where White creates "lifestyle" boards that combine products from Caron's Beach House with images found on other sites (blogs, travel sites, and online magazines). "This is such a great visual way to express our beach style to potential customers," she says.

Caron White maintains more than a hundred Pinterest boards with different decorating ideas and themes ranging from seashells to coastal gourmet recipes. A particularly successful Pinterest board is the one labeled "Beach Living," which was created as a community board for the sharing of any coastal-related ideas, tips, or pictures. Instead of it being a board to which only she posts, it was designed with the intent of encouraging other users to post content to it; this really helps broaden its visibility since the people who are pinning to it are also more likely to share those pins with their followers. Currently, it has almost 100 contributors and more than 13,000 followers, and growing rapidly. (That's a whole bunch of followers, if you're not Beyoncé or Brad Pitt!) In fact, the number of followers for this board seems to be growing at a rate of nearly 500 (or more) followers per month. By the time you read this, it may have two to three times the amount mentioned here!

While pinning pretty pictures of the beach may seem like child's play, these social sharing activities directly translate into sales. In fact, White tracks all of her sales and activities related to her posts or to any social media activity using Google analytics and Lexity.com, a free service.

The results aren't too shabby. While White didn't want to offer specific dollar amounts, she said she receives sales every single day that are tracked back to a Pinterest image that was shared or to another piece of shared social media content. As for the other social selling objectives White set for her business? Pinterest is not only sending sales to her website, but more traffic, too—even if all that traffic doesn't immediately translate to sales. It currently ranks number two in Web traffic referral sites (behind Google Search) and it has over 20,000 followers! The blog is also the third-ranking source for sending referrals.

Despite White's social selling success for her products, she offers a warning to would-be online businesspeople. "Do not expect to post a link to a product and then sell it," White says. "Social media is [only one] part of your entire marketing strategy." She also offers the following tips:

> ➤ **Be consistent:** Post something a few times every day. Using social media is like any other media; sometimes potential customers need to see your message as many as ten times before they actually take any action—and that action may only be to click on a link to your site, not click to make a purchase.

> ➤ **Make content easy to share:** Add *share* buttons everywhere feasible, particularly if you sell a product. White's product pages have "Pin-It," "Tweet," and "Like" buttons.

> ➤ **Test content and share buttons:** It's dangerous to set social media on autopilot and not go back and check on things occasionally. White said that the Pinterest Pin It button broke just after she launched her updated website, but she wasn't immediately aware of it. The result was a severe drop-off in repins.

Company: Bizo, a marketing services firm
Target Market: B2B

Bizo is not new to the concept of identifying a target audience and pulling those prospects through the various stages of the sales funnel. This is in large part the type of online service that Bizo provides its clients—brands like American Express, Mercedes Benz, Salesforce.com, Microsoft, AT&T, and UPS. Using the Bizo proprietary marketing platform, a custom data management and targeting tool, the company can reach prospective customers and identify them by specific business- or company-related demographic criteria such as job role or industry sector. The brands can then deliver their message to the hyper-defined audience and start converting them into buyers. Bizo uses a similar approach as part of its social selling strategy to reach prospective customers that include not only big-name brands but small and medium-sized businesses too.

Bizo's social strategy is carefully aligned with the sales funnel. "We approach all programs with a focus on where they fit in the marketing and sales funnel," said Jennifer Agustin, senior director of marketing for Bizo and head of the company's small social media team.[2] "We use the best (social media) channel to meet the best objective." For example, the objectives used for those social media prospects that show up at the top and mid-level of the funnel include:

> Building awareness.

> Engaging the prospects.

> Showcasing thought leadership.

The ultimate goal is to not only influence prospects, but to convert them. Agustin said the company has always

approached every social media channel with lead generation in mind. For that reason, they use a hybrid social selling strategy that incorporates both organic (no fee) tactics
and paid tactics that use social media ads. The organic
interactions (tweets, posts, and comments) help "prep," or
warm up, the prospects, while the paid ads allow them to
use a more aggressive approach with a lead-generating
offer attached or embedded. Agustin said that LinkedIn,
particularly when using LinkedIn ads delivered through
Bizo, is an ideal platform for social selling because it is a
database rich with their target audience of professionals
and businesses. Plus, LinkedIn ads have performed
extremely well, making it a good place to implement their
hybrid approach. "We are seeing phenomenal results from
it," she said. "It's a sweet spot for us for where our prospects are."

From a purely organic perspective, Bizo adds Twitter
and Facebook to its list (along with LinkedIn) of top social
media channels for reaching prospective customers. To
make the most of each of these channels, Bizo distributes
content that matches a prospect's movement through the
sales funnel. Ultimately, says Agustin, you have to ask,
"Can we see social as being part of the buyer's journey?
Did it carry through to a possible conversion?" So far, the
answer for Bizo has been yes. But to make sure, Bizo
tracks all of its social selling efforts. One measurement is
through the use of custom landing pages created in Eloqua, Bizo's marketing automation program for email. In
that case, any links that are included with tweets, posts, or
shares will send prospects to the custom landing page
where their actions (or inactions) are closely tracked. Bizo
will know the conversion rate for the form (whether people
completed the offer or not). Of course, Agustin points out
that not all social media posts can "be about you." She prefers to follow a 4/1/1 rule, where you retweet or share others' posts (four times), then you send one original post of

your own—and only then follow with an offer or sales pitch.

Bizo also pays attention to Likes, follows, and retweets, though Agustin says they are considered more of a sign of reach rather than popularity, because the greater the number of eyeballs on a piece of content, the more likely that content will be shared. Boosting awareness also means there's a greater possibility the content will be shared within your target audience. In an effort to do just that and increase its bump in eyeballs, Bizo has adopted a new approach for Twitter that takes a different spin on the customer testimonial. Instead of going through the hassle of trying to get a formal case study or testimonial written and approved by a new customer, Agustin asks the customer if Bizo can tweet about their new relationship! This is great exposure for Bizo, especially as a credibility factor, and it's an interesting new way to use Twitter with existing customers while still potentially being shared with and seen by prospective customers.

Bizo also uses Twitter to reach out to prospective customers who are a bit further along in the sales process. In this case, Bizo or the sales representative will follow the prospective customer on Twitter. For example, Bizo may follow the customer's company account as a way to learn more about the brand's values, recent news, and other information that the brand tweets out to the world. Following a brand in this way also means the brand might follow Bizo back (let's hear it for reciprocity!) and have the opportunity to receive additional content that could help further educate or move forward the decision to buy. Similarly, a Bizo salesperson may decide to follow her or his primary contact person for the account on Twitter (if the relationship is far enough along). This gives the salesperson another level of communication with the prospect while the prospect moves through the buying process (connecting with the prospect on LinkedIn is also a common strategy today). These are all great examples of how you can use social media to build upon your relationships with customers and prospects.

Company: Shopify, an e-commerce platform for online retailers
Target Market: B2B

Shopify has come a long way since it first launched in 2006. The e-commerce solution provider offers everything an online retailer needs to start, open, and manage a Web-based store. Today, the company has more than 50,000 online stores running on its platform in over 100 different countries. It also has the resources and employees to make sure all areas of the company are run like a well-oiled machine.

That wasn't always the case, and the difference between the two time periods is particularly noticeable when it comes to the social media efforts for Shopify. When operations were much more streamlined and staff was limited, Shopify's social media efforts were focused on reacting to what was posted on their social networking sites. It really didn't have a good plan for how to proactively use social media to benefit the company or its customers—nor the time to implement it. Jump forward a couple of years and things have really changed!

"Our number one and most important goal is to use social media to establish relationships with our online community," said Mark Hayes, head of public relations for Shopify.[3] "Platforms like Facebook and Twitter provide an effective way to communicate directly with our customers in an environment they are familiar with. We promote their stores and products, answer questions, share educational content to help them sell online, and even share some inspiration every now and then."

Shopify has also developed a "multifaceted social media strategy" that addresses both short- and long-term goals for the e-commerce leader. While social selling is certainly at the top of that goal list, just about every other area of the company is addressed, too. Its goals include:

> ➢ Customer acquisition

> ➢ Customer service

> ➢ Employee recruitment

> ➢ Thought leadership

> ➢ Content promotion

The social media team takes social selling seriously and seemingly recognizes the potential revenue dollars it means to the company. "Social media can also be used as a powerful customer acquisition tool," said Hayes. "Shopify is a DIY online store builder, so our potential customers are anybody who is interested in selling online."

Shopify's social media team has two social media strategies for identifying and talking with prospective customers. The first is to identify discussions on other social platforms. There's nothing better than finding an existing conversation that pertains to you and jumping in to offer some guidance. That's why Shopify's team spends lots of time searching through online conversations across all social platforms. They are looking for individuals or businesses in the consideration phase—people who know what they want to sell but don't necessarily know how to build an e-commerce store or which platform to use. Its social media team is then able to join the conversation and gently help educate or provide a few answers about e-commerce options. (Sounds a lot like our good friend *un*-selling, from Chapter 4, doesn't it?) "It's not a heavy sale," explains Hayes. "We just provide valuable information about selling online with our platform and offer to help in any way." Typical places where these types of conversations with potential merchants are found include e-commerce forums, comment sections of blogs, and Twitter.

Shopify's second social media strategy is to generate blog content to drive customer engagement. According to Hayes, the Shopify blog is one of the most popular e-commerce blogs in the world and is a huge driver in sign-ups for Shopify. As you might expect, quality content and social media go hand in hand to make this approach successful. By regularly publishing first-rate content and then distributing it via Shopify's social media channels, its blog gets lots of referral traffic from social media. Because Shopify is constantly creating content that appeals both to prospective customers and existing customers, the content on the blog is structured the same way—to help current Shopify merchants and non-Shopify merchants sell online.

For these reasons, social media plays a huge role in generating traffic to the Shopify blog. According to Hayes, last year 37 percent of referral traffic to the blog came from social media sites, primarily Facebook, Twitter, Reddit, and Hacker News. "Our blog has become the go-to place for e-commerce merchants selling on any platform, including our competitors, to learn about selling," says Hayes. "So not only is it an educational resource, we also convert readers to become customers."

Part of knowing whether or not social media strategies are working is being able to measure results. When it comes to social selling, those results are often more clear—especially if you are able to accurately track traffic from social conversations to lead-generation forms or other conversion points. This is the approach Shopify takes when it comes to account and trial sign-ups. "With our ongoing Facebook and Twitter ad campaigns, we measure sign-ups," Hayes says. "Both platforms provide excellent analytics tools that allow us to see exactly how many new merchants sign up from the ads we post." The measurement can get a bit muddled with community engagement projects, however. In that case, Hayes says that Shopify's team has to "rely less on hard metrics and more on intuition." They also evaluate the sentiment (pro or con) of comments and consider how many Likes or shares or retweets a post gets.

Shopify doesn't appear to have a shortage of successful social strategies, but one in particular is a good example of how you can target anyone in your community and end up getting kudos from prospects, customers, or vendors.

On February 13, 2013, Shopify surprised its community of Facebook fans by offering everyone a free coffee from Starbucks (while supplies lasted). Using the Starbucks iOS app, Hayes personally added $200 to a Starbucks card and took a screenshot of the barcode and posted it to Facebook, as you can see in Figure 16–1. Along

FIGURE 16–1

A surprise offer on Facebook went viral and made lots of customers happy.

with the image of the barcode, the following message was posted:

> For our merchants working out of Starbucks this morning, have a coffee on us. We put $200 on this card, just hold your phone up at the register to scan. First come first serve. If you want to pay it forward, feel free to put money on it. Have a great day!

The goal of the promotion was to show Shopify's appreciation to its customers. Since many of these online retailers conduct business out of Starbucks stores across the country, the Shopify team thought a free cup of Joe would be lapped up! And they were right. The post received over 225 likes, 52 shares, and most importantly 70 positive comments. It was such a success that Shopify decided to add money to the card several times. Some of the comments they received included:

> "I'm not at Starbucks now (actually the only Starbucks in Stockholm is at the airport) but it feels super awesome to be working on such a great platform as Shopify!"

> "It works! Thanks for the free coffee, Shopify! Things like this make me proud to be a customer!"

> "I haven't used it, but this is very thoughtful and I applaud you guys for doing such a nice thing for your clients! I especially love the idea of paying it forward, this I will do! Thanks again!"

Now those are positive interactions that go a long way—and well beyond just existing customers. Remember, these are comments publicly posted to and share in social media, so everyone, even prospective customers, get to see them. That's how you do social!

NOTES

CHAPTER 1

1. Number of active or registered users is according to published data from each social network, including LinkedIn (238 million), Google + (235 million), Twitter (200 million), and Facebook (699 million), as of August 2013.
2. Sales Benchmark Index; Sales & Marketing Effectiveness Blog: "The Next Big Prediction in B2B Sales," by Greg Alexander, January 2013; www.sales benchmarkindex.com/bid/93649/The-Next-Big-Prediction-in-B2B-Sale.
3. Discussed in the Research Brief: "Social Selling: Leveraging the Power of User-Generated Content to Optimize Sales Results," February 2013; busi ness.linkedin.com/content/dam/business/sales-solutions/global/en_US/site/ pdf/ti/linkedin_social_selling_impact_aberdeen_report ...us_en_1 30702.pdf.

CHAPTER 2

1. Aberdeen Group, "Sales and Marketing Alignment: Collaboration + Co-operation = Peak Performance," by Chris Houpis; September 2010; reported by Pamela Vaughan on HubSpot, "The Steps You Need to Define the Stages of Your Sales & Marketing Funnel," October 2012; blog.hub spot.com/blog/tabid/6307/bid/33711/The-Steps-You-Need-to-Define-the-Stages-of-Your-Sales-Marketing-Funnel.aspx.
2. Nielsen Research, "Social Media Report 2012," December 2012; www .nielsen.com/us/en/reports/2012/state-of-the-media-the-social-media-re port-2012.html.
3. Edison Research, "The Social Habit, 2012 Q4 Research Report," December 2012; socialhabit.com/secure/wp-content/uploads/2012/07/The-Social-Habit-2012-by-Edi son-Research.pdf.

4. Oracle, "Customer Experience Impact Report," commissioned by Right-Now, 2011; www.oracle.com/us/products/applications/cust-exp-impact-report-ep ss-1560493.pdf (www.slideshare.net/jperezpgi/2011-rightnow-customer-experience-impact-report).

CHAPTER 3

1. Truett Cathy is founder of Chick-fil-A. His website, www.TruettCathy.com, details how his personal commitment to biblical principles and how those principles shaped Chick-fil-A, including the decision to close the restaurants on Sundays as a way to "honor God." Dan Cathy, COO of Chick-fil-A, is Truett Cathy's son.

CHAPTER 4

1. Nielsen Global Survey of Online Shopping: Third Quarter, 2011; pt.nielsen.com/documents/tr_201011_Q3_2010_CCI_Final_ Client_Report.pdf.
2. According to research from Nielsen: "Global Trust in Advertising Report," 2012; www.nielsen.com/us/en/reports/2012/global-trust-in-advertising-and-brand-messages.html.
3. *The Thank You Economy,* by Gary Vaynerchuk (HarperBusiness, 2011), p. 63.

CHAPTER 5

1. comScore, "It's a Social World: Top 10 Need-to-Knows About Social Networking and Where It's Headed," 2011; www.comscore.com/Insights/Presentations_and_Whitepapers/2011/it_is_aesocial_world_top_10_need-to-knows_about_social_networking.
2. Nielsen, "Global Survey of New Product Purchase Sentiment," Q3, 2012; www.nielsen.com/content/dam/corporate/us/en/reports-downloads/2013%20Reports/Nielsen-Global-New-Products-Report-Jan-2013.pdf.
3. From Newswire on Nielsen.com, "Digital Influence: How the Internet Affects New Product Purchase Decisions," February 2013; www.nielsen.com/us/en/newswire/2013/digital-influence-how-the-internet-affects-new-product-purchase-decisions.html.

4. LinkedIn, Forrester, and Research Now, "IT Purchasing Goes Social," August 2012; www.iab.net/media/file/IT_Purchasing_Goes_Social-Best_Practices_Final.pdf.

5. Nielsen, "Global Trust in Advertising Report," 2012.

6. BazaarVoice, "Social Trends Report 2012," June 2012; www.hashdoc .com/document/8246/four-social-trends-already-changing-your-business-2012-trends-report.

7. "2013 Digital Influence Report, TechnoratiMedia"; technorati.com/busi ness/article/technorati-medias-2013-digital-influence-report/; p. 13.

CHAPTER 6

1. "The Digital Evolution in B2B Marketing;" a survey published by Google and CEB, 2012; www.executiveboard.com/exbd-resources/content/digital-evolution/content-marketing/index.html.

2. "Buyer Behavior Helps B2B Marketers Guide the Buyer's Journey," from the Forrester Research blog, by Lori Wizdo, October 2012; blogs.for rester.com/lori_wizdo/12–10–04-buyer_behavior_helps_b2b_marketers_ guide_the_buyers_journey.

3. "Buyer Behavior"; blogs.forrester.com/lori_wizdo/12–10–04-buyer_be havior_helps_b2b_marketers_guide_the_buyers_journey.

CHAPTER 7

1. With the rise of mommy bloggers, companies often send free products and other gifts to the influential bloggers in exchange for (or at least in hopes of) a positive review, recommendation, or mention of the company's products. Mommy bloggers are recognized as one of the first major groups of online influencers, at least in the B2C market. The response by companies was so strong and so publicized that it contributed to a couple of important changes. For example, the IRS took notice and mandated that bloggers (and the companies doing the giving) report the value of any gifts, products, travel compensation, or other financial compensation that they receive so that it can be properly taxed. Also, many influential bloggers across all industries now put guidelines on their blog that state how products or samples may be handled and how they may or may not result in a positive review.

CHAPTER 8

1. CSO Insights Sales Performance Optimization Study, 2011; as reported in SellingPower, "How Much Time Do Your Salespeople Spend Selling?" by Gerhard Gschwandtner, www.sellingpower.com/content/article/?i = 1352 &ia = 9271.
2. InsideSales.com, "The Top Problems of the Inside Sales Industry" Executive Summary Report, 2012, as reported on Forbes.com, "Latest Inside Sales Research Shows It's All About the Leads," by Ken Krogue, November 11, 2011; www.forbes.com/sites/kenkrogue/2012/11/11/latest-inside-sales-research-shows-its-all-about-the-leads/.
3. 2012 Social Media Marketing Industry, "How Marketers Are Using Social Media to Grow Their Businesses;" April 2012, by Michael A. Stelzner and sponsored by Social Media Examiner; www.socialmediaexaminer.com/SocialMediaMarketingIndustryReport2012.pdf.

CHAPTER 9

1. Altimeter Group, "How Corporations Should Prioritize Social Business Budgets," February 2011, by Jeremiah Owyang and Charlene Li; www.altimetergroup.com/research/reports/how-corporations-should-prioritize-social-business-budgets. The survey is based on feedback from 140 corporate social strategists at large corporations.
2. "The CMO Survey," February 2012, as reported on its website TheCMO Survey.org, directed by Christine Moorman, the T. Austin Finch, Sr. Professor of Business Administration, The Fuqua School of Business, Duke University. The survey is administered twice a year via an Internet survey; www.cmosurvey.org/blog/social-media-spend-continues-to-soar/.
3. "The CMO Survey," February 2012.
4. "The CMO Survey," February 2013, by Christine Moorman; cmosurvey .org/files/2013/02/The_CMO_Survey_Highlights_and _Insights…Feb-2013-Final2.pdf.
5. Wendy Clark (@wnd6h), Senior Vice President, Integrated Marketing Communications and Capabilities for the Coca-Cola Company, was a guest on the weekly Twitter chat, #MMChat; Sponsored by The Social CMO Blog, speaking about Coca-Cola's social media strategy; www.thesocialcmo.com/blog/events/.
6. Sonoma County, California, supervisors board meeting, March 12, 2013,

reported in *The Healdsburg Tribune*, March 20, 2013; www.sonomawest
.com/the_healdsburg_tribune/news/county-supervisors-triple-social-media-
training-budget/article_be6c1842–91a0–11e2-bfda-001a4bcf887a.htm l.

7. "The Paid Social Media Advertising Report 2013," by Vizu, a Nielsen company; www.nielsen.com/us/en/reports/2013/the-paid-social-media-advertis
ing-report-20 13.html.

8. Bloggers are now required by the Internal Revenue Service (IRS) to report
gifts and free products as part of their income. If you work with bloggers
and other influencers, be sure to follow the IRS guidelines, available from
the website www.IRS.gov.

CHAPTER 11

1. LinkedIn Blog, "200 Million Members!" by Deep Nishar, January 9, 2013;
blog.linkedin.com/2013/01/09/linkedin-200-million/.

2. Personal interview, Koka Sexton, senior social marketing manager for
LinkedIn. April 2013.

3. Sexton interview.

4. "8 Mistakes You Should Never Make on LinkedIn," by Libby Kane, Forbes
.com, March 2013; www.forbes.com/sites/learnvest/2013/03/04/8-mis
takes-you-should-never-make-on-linkedin/.

5. "Top Salespeople Use LinkedIn to Sell More," by Steve W. Martin, *Harvard
Business Review*, April 2013; blogs.hbr.org/cs/2013/04/top_salespeople_
use_linked.html.

6. LinkedIn Blog, "How Large Is Your Network? The Power of 2nd and 3rd
Degree Connections" by Reid Hoffman, December 2012; www.linkedin
.com/today/post/article/20121206195559–1213-how-large-is-your-network-
the-power-of-2nd-and-3rd-degree-connections.

CHAPTER 12

1. "Celebrating #Twitter7" by Karen Wickre; March 21, 2013; blog.twitter
.com/2013/celebrating-twitter7.

2. "When Twitter Rogues Move Markets: A Timeline," Bloomberg Business-
Week Technology, April 25, 2013, by Jared Keller and Evan Applegate;
www.businessweek.com/articles/2013–04–25/when-twitter-rogues-move-
markets-a-timeline.

3. "How Many B2B Leads Can You Get from Twitter?" by Vernon Niven, NeedTagger, April 2013; www.needtagger.com/how-many-b2b-leads-can-you-get-from-twitter/.

CHAPTER 13

1. "2013 Digital Influence Report," p. 13.
2. newsroom.fb.com/Key-Facts.
3. Facebook Marketing channel; SlideShare presentations posted on www.SlideShare.net.
4. Small Business Saturday Consumer Insights Survey, conducted by the National Federation of Independent Business (NFIB) and American Express, November 2012; www.nfib.com/press-media/press-media-item? cmsid = 61348.
5. "Suddenly, Google Plus Is Outpacing Twitter to Become the World's Second Largest Social Network," by Thomas Watkins; Business Insider, May 2013; www.businessinsider.com/google-plus-is-outpacing-twitter-2013–5.
6. "2013 Digital Influence Report," p. 15.
7. "2013 Digital Influence Report," p. 12

CHAPTER 14

1. Stats reported by YouTube; www.youtube.com/yt/press/statistics.html.
2. "The Power of Visual Content Marketing and Brand Visuals in Action," by Miranda Miller for Top Rank blog, May 2013; www.toprankblog.com/2013/05/visual-social-content/.
3. "How Oreo Won the Marketing Super Bowl With a Timely Blackout Ad on Twitter," by Angela Watercutter for *Wired Magazine*, February 2013; www.wired.com/underwire/2013/02/oreo-twitter-super-bowl/.
4. "What Makes a Link Worthy Post—Part 1," by Casey Hen for SEOMoz .com, October 19, 2009; moz.com/blog/what-makes-a-link-worthy-post-part-1.
5. "Facebookers Feed Graph Search And Set A Record By Uploading 1.1B Photos On New Year's Day/Eve" by Josh Constine for TechCrunch, January 17, 2013; techcrunch.com/2013/01/17/facebook-photos-record/.
6. Based on research from online news organization, Bit Rebles, as reported in the article, "Infographics Shared on Twitter Get 832% More Retweets

Than Images and Articles," by Lauren Dugan for MediaBistro.com, August 2012; www.mediabistro.com/alltwitter/infographics-on-twitter_b26840.

7. Statistics collected and released by Instagram, "Instagram in Statistics," available from the Instagram Press Center; instagram.com/press/#.

8. Pew Research: "The Demographics of Social Media Users – 2012," by Maeve Duggan, Joanna Brenner; taken from the excerpt: Social Networking Site Users Report, released February 2013; pewinternet.org/Commentary/2012/March/Pew-Internet-Social-Networking-full-detail.aspx.

9. Stats reported by YouTube, from Snapchat blog on June 24, 2013, entitled "Recent Additions to Team Snapchat"; blog.snapchat.com.

10. Stats reported by YouTube.

11. "Social Network Demographics: Twitter, Pinterest, Instagram, Facebook," by Lenna Garibian for MarketingProfs.com; February 2013; www.marketingprofs.com/charts/2013/10139/social-network-demographics-twitter-pinterest-instagram-facebook; also references Pew Research: "The Demographics of Social Media Users – 2012," by Maeve Duggan, Joanna Brenner.

12. Based on research from Unmetric and presented in the article, "The Most Popular Branded Boards on Pinterest," by Laura Indvik for Mashable; May 2013; mashable.com/2013/05/08/pinterest-most-popular-brand-boards/.

13 Statistics reported by SlideShare "Quick Trivia," and attributed to comScore, 2012; www.slideshare.net/about.

14. SlideShare, as reported in The Social Media Examiner, "How To Generate Leads with Slideshare" by Barry Feldman, January 10, 2013; www.socialmediaexaminer.com/how-to-generate-leads-with-slideshare/.

CHAPTER 15

1. "U.S. Mobile, Future in Focus," comScore; February 2013; www.comscore.com/Insights/Presentations_and_Whitepapers/2013/2013_Mobile_Future_in_Focus.

2. "Social Media Behaviors: What Do People Do?" The Media Behavior Institute, May 2013 (as reported by eMarketer, "How Do Internet Users Divvy Up Their Desktop, Mobile Web Time?" April 25, 2013; www.emarketer.com/Article/How-Do-Internet-Users-Divvy-Up-Their-Desktop-Mobile-Web-Time/1009841).

3. "U.S. Mobile, Future in Focus," comScore.

4. "KPCB Internet Trends Report 2013," by Mary Meeker, May 2013 (distributed on SlideShare; www.slideshare.net/kleinerperkins/kpcb-internet-trends-2013?ref=http://www.kpcb.com/insights/2013-internet-trends).

5. "Eight Percent of Amazon's Sales Are Coming From Mobile," by Tricia Duryee, on AllThingsD, January 4, 2013; allthingsd.com/20130104/eight-percent-of-amazons-sales-are-coming-from-mobile/.

6. "Eight Percent of Amazon's Sales Are Coming from Mobile," by Tricia Duryee.

7. "Smartphones, Tablets Drive Faster Growth in Ecommerce Sales," eMarketer; April 2013; www.emarketer.com/Article/Smartphones-Tablets-Drive-Faster-Growth-Ecommerce-Sales/1009835.

8. "Small Business Mobile Survey 2012," from Web.com referenced in "Small Businesses That Use Mobile Marketing See Their Sales Soar, Survey Shows," from NetworkSolutions, May 2012; www.networksolutions.com/smallbusiness/2012/05/small-businesses-that-use-mobile-marketing-see-their-sales-soar-survey-shows/.

9. "Forrester: U.S. Mobile Payments Market Predicted To Reach $90B by 2017, Up From $12.8B in 2012," by Darrell Etherington on TechCrunch, January 2013; techcrunch.com/2013/01/16/forrester-u-s-mobile-payments-market-predicted-to-reach-90b-by-2017-up-from-12–8b-in-2012/.

CHAPTER 16

1. Online Q&A interviews, Facebook messaging, and email May 9–19, 2013.

2. Phone interview, May 13, 2013.

3. Phone and email interviews, May 9–13, 2013.

INDEX